U.S. POWER IN INTERNATIONAL HIGHER EDUCATION

U.S. POWER IN INTERNATIONAL HIGHER EDUCATION

EDITED BY
JENNY J. LEE

RUTGERS UNIVERSITY PRESS
New Brunswick, Camden, and Newark, New Jersey, and London

Library of Congress Cataloging-in-Publication Data
Names: Lee, Jenny J., editor.
Title: U.S. power in international higher education / edited by Jenny J. Lee.
Description: New Brunswick, New Jersey: Rutgers University Press, 2021. |
   Includes bibliographical references and index.
Identifiers: LCCN 2020043923 | ISBN 9781978820777 (paperback) |
   ISBN 9781978820784 (hardcover) | ISBN 9781978820791 (epub) |
   ISBN 9781978820807 (mobi) | ISBN 9781978820814 (pdf)
Subjects: LCSH: International education—Political aspects—United States. |
   Education, Higher—Political aspects—United States. | Education, Higher—
   International cooperation. | Education and globalization—United States.
Classification: LCC LC1090 .U5 2021 | DDC 378.73—dc23
LC record available at https://lccn.loc.gov/2020043923

A British Cataloging-in-Publication record for this book is available from the British Library.

This collection copyright © 2021 by Rutgers, The State University of New Jersey
Individual chapters copyright © 2021 in the names of their authors
All rights reserved

No part of this book may be reproduced or utilized in any form or by any means, electronic or mechanical, or by any information storage and retrieval system, without written permission from the publisher. Please contact Rutgers University Press, 106 Somerset Street, New Brunswick, NJ 08901. The only exception to this prohibition is "fair use" as defined by U.S. copyright law.

♾ The paper used in this publication meets the requirements of the American National Standard for Information Sciences—Permanence of Paper for Printed Library Materials, ANSI Z39.48-1992.

www.rutgersuniversitypress.org

Manufactured in the United States of America

CONTENTS

1	International Higher Education as Geopolitical Power JENNY J. LEE	1

PART I: GEOPOLITICS AND THE REGULATION OF HIGHER EDUCATION

2	International Education as Soft Power: A History of Changing Governments, Shifting Rationales, and Lessons Learned ROOPA DESAI TRILOKEKAR	23
3	What Do Global University Rankings Tell Us about U.S. Geopolitics in Higher Education? ELLEN HAZELKORN	42
4	International Accreditation as Geopolitical Space: U.S. Practices as "Global Standards" for Quality Assurance in Higher Education GERARDO L. BLANCO	60

PART II: NATIONAL AND GLOBAL RESEARCH

5	Geopolitical Tensions and Global Science: Understanding U.S.-China Scientific Research Collaboration through Scientific Nationalism and Scientific Globalism JOHN P. HAUPT AND JENNY J. LEE	77
6	Concepts for Understanding the Geopolitics of Graduate Student and Postdoc Mobility BRENDAN CANTWELL	94

PART III: UNIVERSITY INTERNATIONALIZATION STRATEGIES

7	Exploring Geopolitics in U.S. Campus Internationalization Plans CHRYSTAL A. GEORGE MWANGI, SEAN JUNG-HAU CHEN, AND PEMPHO CHINKONDENJI	113

8	The Life Cycle of Transnational Partnerships in Higher Education DALE LAFLEUR	131

PART IV: STUDENTS AND INTERNATIONAL LEARNING

9	Global Positional Competition and Interest Convergence: Student Mobility as a Commodity for U.S. Academic Imperialism CHRISTINA W. YAO	151
10	Global Competence: Hidden Frames of National Security and Economic Competitiveness CHRIS R. GLASS	170
11	Internationalizing the Curriculum: Conceptual Orientations and Practical Implications in the Shadow of Western Hegemony SHARON STEIN	187

PART V: CONCLUDING THOUGHTS

12	Where Do We Go from Here? JENNY J. LEE AND SANTIAGO CASTIELLO-GUTIÉRREZ	207
	Notes on Contributors	219
	Index	225

U.S. POWER IN INTERNATIONAL HIGHER EDUCATION

1 ◆ INTERNATIONAL HIGHER EDUCATION AS GEOPOLITICAL POWER

JENNY J. LEE

Internationalization has become indispensable to higher education institutions' core functions and strategies. While formerly on the fringe of university programming, internationalization is more integrated and central than ever before. Terminal degrees, short-term programs, and educational exchange have all expanded to meet the needs of a growing global market. International student enrollment in particular has been a major target area with undisputed benefits. The over 5 million students currently studying outside their home countries (United Nations Educational, Scientific and Cultural Organization [UNESCO], 2020) foster a more diverse student body while providing a necessary revenue stream for their host universities, especially in places in the world where higher education is experiencing decreasing domestic supply and declining public funds. With international travel reaching a record high of 1.5 billion during 2019 (United Nations World Tourism Organization, 2020) and the unprecedented expansion of technology-driven innovation, educational programs have also broadened in scope to provide more flexible options for both students from abroad and students from home. The rise of transnational education (TNE), which can allow for an international education without crossing borders, demonstrates an imminent "post-mobility world" (White and Lee, 2020). Beyond a formal degree or certificate, student demand for international exposure and cross-cultural knowledge is also growing. Global awareness and intercultural skills have become requisites to work in and be part of today's highly interconnected global society.

Successful internationalization is not segmented to the enrollment and education of students alone. Internationalized faculty are essential, contributing to the geographic mobility and professional development of international educators.

There is also the cross-border movement and collaboration of scholars for research purposes. Knowledge creation between countries tends to strengthen the quality of the work. It also naturally expands academic networks to facilitate far-reaching dissemination and impact. University administrative duties are also globalizing to include the initiation and facilitation of student and scholarly exchange, transnational programs, and other cross-border activities. The growth of international education is further evidenced by global professional associations, such as NAFSA: Association for International Educators, with over 10,000 members representing over one hundred countries worldwide, as well as the proliferation of regional associations in every major region of the world. Clearly, internationalization is progressively central to higher education, and its integration in university core functions is a mainstay.

Regardless of internationalization's form, there is also the indisputable and unstoppable force of globalization on the broader higher education field. We have witnessed higher education's response based on particular attention to global markers, including "world class university" status, multinational benchmarks (i.e., United Nations' Sustainable Development Goals), global rankings, and international publication outlets, to name some examples. And the curriculum, whether delivered at home or abroad, is also internationalizing to consider the highly varied contexts in which disciplinary fields operate and the diverse cultural frameworks from which to draw meanings and interpretations. This common global sphere in which higher education institutions function is inseparable from an evolving sense of legitimacy that is also becoming international. For an institution to isolate from globalized standards and pressures would mean risking its own reputation as a perceived "quality" institution.

CHANGING GLOBAL FORCES

Globalization is commonly understood as a persisting force, but global crises are possible and the ways that higher education responds are intricately tied to global events. Starting in early 2020, the world underwent a massive halt in travel and in-person gatherings due to the coronavirus disease 2019 (COVID-19). Immediate pivots to distance learning, online-adapted meetings and conferences, and other sudden diverting of higher education activities were unprecedented. COVID-19 had, in many ways, made clear that higher education cannot operate in a silo, despite past attempts to study and address it as such, but rather has always been highly subject to external social, economic, and political forces. The pandemic also revealed the ability of universities to quickly and flexibly transform in the midst of crisis and uncertainty. In the medium term, COVID-19 has most notably impacted student mobility, forms of educational delivery across borders, and other face-to-face activities, but will likely also have lasting effects in the new post-pandemic world. What international higher education will look like in the more distant future will at least partly be subject to varying and shifting relations with countries abroad.

While higher education organizations were busy managing their reduced international deliveries in response to the pandemic, bigger changes were occurring on a geopolitical scale. During the writing of this book, the two global superpowers, the United States and China, were entering into a "new cold war." Given that the United States and China are also the biggest players in the mobility of students and research collaboration, this rivalry created further challenges in university operations and planning. Even before COVID-19, escalating tensions between these two countries had already led to numerous U.S. proposals and enactments related to limiting student visas, withholding research funding, and surveilling scientists, as well as furthering an inhospitable climate for internationals in the United States, all of which directly impact university activities (Lee, 2019). Thus, as the book aims to demonstrate, international higher education has long been a reflection of, and will continually be shaped by, geopolitical interests.

INTERNATIONALIZATION AS GLOBAL POWER

A new conceptualization of internationalization is needed to acknowledge and to center the role of power in international higher education. Internationalization, commonly referred to as a process, is hardly neutral. Both globalization and internationalization have become synonymous with Westernization (Mok, 2007; Yang, 2002). To approach internationalization without critical awareness, one overlooks the relative power dynamics between participating countries, institutions, and individuals and inadvertently maintains the global status quo. Rather than placing energies on programmatic efficiencies and immediate revenue gains, internationalization has the potential to transform the global higher education system, with far-reaching benefits for broader society. Yet doing so first requires an acknowledgment that the world is vastly unequal and oftentimes unfair.

Inequalities throughout the world are indisputable, with clear regional differences in wealth (Credit Suisse, 2019). While between-country inequality has modestly declined, the increasing within-country inequality could lead to global inequality rising again (Qureshi, 2017), especially in the post-pandemic era. Differentiating terms such as the Global North and Global South, or centers and peripheries, although overly sweeping, are still used today to make plain the vast disparities in wealth and influence between predominantly Anglo regions and the rest. Such inequalities have spilled over to higher education, with institutions throughout the world facing vast differences in resources, including resources to internationalize. Even capacity-building projects have been observed as reproducing coloniality when quality is determined by Western norms (Madsen and

Adriansen, 2020). Dependency is furthered when universities or organizations, typically from the Global North, position themselves as providers by identifying and creating a market for what the rest of the world "needs." In effect, academic capitalism has largely determined the extent to which, but especially how, internationalization operates (Cantwell and Kauppinen, 2014). While internationalization is seemingly and idealistically portrayed as cooperation between nations, neoliberal agendas, in reality, have fueled competition over collaboration, especially when quality is associated with rank, selectivity, or other zero-sum criteria on the global stage. University partnerships in the globalizing world can reflect strategic tactics to make organizational gains in the pursuit of "excellence." In short, international education activities, including those who participate in them, are seldom on a level playing field or without self-interested agendas, whether they be in accumulating resources or raising reputations. As this book will demonstrate, the global imbalance of resources and power can be preserved or even furthered through existing higher education practices.

In essence, power is central to social science and particularly evidenced in international affairs (Hearn, 2012). As stated by Bertrand Russell (2004), "The fundamental concept of social science is Power, in the same sense in which Energy is the fundamental concept in physics" (p. 4), or as simply put by Michel Foucault (1998), "Power is everywhere" and "comes from everywhere" (p. 63). The dominance of the English language is the clearest example of "Western" power in international education, with major implications on where and what students study, the location of institutional partners, and the research enterprise. Universities in Anglophone countries are clearly advantaged. The mobility of international students and scholars and TNE programs have favored the United States, the United Kingdom (UK), Australia, and Canada for individuals seeking to learn or improve their English as well as fluent English speakers who prefer to study in their primary or sole language. Universities based in Anglophone countries are preferred for international partnerships and exchange as well, facilitating their accumulating advantage in resources, reputation, and networks. The world's majority are thereby not just on a lower playing field but further penalized. For non-Anglophone countries seeking to globalize, English as the dominant linguistic medium impacts country language policies but with costly limitations related to the extent and quality of English language delivery (Byun et al., 2010). For some of these countries, extensive English usage represents a perceived threat to national identity and culture (Saarinen, 2020). Despite these and other hurdles, English remains the uncontested global platform of communication.

Yet, English did not just happen to be the world's lingua franca without centuries of linguistic imperialism that is still in effect today (Phillipson, 2018). While English is the most commonly spoken language in academia, it is only the third-most-spoken language on the planet, following Mandarin Chinese and Spanish. And although a third of the 27,000 peer-reviewed scholarly journals are being published in languages other than English, they are excluded from prestigious journal indexes, such as the prominent Science Citation Index (Curry and Lillis, 2018). The implications of English as the single global language of scholarly publishing are several. Most notably, Anglophone countries are privileged in the global rankings given that indexed publications are a key criteria metric. The rest of the world's majority are thereby disadvantaged with the added workload and expenses in translating their work. More worrisome than the hegemony of the language is the hegemony of ideas (Tietze and Dick, 2013), in which hegemonic discourses are being reinforced in Anglophone journals (Meriläinen, Tienari, Thomas, and Davies, 2008; Paasi, 2005). As stated by Tietze and Dick (2013), "Whenever English is used, meaning is shaped in such a way that it privileges the worldview and the economic–political interests of (United States) English-speaking groups by 'glossing over' alternate meaning systems" (p. 123). Loss of local knowledge can result. Research based on local contexts outside the West and then exported for global, English-speaking audiences may be compromised and offer less value to the originating research communities (Curry and Lillis, 2018). Moreover, a hierarchy of "Englishes" exist, with a preference for Anglo-American varieties, including those of the United States, Canada, UK, Australia, New Zealand, and Ireland (Saarinen and Nikula, 2013). Native English speakers from any of the approximately fifty countries where English is also an official language, such as India, Pakistan, Nigeria, or South Africa, are not always accepted as meeting English language proficiency requirements (Saarinen and Nikula, 2013). In sum, the use of English is not simply a neutral or convenient vehicle for internationalization. Rather, as invoked by Antonio Gramsci, global English is intricately tied to power dynamics and global politics (Ives, 2009). This book, as written in English, is no exception.

A REVISED DEFINITION OF INTERNATIONALIZATION

Therefore, power must be made explicit in how internationalization is defined. As among the most cited definitions in the field, internationalization in higher education has been commonly referred to as "the process of integrating an international, intercultural or global dimension into the purpose, functions or delivery of post-secondary education" (Knight, 2004, p. 11). This "more generic" definition by Jane Knight evolved from earlier versions (Arum and van de Water, 1992; Knight, 1994) to provide greater relevance to a wider range of sector/national levels and providers (Knight, 2004, p. 12). Since then, Hans de Wit and Fiona Hunter (2015) called for an extension of the concept to indicate "the *intentional* process of integrating an international, intercultural or global dimension into the purpose, functions *and* delivery of post-secondary education, *in order to enhance the quality of education and research for all students and staff, and to make a meaningful contribution to society*" (p. 3). Among their proposed contributions were to indicate greater intentionality, more inclusivity and less elitism, and a greater emphasis on outcomes to include quality within and beyond the institution (Hunter, 2015).

Yet, this also highly cited and seemingly benign extended definition was the subject of debate. In response to the authors' attempt to suggest a moral compass, questions about its universality arose. Damtew Teferra (2019a) argued that internationalization is more than an "intention" but can be a form of "coercion and contestation" for African countries as well as the broader Global South. Indeed, not all international education processes have benefited all of society. Much of international education's early history from the Global North to the Global South was rooted in settler colonialism (White, 1996), and these colonial legacies remain (Majee and Ress, 2020). Teferra (2019b) further warned that the foregrounding of "internationality" reinforces "internationalisation as a continuation of the neo-colonial project which the Global South needs to do away with, as part of the struggle against neo-colonialism and colonisation" (para. 11). In short, whose "intention" is being served? De Wit and Hunter's (2015) proposed addition opened up important questions about the ethical purposes of internationalization, which Teferra (2019a; 2019b) suggests necessitates a consideration of where power lies.

Thus, power must be acknowledged in defining internationalization. By making explicit the role of power over assuming any particular intention, the revised conceptualization asserts that disparities exist and that recognizing power is fundamental to understanding as well as addressing internationalization. Without this essential component, internationalization can also include colonialism, imperialism, and exploitation. Thus, in addition to a process, internationalization is also an object of influence (and sometimes dominance), but is all too often left uninterrogated. A proposed updated definition of internationalization is a simple but potentially transformative one: "*the power* and process of integrating an international, intercultural or global dimension into the purpose, functions or delivery of post-secondary education." A key assumption that this book elucidates is that *power is embedded in international higher education regulation, strategies, and activities.*

While the book's reference to power will mostly refer to geopolitical power, stemming from the nation-state or region, power in international higher education can also extend across geographic borders to include international, multinational, and transnational entities and networks. For example, international organizations such as the World Bank, Organisation for Economic Co-operation and Development (OECD), and UNESCO are influential in globalizing higher education policy (Shahjahan, 2012) and potentially reproducing global inequities (Collins and Rhoads, 2010; Shahjahan, 2016). Power can also be observed within a single geographic location, depending on, for instance, forms of government or social group positions, thereby influencing the goals and process of internationalization. Even within a single organizational unit, power dynamics shape which international activities are prioritized, delivered, and measured. The point is that as the original definition makes clear, internationalization encompasses a wide range of actions. The addition of "power" brings attention to whose agenda, whether by regions, countries, organizations, or players, is being advanced, which brings added light on the particular forms of internationalization that are emphasized and how they are enacted.

THE LEADING POWER OF THE UNITED STATES (FOR NOW)

The book's deliberate focus is on the United States. A key indicator of U.S. power in the higher education field is its dominant presence in the major global ranking systems (Hazelkorn, 2016). The United States is home to eight of the ten most highly ranked universities in the world, according to both the Academic Ranking of World Universities (ARWU, 2020), also known as the Shanghai Ranking, and the list of Best Global Universities published by U.S. News and World Report (USNWR, 2020). The United States also occupies forty-one of the top one hundred positions in the ARWU (2020) and forty of the top one hundred places in the Times's World University Rankings, which is about four times as many as the second leading country, the UK (Times Higher Education, 2020). These rankings correspond with the ability of the United States to attract top students and scholars from abroad. The United States is the largest host of international students in the world, educating over 1 million students from abroad (Institute of International Education [IIE], 2020). International scholars are also drawn to the country as U.S. universities lead in top research-producing institutions (top twenty-two of fifty, top forty-four of one hundred) (Nature Index, 2020). The United States is also the world's leading international collaborator (Nature Index, 2020). As the rankings criteria further reflect, the United States has long been the world's top research and development (R&D) performer and leads in scientific impact, as measured by publication citations (NSB, 2020).

Besides the United States drawing talent and international networks throughout the world, the country's positional power strongly dictates what internationalization should look like, how it is measured, and who participates. Past research has found that universities all over the world are building legitimacy via external criteria (i.e., global rankings metrics), likening their strategies to those at the highest ranks (Liu, 2020; Stensaker et al., 2019), which are largely dominated by U.S. institutions (ARWU, 2020; Times Higher Education, 2020; USNWR, 2020). A related study further found that this pursuit toward global status can come at the cost of local needs (Lee, Vance, Stensaker, and Ghosh, 2020). Internationalization that is narrowly determined by neoliberal values allows particular countries and their institutions access (see chapter 8 by Dale La Fleur).

Emerging economies, notably China, India, and South Korea, are the biggest buyers when it comes to the selling of U.S. higher education abroad, at least in the form of international student enrollment. Meanwhile, internationalization in African countries has been described as a product "not by participation but by omission" that is largely determined by the Global North (Teferra, 2019a; 2019b). The United States also influences how quality is measured (i.e., accreditation) (see chapter 4 by Gerardo L. Blanco) and even what is considered to be "internationally competent" (see chapter 8 by Chris Glass and chapter 9 by Sharon Stein).

Despite the supremacy of the United States, its number one position is not guaranteed. A global population study reveals that China is on course to replace the United States as the country with the largest total gross domestic product (GDP) globally by 2035 (Vollset et al., 2020). According to the authors, the decline in the population of working-age adults alone will reduce GDP growth, resulting in major shifts in global economic power. The United States' place as the largest host of the world's top universities is also not permanent. The UK's high status is also vulnerable. According to the Times's longitudinal analysis (Bothwell, 2019), the United States' and the UK's shares in the global rankings are shrinking while those of other countries are emerging. China was the sixth-most-represented country among the top 200 global university rankings, despite not being in the top 10 five years ago, and South Korea rose as well. According to the Quacquarelli Symonds (QS, 2020) World University Rankings, most U.S. and UK universities fell from their previous positions. This drop was mostly attributable to their relative decline in measures of academic standing and research impact (University World News, 2020). Universities located in Asian and Middle Eastern countries, on the other hand, rose (QS, 2020). These patterns are not simply a matter of internal efforts but reflect changing geopolitical dynamics (see chapter 3 by Ellen Hazelkorn).

Another area in which the United States has suffered is the extent of U.S. students obtaining an international education. While it is arguable that being the leading destination for the world's internationals would support internationalization efforts at home, international students make up only 5 percent of all students at U.S. universities, whereas the percentages are much higher elsewhere, such as in Luxembourg (48%), Australia (27%), and New Zealand (20%) (OECD, 2020). There is also ample evidence indicating that internationals do not fully integrate with locals, experiencing challenges in forging relationships with domestic peers and social isolation in classroom settings (Lee and Rice, 2007; Wu, Garza, and Guzman, 2015). Furthermore, in comparison with the inbound numbers from abroad, U.S. students tend not to study abroad at the same rate. The proportion of U.S. students studying outside the country is less than a third of the total number of internationals studying in the United States (347,099), with over half going to Europe for a few weeks or for the summer

(IIE, 2020). As a collective, the European Union (EU) hosts far more students (1.7 million), with over a third from within Europe (657,900) (Eurostat, 2020). These outbound numbers for both the United States and EU pale in comparison with China, which sends almost a million students abroad (UNESCO, 2020).

China has also outpaced the United States and the EU in scientific knowledge production. Though the EU's twenty-eight countries lead the world in research output (NSB, 2020), the United States has been the top single-country producer of research publications for decades. In 2017, China surpassed the United States and is now the top country in generating scientific knowledge (NSB, 2020). And although the United States and the UK also produce a substantial volume of the world's publications, numerous countries exceed the two countries' average growth rate of about 1 percent, such as Iran (11%), India (11%), Russia (10%), China (8%), Brazil (5%), and South Korea (4%) (NSB, 2018). China's citation measure remains less than that of the United States or the EU, but it is climbing (NSB, 2020). These trends mirror similar patterns based on a country's level of economic development. The publication rates of high-income countries have mostly flattened (1% increase per year), and those of upper-middle-income countries have been steadily climbing (9% increase per year) (NSB, 2019). R&D spending reflects similar patterns. U.S. R&D spending accounted for twenty percent of the global growth between 2000 and 2017 whereas China's contribution rose to almost one-third (32%) (NSB, 2020). When it comes to research collaboration between the United States and China, the United States trails China in first authorship and funding (see chapter 5 by John Haupt and Jenny Lee).

Given China's fast-rising status as a global superpower and now leader in the world's scientific research production, China is in a unique position to challenge a global system that has long been dominated by the West (i.e., Anglo America and Western Europe). During February 2020, China's Ministry of Education and Ministry of Science and Technology issued a joint announcement related to reforming research evaluations, including de-emphasizing the number of publications or citations in the Science Citation Index (SCI), as well as any publishing bonuses, in an effort to more directly address concerns within the country's context ("China changes tack," 2020; Huang, 2020). China has long criticized the "blind pursuit of rankings" and an overreliance on "papers only, professional titles only, academic qualifications only, or awards only," in favor of a more holistic review to assess quality (Yan, 2020, p. 2). Before this reform announcement, China, as well as other countries, had expressed dissatisfaction with how governmental and university funds were being used toward mostly Western European and U.S. publishers, and then spent additional funds to access their own research articles at full price (Schiermeier, 2018). For lower-income countries, the unaffordability of journal subscriptions placed them even further toward the scientific "periphery" (Chan, Kirsop, and Arunachalam, 2008). These new geopolitical realities will undoubtedly shape the international higher education field. Not just in the *process* by which internationalization happens, but also in the *power dynamics* between participating countries. U.S. dominance is not ensured, which also helps explain how and why international education became a geopolitical concern.

U.S. GEOPOLITICAL STRATEGIES IN INTERNATIONAL EDUCATION

International education activities have long been operated by the U.S. State Department rather than the U.S. Department of Education. Simply put, international education is not solely a traditional education pursuit. U.S.-sponsored international education exchange programs, such as the highly regarded U.S. Fulbright Program since 1946, are overseen by the Bureau of Educational and Cultural Affairs (ECA), which is in the Public Diplomacy and Public Affairs branch in the U.S. State Department. The ECA's mission is "to increase mutual understanding between the people of the United States and the people of other countries by means of educational and cultural exchange that assist in the development of peaceful relations" (U.S. Department of State, 2020). Other offices within the ECA include the Office of Academic Exchange Programs, the Office of English Language Programs, and the Office of Global Educational Programs, including the U.S. Study Abroad branch, all supporting international education activities that would normally be considered within Education but instead are within Public Affairs. This distinction is important in recognizing that in the case of the United States especially, international education is key to fostering positive U.S. relations abroad over the education of students. And yet, international education tends to be narrowly understood by universities and professional associations as an educational rather than a geopolitical endeavor.

Education in the United States is decentralized, meaning schooling responsibilities, including whether or how internationalization is carried out, are left to the states and local districts. On the federal level, the specific role of the U.S. Department of Education is fourfold, including setting federal financial aid policies, collecting national data and overseeing research, identifying and bringing awareness to national problems, and enforcing civil rights statutes to ensure equal educational opportunities (U.S. Department of Education, 2020). In 2012, the U.S. Department of Education took on a more geopolitical role from its previous domestic focus. The department released its first-ever international strategy, which stressed the importance of "a globally competent citizenry" with a focus on U.S. economic competitiveness. The report stated:

> The international strategy for 2012–16 affirms the Department's commitment to preparing today's youth, and our country more broadly, *for a globalized world, and to engaging with the international community to improve education.*

> ... It is no longer enough to solely focus on ensuring that students have essential reading, writing, mathematic and science skills. Our hyper-connected world also requires the ability to think critically and creatively to solve complex problems, *the skills and disposition to engage globally*, well-honed communication skills, and advanced mathematics, science and technical skills. Such competencies will prepare students, and our nation, for a world in which the following are the reality. (U.S. Department of Education, 2012, p. 2, emphasis added)

According to the report, disposition and skills for global engagement are introduced as newly added educational competency goals for U.S. students. The department also introduced an internationalization framework, with two primary goals: strengthening U.S. education and advancing the nation's international priorities. The national agenda here is clear: international education is to serve national advancement interests.

International education as a geopolitical tool has not been pursued by the federal government alone. International education organizations have long pushed for a comprehensive national policy on internationalization, dating back to 1999. According to a joint statement by NAFSA and the Alliance for International Education and Cultural Exchange, titled "An International Education Policy for US Leadership, Competitiveness, and Security,"

> international education is more important than ever for U.S. international leadership and security. Alliances matter. International relationships matter. European leaders worry about the implications for the Atlantic Alliance as the United States loses its decades-old status as the preferred destination for Europeans to study abroad. Leaders of friendly countries in the Middle East worry about a "lost generation" of future Arab leaders who will not be educated in the United States because of post-September 11 visa issues. We should worry too. These leaders understand that exchange relationships sustain political relationships; if one atrophies, sooner or later the other will too. Having fewer future world leaders study in the United States will inevitably translate into a loss of U.S. international influence down the road. (NAFSA, 2006, p. 2)

Such geopolitical intentions, combined with the vast educational resources and opportunities as an international host and partner, create the conditions for the exercise of soft power, commonly referred to as a persuasive, rather than coercive, approach to international relations, typically involving the use of economic or cultural influence (Nye, 2004). As Roopa Desai Trilokekar delves further in chapter 2, international education and foreign policy have long been closely linked. International education becomes a form of soft power to promote national interests abroad as well as position the host country as a global leader in international higher education. Chrystal George Mwangi, Sean Jung-Hau Chen, and

Pempho Chinkondenji observe that one-sided U.S. interests were predominant in university internationalization plans (see chapter 7). The problem with this approach is that nationalism, which prioritizes a particular political agenda over discovery, not only runs counter to the spirit of internationalization but also downgrades higher education (Cantwell and Lee, 2020). For example, competition for international students as "commodities," as Christina Yao criticizes in chapter 9, dehumanizes students and undermines the social purposes of international education.

International higher education has also taken on new challenges. As nation-states are globalizing, they are also retracting. The rise in populism, along with protectionist ideologies, has fueled a wave of nationalism throughout the world that has sought to secure migration borders, figuratively and physically. Immigration reform is a leading political concern, with hotly contested policies and proposals to limit particular groups, oftentimes positioned as scapegoats for the failed promises of globalization. According to Stein Emil Vollset and colleagues (2020), U.S. population declines, and the United States' number one global position, could be offset by immigration as well as reverse the trend that has China's economy surpassing that of the United States by 2035. Yet despite the overwhelming evidence that this and countless studies have demonstrated regarding the benefits that migrants offer, political rationales have superseded economic ones.

The concept of neo-racism, introduced to the field of higher education over a decade ago (Lee and Rice, 2007), is now clearly evidenced in federal policies. Neo-racism refers to discrimination against particular populations on the basis of culture between ethnic groups. Beyond biological racism, neo-racism is tied to national superiority and used to justify maintaining a particular culture in which some internationals are posed as a threat (Balibar, 2005). Ultimately, neo-racism is rooted in white supremacy on a global scale (Stein & de Andreotti, 2016; Suspitsyna, & Shalka, 2019). In the United States, this includes travel bans against those from Muslim-majority countries, limiting the duration of study visas for Chinese students, and more recently, the proposed deportation of international students at universities that are fully online, in response to COVID-19. There is also rising suspicion about malicious intent from abroad. The U.S. Justice Department launched the China Initiative, aiming to investigate the transfer of U.S. knowledge to China (U.S. Department of Justice, 2018). In the years that followed, Chinese scientists have been closely monitored out of fear that they are engaging in espionage. Such concerns position universities as "vulnerable" knowledge producers in the current geopolitical climate (Lee, 2019). Bibliometric evidence suggests that such neo-racist fears about the "China Threat" could impede global scientific advancement between the two global superpowers and that the United States has much more to gain than lose in collaborating with China (see chapter 7 by John Haupt and Jenny Lee). International postdocs and graduate students as imported scientific labor have furthered the United States' national advantage but may decline as anti-immigration policies continue (see chapter 8 by Brendan Cantwell). Internationalization will thus likely take on different forms in the years to come, particularly in light of potential pandemics, such as COVID-19, which is having a drastic effect on international meetings, travel, and in-person classes and will undoubtedly spill over into the postpandemic world. In light of these simultaneous factors, there will likely be more selective international engagement, combined with increasing outside dependencies amid rising suspicions.

For these reasons, the book's focus on the United States is intended to caution U.S. readers that the country's dominant position is not guaranteed and, more importantly, to inform all readers about the ways that national power can surface in international higher education policy and practices. The geopolitical phenomena and associated implications are not limited to the United States alone. Rather, the United States' concentration of geopolitical power makes the arguments quite clear and leaves it up to readers in other countries to draw similar parallels based on their own insider experiences and local expertise.

AIMS AND OVERVIEW OF THE BOOK

The book is based on the premise that internationalization in higher education is not only an educational endeavor but also a geopolitical one. Unlike many academic texts in the market today, the book's aim is not to advance a single theory. There is no one-size-fits-all theoretical or conceptual frame that encompasses all the complexities of internationalization, although there have been past attempts to do so. Rather, the book proposes a range of critical outlooks across a range of activities to make the broader case for the need to more critically examine *how power shapes the international higher education field*. In asserting the role of power in internationalization, we "carve the boundaries, practice, paradigm and discourse of that phenomenon," as Teferra (2019b, para. 4) advocates in defining internationalization. The broader sociological frames, such as postcolonial theory, neo-nationalism, and others, are not intended to limit but rather expose a range of critical viewpoints on activities that are approached or reported all too often neutrally. In essence, this book seeks to problematize rather than offer pat solutions.

While there is no denying that global inequalities exist, there has been a disregard for the role and relative power of universities in particular countries over their international so-called partners in policy and implementation. International higher education professionals are among the targeted audience for this book as they play an essential part in addressing issues of power in practice directly in the field. Individual actions have the potential to become collective actions, whether intentional or not. There is a dearth of acknowledgment in the professional field, especially within university international affairs, about the ways that higher education actors might unintentionally perpetuate existing power imbalances or even further them. Part of the reason may have to do with how internationalization has been framed as a neutral process rather than a political one. In their study of how internationalization was conceptualized by the leading professional associations, NAFSA, the International Association of Universities, and the European Association of International Education (EAIE), Elizabeth Buckner and Sharon Stein (2020) observed a "blind spot" on unequal relations of power, with current approaches focusing on technical implementation over ethical engagement. Yet even among the most critically minded professionals, organizational interests may not always align (Deschamps and Lee, 2015). Put another way, at-will employees' survival is dependent on the employing organization's agenda, which may not always reflect equity concerns. Rather than being critical areas of inquiry, power and resources become functional tools to meet institutional objectives such as the financial bottom line, enrollment counts, and expanded programs (Deschamps and Lee, 2015). Critical debate may be silenced or objection to an organization's goals may be frowned on. Administrators' agency only goes so far as to the reaches of the employer's interests. Professional development is largely tied to the delivery of services but very little to moral responsibility, which is left to institutional agendas. The danger is that unless power is made explicit and recognized, particularly by those on the front lines of international education, the global status quo is left unchecked and perpetuated.

Thus, as international activities broaden and proliferate, it is high time to remove the blinders and make plain the unevenness of internationalization and call for greater moral responsibility in the process. This is not the first text to do so as there have been mounting calls to promote balanced and ethical international higher education approaches (Castiello-Gutiérrez, 2019; de Wit, 2020; International Education Association of South Africa [IEASA], 2014). Rather, this book centers the role of power as a requisite to meaningful change, especially in the post-COVID world. To accomplish this objective, the book provides in-depth accounts of the varied ways that power operates in policy, the international higher education field, and universities in commonly known forms of international higher education today. Thus, in order to be kind, inclusive, and respectful, we must first be critically aware. By embracing questions of power, we are able to gain a more empathetic understanding of others and facilitate social change (Hearn, 2012).

Using the United States as a case example, this book uncovers existing power dynamics in international higher education, which have yet to be fully taken into account when promoting internationalization programs or recognizing the responsibilities of internationalization actors. In the following chapters, ten key international higher education topics (as they relate to power) will be showcased. The overarching questions include: How is power evident in U.S. higher education internationalization activities? What are the various geopolitical forces and how do they contribute to U.S. dominance? The chapters are organized on a scale from the global, to the institutional, and then to the individual, while offering a range of perspectives from inside and outside the United States, including postcolonial, neo-national, and other critical frameworks that examine dominant power relations.

Part I is "Geopolitics and Regulation of Higher Education" and provides evidence of past and current U.S. soft power. First, Roopa Desai Trilokekar outlines the ways that international education and soft power are intertwined, based on her analysis of U.S. governmental policies throughout history. She demonstrates the usage of international education as a soft power foreign policy tool. Next, Ellen Hazelkorn discusses how rankings are not just a tool to compare institutions but a reflection of "historical competitive advantage," with powerful influence at all levels of government and institutional governance. In the final chapter of this section, about accreditation, Gerardo L. Blanco discusses how U.S. accreditation has become a global standard for quality assurance, which in turn promotes the United States' role in setting the standards of best practices.

Part II, "National and Global Research," examines the geopolitical landscape of scientific knowledge production. In the first chapter of this section, John P. Haupt and Jenny J. Lee provide a more recent case of how the current U.S.-China trade war has spilled over into the higher education sector, with negative implications not only for STEM (science, technology, engineering, and mathematics) scholars but also for U.S. knowledge production. Next, Brendan Cantwell writes about the geopolitical implications of international graduate education and postdoctoral training in the United States. He argues that internationalization of graduate education and scientific training is an example of the way U.S. institutions have exploited globalization processes to leverage individual, institutional, and, national advantages from the labor and expertise of internationally mobile researchers.

Part III, "University Internationalization Strategies," begins with Chrystal A. George Mwangi, Sean Jung-Hau Chen, and Pempho Chinkondenji's critical analysis of campus internationalization strategies. They demonstrate ways that international strategies serve as geopolitical tools that reflect one-sided benefits in favor of U.S. universities and their states/regions, with limited mention of possible benefits for their international partners. Among these tactics is the establishment of university partnerships and dual degrees. In the next chapter, Dale LaFleur observes that U.S. institutions are often sought for prestige by international institutions seeking to heighten their global rankings. In exchange, the U.S. institutions gain access to new student markets. She identifies ways that neoliberalism has shaped international university partnerships.

In the first chapter of part IV, "Students and International Learning," Christina W. Yao discusses the commodification of students and how their mobility contributes to the United States' overall pursuit of academic imperialism through economic gain, institutional visibility, and international prestige. She critiques the current discourse that commodifies students as imports and exports, all of which contributes to the United States' academic imperialism. Another area that has received increasing attention is how student learning is evaluated. Chris R. Glass provides a critical examination that explores ways that U.S. economic competitiveness and national security have tied into the global competency discourse. He then discusses what he refers to as the "hidden frame of global competence," which lacks reference to geography, stratification, politics, and non-Western views of the self. A popular approach in addressing global competency has been through internationalizing the curriculum. In the final chapter of this section, Sharon Stein argues that such efforts can serve as an extension of U.S. power, making the U.S. curriculum "universal." She then offers a critical framework for distinguishing between and assessing different orientations to internationalizing the curriculums.

Finally, the book ends with some reflections of moving forward toward more inclusive and equitable forms of internationalization. Reflecting on the historical contexts and on the unintended (or intended) consequences of U.S. geopolitical influence in the field as demonstrated in the book, the final chapter, by Jenny J. Lee and Santiago Castiello-Gutiérrez, calls for critical action toward more equitable forms of global engagement. Such actions must stem from collective voices, both from those in contexts that have perpetuated current inequities and from those whose voices, knowledges, and forms of knowing have been marginalized. Actors at both ends and across all of the power spectrum should jointly reimagine policies and practices of internationalization beyond national interests. We are facing unprecedented times that require unprecedented actions to transform ourselves and our institutions in preparation for a new era.

REFERENCES

Academic Ranking of World Universities. (2020, August 15). Shanghai Ranking's Academic Ranking of World Universities 2020 [Press release]. Retrieved from http://www.shanghairanking.com/Academic-Ranking-of-World-Universities-2020-Press-Release.html

Arum, S., and van de Water, J. (1992). The need for a definition of international education in U.S. universities. In C. Klasek (Ed.), *Bridges to the future: Strategies for internationalizing higher education* (pp. 191–203). Carbondale, IL: Association of International Education Administrators.

Balibar, E. (2005). Racism and nationalism. In P. Spencer and H. Wollman (Eds.), *Nations and nationalism: A reader* (pp. 163–172). New Brunswick, NJ: Rutgers University Press.

Bothwell, E. (2019, September 11). THE World University Rankings 2020: China powers up. *Times Higher Education*. Retrieved from https://www.timeshighereducation.com/world-university-rankings/world-university-rankings-2020-china-powers

Buckner, E., and Stein, S. (2020). What counts as internationalization? Deconstructing the internationalization imperative. *Journal of Studies in International Education*, 24(2), 151–166.

Byun, K., Chu, H., Kim, M., Park, I., Kim, S., and Jung, J. (2010). English-medium teaching in Korean higher education: Policy debates and reality. *Higher Education*, 62(4), 431–449.

Cantwell, B., and Kauppinen, I. (2014). *Academic capitalism in the age of globalization.* Baltimore, MD: Johns Hopkins University Press.

Cantwell, B., and Lee, J. J. (2020). The impossibility of the nationalist university. *University World News*. Retrieved from https://www.https://www.universityworldnews.com/post.php?story=20200724132403482

Castiello-Gutiérrez, S. (2019, March 1). Reframing internationalisation's values and principles. *University World News*. Retrieved from https://www.universityworldnews.com/post.php?story=20190225085141576

Chan, L., Kirsop, B., and Arunachalam, S. (2008). Open access archiving: The fast track to building research capacity in developing countries. *Science Development Network*. Retrieved from https://www.scidev.net/global/communication/feature/open-access-archiving-the-fast-track-to-building-r.html

China changes tack: A new researcher-evaluation system must not reduce international collaborations [Editorial]. (2020). *Nature*, 579, 8.

Collins, C. S., and Rhoads, R. A. (2010). The World Bank, support for universities, and asymmetrical power relations in international development. *Higher Education*, 59(2), 181–205.

Credit Suisse (2019). Global wealth report 2019. Retrieved from https://www.credit-suisse.com/about-us/en/reports-research/global-wealth-report.html

Curry, M. J., and Lillis, T. (2018, March 13). The dangers of English as lingua franca of journals. *Inside Higher Education*. Retrieved from https://www.insidehighered.com/views/2018/03/13/domination-english-language-journal-publishing-hurting-scholarship-many-countries

de Wit, H. (2020). Internationalization of higher education: The need for a more ethical and qualitative approach. *Journal of International Students*, 10(1): i–iv.

de Wit, H., and Hunter, F. (2015). The future of internationalization of higher education in Europe. *International Higher Education*, 83, 2–3.

Deschamps, E., and Lee, J. J. (2015). Internationalization as mergers and acquisitions: Senior international officers' entrepreneurial strategies and activities in public universities. *Journal of Studies in International Education*, 19, 122–139.

Eurostat (2020). Learning mobility statistics. Retrieved from https://ec.europa.eu/eurostat/statistics-explained/index.php/Learning_mobility_statistics#Number_and_share_of_students_from_abroad

Foucault, Michel (1998) *The history of sexuality: The will to knowledge.* London, England: Penguin.

Hazelkorn, E. (Ed.). (2016). *Global rankings and the geopolitics of higher education: Understanding the influence and impact of rankings on higher education, policy and society.* https://doi.org/10.4324/9781315738550

Hearn, J. S. (2012). *Theorizing power.* London: Palgrave Macmillan.

Huang, F. (2020, February 26). China is choosing its own path on academic evaluation. *University World News*. Retrieved from https://www.universityworldnews.com/post.php?story=20200226122508451

Hunter, F. (2015, October 5). What's in a name? Refocusing internationalisation of higher education. *EAIE Blog*. Retrieved from https://www.eaie.org/blog/whats-in-a-name-refocusing-internationalisation-of-higher-education.html

Institute of International Education. (2020). Open doors: Fast facts 2020. Retrieved from https://www.iie.org/Why-IIE/Announcements/2020/11/2020-Open-Doors-Report

International Education Association of South Africa. (2014). *Nelson Mandela Bay global dialogue declaration on the future of internationalisation of higher education.* Retrieved from https://www.eaie.org/dam/jcr:86722ac9-fc8f-44c7-bc41-8dce7e290258/Global%20Dialogue%202014%20Declaration.pdf

Ives, P. (2009). Global English, hegemony and education: Lessons from Gramsci. *Educational Philosophy and Theory,* 41(6), 661–683.

Knight, J. (1994). *Internationalization: Elements and checkpoints* (Research Monograph, No. 7). Ottawa, Canada: Canadian Bureau for International Education.

———. (2004). Internationalization remodeled: Definition, approaches, and rationales. *Journal of Studies in International Education,* 8(1), 5–31.

Lee, J. J. (2019, November 9). Universities, neo-nationalism and the 'China threat.' *University World News.* Retrieved from https://www.universityworldnews.com/post.php?story=20191105074754722

Lee, J. J., and Rice, C. (2007). Welcome to America? International student perceptions of discrimination. *Higher Education,* 53(3), 381–409.

Lee, J. J., Vance, H., Stensaker, B., and Ghosh, S. (2020). Global rankings at a local cost? The strategic pursuit of status and the third mission. *Comparative Education.* doi:10.1080/03050068.2020.1741195

Liu, W. (2020). The Chinese definition of internationalization in higher education. *Journal of Higher Education Policy and Management.* doi:10.1080/1360080X.2020.1777500

Madsen, L. M., and Adriansen, H. K. (2020): Transnational research capacity building: Whose standards count? *Critical African Studies.* doi:10.1080/21681392.2020.1724807

Majee, U. S., and Ress, S. B. (2020). Colonial legacies in internationalisation of higher education: Racial justice and geopolitical redress in South Africa and Brazil. *Compare: A Journal of Comparative and International Education,* 50(4), 463–481.

Meriläinen, S., Tienari, J., Thomas, R., and Davies, A. (2008). Hegemonic academic practices: Experiences of publishing from the periphery. *Organization,* 15(4), 584–597.

Mok, K. H. (2007). Questing for internationalization of universities in Asia: Critical reflections. *Journal of Studies in International Education,* 11(3–4), 433–454.

NAFSA: Association of International Educators. (2006). *An international education policy for US leadership, competitiveness, and security.* Retrieved from https://www.nafsa.org/sites/default/files/media/document/NIEP2006.pdf

National Science Board (2020). *The State of U.S. Science and Engineering 2020.* National Science Board: Science and Engineering Indicators. Retrieved from https://ncses.nsf.gov/pubs/nsb20201

———. (2019). *Publications Output: U.S. Trends and International Comparisons.* National Science Board: Science and Engineering Indicators. Retrieved from https://ncses.nsf.gov/pubs/nsb20206/publication-output-by-region-country-or-economy

———. (2018). *Science and engineering indicators 2018.* . National Science Board: Science and Engineering Indicators. Retrieved from https://www.nsf.gov/statistics/2018/nsb20181/report.

Nature Index (2020). Connected world: Patterns of international collaboration captured by the Nature Index. Retrieved from https://www.natureindex.com/annual-tables/2020

Nye, J. S., Jr. (2004). *Soft power: The means to success in world politics.* New York: Public Affairs.

Organisation for Economic Co-operation and Development (2020), *Education at a Glance 2020: OECD Indicators*, OECD Publishing, Paris, https://doi.org/10.1787/69096873-en

Paasi, A. (2005). Globalisation, academic capitalism, and the uneven geographies of international journal publishing spaces. *Environment and Planning A,* 37(5), 769–789.

Phillipson, R. (2018). Linguistic imperialism. In *The encyclopedia of applied linguistics*, C.A. Chapelle (Ed.). https://doi.org/10.1002/9781405198431.wbeal0718.pub2

Quacquarelli Symonds. (2020). QS world university rankings 2021. Retrieved from https://www.topuniversities.com/university-rankings/world-university-rankings/2021

Qureshi, Z. (2017). Trends in income inequality: Global, inter-country, and within countries. Retrieved from https://www.brookings.edu/wp-content/uploads/2017/12/global-inequality.pdf

Russell, B. (2004). Power: A new social analysis. https://doi.org/10.4324/9780203506530

Saarinen, T. (2020). Higher education, language and new nationalism in Finland: Recycled histories. Palgrave-Macmillan.

Saarinen, T., and Nikula, T. (2013). Implicit policy, invisible language: Policies and practices of international degree programmes in Finnish higher education. In A. Doiz, D. Lasagabaster, and J. Sierra (Eds.), *English-medium instruction at universities: Global challenges* (pp. 131–150). Bristol, England: Multilingual Matters.

Schiermeier, Q. (2018). China backs bold plan to tear down journal paywalls. *Nature, 564*, 171–172. doi:https://doi. org/10.1038/d41586-018-07659-5

Shahjahan, R. A. (2012). The roles of international organizations (IOs) in globalizing higher education policy. In J. Smart and M. Paulsen (Eds.), *Higher education: Handbook of theory and research* (pp. 369–407). Dordrecht, Netherlands: Springer.

———. (2016). International organizations (IOs), epistemic tools of influence, and the colonial geopolitics of knowledge production in higher education policy. *Journal of Education Policy, 31*(6), 694–710.

Stein, S., & de Andreotti, V. O. (2016). Cash, competition, or charity: International students and the global imaginary. *Higher Education, 72*(2), 225–239.

Stensaker, B., Lee, J. J., Rhoades, G., Ghosh, S., Castiello-Gutiérrez, S., Vance, H., . . . , and Peel, C. (2019). Stratified university strategies: The shaping of institutional legitimacy in a global perspective. *The Journal of Higher Education, 90*(4), 539–562.

Suspitsyna, T., & Shalka, T. R. (2019). The Chinese international student as a (post) colonial other: An analysis of cultural representations of a US media discourse. *The Review of Higher Education, 42*(5), 287–308.

Teferra, D. (2019a, August 23). Defining internationalisation—intention versus coercion. *University World News*. Retrieved from https://www.universityworldnews.com/post.php?story=20190821145329703

Teferra, D. (2019b, September 21). Internationalisation—The search for a definition continues. *University World News*. Retrieved from https://www.universityworldnews.com/post.php?story=20190920065921180

Tietze, S., & Dick, P. (2013). The victorious English language: Hegemonic practices in the management academy. *Journal of Management Inquiry, 22*(1), 122–134.

Times Higher Education. (2020). World University Rankings 2020. Retrieved from https://www.timeshighereducation.com/world-university-rankings/2020/world-ranking

United Nations Educational, Scientific and Cultural Organization. (2020). Education: Outbound internationally mobile students by host region. Retrieved from http://data.uis.unesco.org/Index.aspx?queryid=172

United Nations World Tourism Organization. (2020). International Tourism Growth Continues to Outpace the Global Economy. Retrieved from https://www.unwto.org/international-tourism-growth-continues-to-outpace-the-economy

University World News. (2020, June 10). Asia rises, US, UK, Europe decline in new QS rankings. Retrieved from https://www.universityworldnews.com/post.php?story=20200610154557289

U.S. Department of Education. (2012). Succeeding globally through international education and engagement. Retrieved from https://www2.ed.gov/about/inits/ed/internationaled/international-strategy-2012-16.pdf

———. (2020, February 12). U.S. Department of Education launches investigation into foreign gifts reporting at ivy league universities. Retrieved from https://www.ed.gov/news/press-releases/test-0

U.S. Department of Justice. (2018, December 20). Department of Justice China initiative fact sheet. Retrieved from https://www.justice.gov/opa/page/file/1122686/download

U.S. Department of State. (2020). About educational and cultural affairs. Retrieved from https://eca.state.gov/about-bureau

U.S. News and World Report. (2020). 2021 Best Global Universities Rankings. Retrieved from https://www.usnews.com/education/best-global-universities/rankings?int=a27a09

Vollset, S. E., Goren, E., Yuan, C. W., Cao, J., Smith, A. E., Hsiao, T., . . . & Dolgert, A. J. (2020, July 14). Fertility, mortality, migration, and population scenarios for 195 countries and territories from 2017 to 2100: A forecasting analysis for the Global Burden of Disease Study. *The Lancet*, 396(10258), 1285–1306. https://www.thelancet.com/journals/lancet/article/PIIS0140-6736(20)30677-2/fulltext

White, B. T., and Lee, J. J. (2020, April 19). The future of international higher education in a post-mobility world. *University World News*. Retrieved from https://www.universityworldnews.com/post.php?story=20200417105255362

White, B. W. (1996). Talk about school: Education and the colonial project in French and British Africa (1860–1960). *Comparative Education*, 32(1): 9–25.

Wu, H. P., Garza, E., and Guzman, N. (2015). International student's challenge and adjustment to college. *Education Research International*, 2015:1–9. https://doi.org/10.1155/2015/202753

Yan, S. (2020, May 19). China's latest policies: Some backgrounds and major influences on research evaluation and scientific publishing. *KeAi webinar: Changing research evaluation policies in China—insights and impact*.

Yang, R. (2002). *Third delight: The internationalisation of higher education in China*. New York, NY: Routledge.

PART 1 GEOPOLITICS AND
THE REGULATION OF
HIGHER EDUCATION

2 • INTERNATIONAL EDUCATION AS SOFT POWER

A History of Changing Governments, Shifting Rationales, and Lessons Learned

ROOPA DESAI TRILOKEKAR

In 1989, Nye introduced "soft power" as a concept in the field of international relations. Higher education has since been recognized as a crucial soft power tool to heighten the attractiveness of a given country or culture in world politics (Altbach and Peterson, 2015; Bertelsen, 2014; Byrne and Hall, 2014; Nye, 2005, 2007; Peterson, 2014; Wojciuk, 2018). America's higher education soft power is well recognized given that the "U.S. boasts the highest number of top universities in the world, attracts the largest number of international students, and contributes significantly to academic research" (McClory, 2017, p. 54). Is it a given that international education (IE) is linked to a nation's foreign policy and cannot operate outside global geopolitical contexts?

Knight (2014) critiques IE for being drawn to the concept of soft power "like bees to honey" (para. 2), while recognizing its multiple interpretations. She objects to the adoption of soft power as a concept for IE because of its motivation to achieve self-interests and its framing within a power and dominance paradigm. This chapter provides a historical analysis of IE federal policy development in the United States starting from 1945 and going through the late 2000s. It asks if the United States is in fact an exemplary case of how foreign policy and the centrality of geopolitics come to dictate government IE agendas, and if IE, as a soft power tool for the United States, is weakening as a result of changed geopolitics. It considers the investments the government has made in IE as part of its soft power diplomacy. What were its rationales then, and how have these rationales changed over time? What domestic and international determinants have caused this change? It concludes with three lessons learned from U.S. history regarding the government's use of IE as soft power, suggesting that perhaps Knight's objection to the notion of soft power is somewhat limiting.

CONTEXT

As a federal government, U.S. higher education is deemed a state responsibility. Further, with institutional autonomy and academic freedom being highly valued, the role of the government, in particular the federal government, is highly circumscribed (Trilokekar, 2007, 2015). IE as a policy arena thus falls through the cracks of federal, state, and institutional responsibilities. However, as de Wit argues, "the fact that by constitution the government's role is limited in educational policy but extensive in foreign affairs, defense, trade and commerce suggests the federal policy on international education will be more linked to these areas than to education itself" (as cited in Miyokawa, 2009, p. 19).

SOFT POWER AND INTERNATIONAL EDUCATION

Soft power is defined as "the ability to get what you want through attraction rather than coercion or payments. It arises from the attractiveness of a country's culture, political ideals, and policies" (Nye, 2004a, p. x). IE, particularly the education of international students, is frequently identified as a strong soft power resource because the free flow of students/scholars has served well the interests of the United States. This is because as an "international student returns to his or her native country and takes over vital positions in the public or private sector, the individual will eventually affect his or her country's trajectory and, in turn, U.S. foreign policy" (Mai, 2015, para. 3). Examples are frequently used to illustrate this advantage. One of the most famous alumni of the Fulbright program is Russian student Alexander Yakovlev. Yakovlev studied at Columbia University in 1958—the period of the Cold War—and is said to be strongly influenced by the political scientist David Truman. Yakovlev would eventually return to the USSR (Union of Soviet Socialist Republics) to become a close ally of Mikhail Gorbachev's and eventually become the "father of glasnost," the political philosophy (along with Perestroika) that eventually brought down the Iron Curtain. A fellow student, Oleg Kalugin, who became a high-level official in the KGB, said "Exchanges were a Trojan Horse for the Soviet Union. They played a tremendous role in the erosion of the Soviet system. . . . They kept infecting more and more people over the years" (Lane, 2017). Similar examples include Nahas Angula, who graduated from Columbia and was appointed Namibia's prime minister in 2005. He defended the decision to sign the multibillion-dollar Millennium Challenge Account Development agreement with the United States. Panama's president,

Ricardo Martinelli, graduated from the University of Arkansas and achieved a free trade agreement with the United States (Mai, 2015). And the list goes on. The impact of IE extends to government programs for international students, the teaching and training of American citizens abroad, the allocation of grants through civil society, and the mass spreading of American educational and research centers in other countries, among many other initiatives (Savin, 2018).

THE HISTORY OF FEDERAL GOVERNMENT INVESTMENT IN IE

With changing governments and associated shifts in U.S. foreign policy, there have been ebbs and flows of investments in IE, with perceptions of IE as a soft power tool shifting dramatically over different time periods. Below is a brief description of these time periods.

1945–1960s: The Beginning of the Golden Years

The U.S. federal government initiated its formal role in IE in 1945. The post–World War II period and the Cold War era heavily shaped the roots of IE (I. Hall, 2018). This period is fondly cherished as the golden era or as a period of euphoria because it was during this era that several major IE initiatives emerged. The "birth" of IE (McAllister-Grande, 2008, p. 4; also Campbell, 2005) is first and foremost linked to Senator James William Fulbright's vision of the "promotion of international good will through the exchange of students in the fields of education, culture and science" (Bureau of Educational and Cultural Affairs, n.d., para. 3) using the proceeds from the sale of surplus war property. Under President Truman (1945–1953), the Fulbright program achieved an "unprecedented size and scope" (Miyokawa, 2009, p. 102) and became an envy of other nations and America's IE flagship initiative. Facilitating the movement of more than 360,000 students/scholars (Lane, 2017), with more than 8,000 annual grants, the program is operational in over 160 countries (Savin, 2018), representing the U.S. view on how IE can support democracy and encourage positive relationships between nations (Altbach and Peterson, 2008).

Contrasting Fulbright's idealism was the new National Defense Education Act (NDEA) of 1958 under President Eisenhower (1953–1961), which introduced the Title VI programs, perhaps the most influential IE policy development in the United States. In responding to Russia's launch of Sputnik, the NDEA proclaimed that "the security of the nation requires the fullest development of the mental resources and technical skills of its young men and women" (Ruther, 2002, p. 60).[1] Among other policy directives within the NDEA, Title VI provided federal funding to U.S. universities to develop language and area studies centers as well as graduate fellowships for advanced international knowledge and expertise (Ruther, 2002, p. 59). Other important initiatives developed during this period include the Smith Act (1948), which resulted in congressional appropriations for international educational exchanges, and the creation of the U.S. Information Agency (USIA), an organization established in 1953 to promote America's image abroad "in the midst of the ideological conflict of the Cold War" (I. Hall, 2018, para. 6; see also Cull, 2010).

In addition, in 1949 the U.S. federal foreign aid agency developed a new role of international technical assistance for the U.S. land grant universities (Ruther, 2002). The academic community welcomed these important initiatives, while also expressing concern over the influence of the government's political agenda on IE. Sensitive to these concerns, the government assured academics that "neither partnership or reciprocity implied government control or any loss of university autonomy" (Ruther, 2002, p. 71).

The governments of Presidents Kennedy (1961–1963) and Johnson (1963–1969) were part of this golden era. Kennedy endorsed the broader rationales for international exchange through the Mutual Educational and Cultural Exchange Act, or the Fulbright Hays Act (1961). He strongly supported the Bureau of International Cultural Relations, established under Eisenhower in 1959 and subsequently renamed the Bureau of Educational and Cultural Affairs (1960) within the Department of State (DOS) (Davis, 1970). One of Kennedy's major legacies was the creation of the United States Agency for International Development (USAID) (1961) and the introduction of the influential Peace Corps program, designed to send young Americans abroad to promote friendship and world peace. A successful program by 1966, it sent the highest number of U.S. volunteers abroad (Snow, 2008).

President Johnson was committed to building America as a "great society," and he believed that "ideas, not armaments, will shape our last prospects for peace; that the conduct of our foreign policy will advance no faster than the curriculum of our classrooms; that the knowledge of our citizens is the one treasure which grows only when it is shared" (Vestal, as cited in McAllister-Grande, 2008, p. 31). He appointed a task force on IE and introduced the International Education Act (IEA) (1966), which recommended a wide range of initiatives, including the setup of a new Center for International Educational Cooperation (to be housed in the Department of Health, Education, and Welfare).[2] Unfortunately, the IEA, although enacted into law, was never funded. However, Vestal contends, the IEA "remains an important landmark of federal *intentions* [emphasis added] in this policy arena" (as cited in Campbell, 2005, p. 138); others suggest that the funding failure signaled a shift away from these golden years (Miyokawa, 2009).

1970s

The waning of interest and a shift in U.S. global leadership. The end of the period of euphoria came as a direct result of several events, including Kennedy's assassination, the fallout from the Vietnam War, a faltering U.S. economy, the oil crisis, and the Watergate scandal (Campbell, 2005; Davis, 1970; Snow, 2008)—events that did not bode well for IE. This was a time of severe budget cuts. Ruther (2002) states that the funding for Title VI centers was cut by almost half, with the program representing less than 1 percent of the Office of Education program funding from its original 8 percent in 1958. Aid funding was also substantially reduced. In 1970, the report of the Advisory Commission on International Education and Cultural Affairs indicated that "expenditures for educational exchanges [were] lowest of any time in recent history" (Davis, 1970, p. 235), causing disappointment and serious doubts about the government's interest in IE. The broader goals of mutual understanding, peace, and humanitarian assistance "failed to garner [the same] major support" within the federal government (Ruther, 2002, p. 110; see also Snow, 2008). This is why Ruther (2002) describes the Nixon (1969–1974) and Ford (1974–1977) IE period as one "from boon to bane" (p. 135), a time when "the nation was in no mood to assume global leadership if it meant more Vietnams" (p. 111). However, according to Snow (2008), the Cold War paradigm continued to provide the rationale for what little federal investment continued. The threat from the Soviet Union resulted in a push toward exchanges and in hosting international students, "who in turn [would] represent a more accurate picture of America to [their] compatriots upon return" (Snow, 2008, p. 207). IE programs that justified a pragmatic and national defense rationale survived.

With President Carter's election (1977–1981) there was new hope for IE. He created a separate Department of Education (DoED); USIA was changed to the U.S. International Communication Agency, absorbing the Bureau of Educational and Cultural Affairs from the DOS, the purpose being to enable the government to fulfill its "public diplomacy" role (Ruther, 2002, p. 121). By 1978, a presidential commission was created to attempt to improve U.S. attention to international concerns and foreign language and international studies (Newell, 1987). The Coalition for the Advancement of Foreign Languages and International Studies was formed under three supportive legislators: Paul Simon, Dante Fascell, and John Buchanan; however, Ruther (2002) suggests that they were ineffective in fulfilling the commission's mandate.

1980s

IE as important for growing national security concerns. The Iranian Revolution and the resulting hostage crisis shifted the perspective on IE, in spite of the overall support for IE under the Carter administration (1977–1981). For most of the 1970s, Iran sent more students to the United States than to any other country; however, after relations between the two nations deteriorated, the number of Iranian students coming to the United States significantly declined (Lane, 2017). Difficulties in tracking Iranian students led to the government taking a series of measures that made visa regulations more complex and burdensome. The government considered introducing a formal immigration tracking system and proposed the Simpson-Mazzoli bills in the mid-1980s to impose a two-year foreign residence requirement for all foreign students after graduation. Strong advocacy from the IE lobby groups prevented the implementation of these strict measures (Miyokawa, 2009, p. 24).

With Reagan elected president (1981–1989), the early 1980s were initially not an optimal time for IE. Enormous budget cuts were made to Higher Education Act Title VI and Fulbright programs, and there was talk of DoED closure and shifting programs from the federal level to the state level (Newell, 1987). Similarly, funding for USAID/international research and technical assistance declined, and the Peace Corps was slashed in size. The shift in international assistance policy also meant less engagement of university faculty/students. Ironically, in spite of this initial lack of support, it was Reagan's conservative foreign policy perspective that changed the tide for IE. The IE lobby, cognizant of Reagan's policy priorities, emphasized the importance of national security goals achieved through IE. Either in response to the lobby's arguments or in response to its own policy priorities, the Reagan administration, quite unexpectedly, provided a fairly large boost to IE. A new title VI was created in the HEA, with NDEA Title VI and the IEA repealed. "There was a need to strengthen course offerings and requirements in foreign languages studies and international studies in the nation's schools, colleges and universities" (Ruther, 2002, p. 129), and international exchanges were seen as an explicit foreign policy tool to combat the influence of the "so called Evil empire" (Campbell, 2005, p. 131). Reagan's aggressive anti-communist foreign policy provided the ideological basis to support international educational exchanges, with the "era of sending and receiving young scholars to build mutual understanding...now a quaint artifact of a bygone era" (Snow, 2008, p. 212). Another IE policy shift occurred as the U.S. economy came to be viewed as core to the long-range security of the nation. New Title VI programs now included business schools, and there was a focus on the research and instructional needs of business students in the area of international affairs and languages (Ruther, 2002).

1990s

Shifting rationales for IE in a post–Cold War era. The end of the Cold War left a policy vacuum as national security had provided a consistently important rationale for the federal government's interests in IE (Campbell, 2005). However, once again, reminiscent of the Reagan era, under the Bush (Sr.) administration, the National Security Education Act in 1991 reinstated the national security agenda as a predominant policy rationale. Re-educating the newly independent countries of the Soviet Union/Eastern Europe provided a new impetus resulting in substantial funding for education exchange programs. Given this new enthusiasm for IE, Vestal concluded that the "logjam of federal funding had indeed been broken and expressed enthusiasm that indeed international education was in a new age perhaps a golden one" (as cited in Campbell, 2005, p. 132).

President Clinton's election (1993–2001) signaled a much anticipated return to the traditional values of IE. But the IE community was disappointed when his administration did not move in this direction, but instead adopted as his doctrine "economic expansion and enlarging markets for US goods and services" (Snow, 2008, p. 216). Under the Clinton administration, the USIA programs were initially reduced by 23–25 percent, and eventually in 1998 the Foreign Affairs Reform and Restructuring Act led to the merger of USIA with the DOS, its responsibilities assigned to a new undersecretary for public diplomacy (Campbell, 2005, p. 142; Miyokawa, 2009). This was reflective of a time when "mutual understanding had no resonance on Capital Hill" (Campbell, 2005, p. 134). The focus on global economic competitiveness led to a heightened interest in developing the global competence of Americans (Campbell, 2005). Study abroad for American students was important, as "globalization requires a cadre of workers in business, academics and the NGO community who are well educated in the history, politics and culture of other nations" (Campbell, 2005, p. 133). The government was concerned with "reinventing diplomacy in the information age" (Campbell, 2005, p. 133) and with engaging higher education with this "new challenge" to strengthen the place of the United States in the post–Cold War world.

The outward-looking policy of sending American students abroad was antithetical to the proposed set of new immigration regulations restricting international student entry and stay in the United States. The 1994 World Trade Center bombings had raised fear about openly welcoming international students. The government introduced the Illegal Immigration Reform and Immigration Responsibility Act (1996) amending the 1952 Immigration and Nationality Act. It proposed a pilot computer-based system to track international students—a system that eventually became the predecessor of the Student and Exchange Visitors Information System (SEVIS) program introduced after 9/11 (Miyokawa, 2009).

Early 2000s

IE as risk to national security. Clinton (1993–2001) eventually rekindled his image as an internationalist through his first-ever 2000 presidential memorandum on an IE policy that called for a "coherent and coordinated international education strategy [that] will help us meet the twin challenges of preparing our citizens for a global environment while continuing to attract and educate future leaders from abroad" (Clinton, 2000). It made specific reference to international students as contributors of "$9 million to the [U.S.] economy," while also serving as facilitators of cultural exchange and "our greatest foreign policy assets"

(Campbell, 2005, p. 134; also Clinton, 2000). This presidential-level support for IE, even if mostly rhetorical, was dramatically challenged with the catastrophic events of September 11, 2001.

September 11, 2001, is often referred to as a "period of crisis" that dramatically changed the landscape of IE in the United States. With 9/11, IE posed a risk to the nation's security. Recoiling back to restrictive immigration policies initiated as a response to the Iranian crisis and the World Trade Center bombings, a new tracking system for international students was introduced by the Bush (Jr.) administration (2001–2009). The passage of the U.S. Patriot Act, the Enhanced Border Security Act, the Homeland Security Act, and the Visa Entry Reform Act facilitated the federal government's restrictive immigration policies and the implementation in 2003 of the controversial SEVIS program, administered by the new Department of Homeland Security (operations were still the DOS's responsibility) (Campbell, 2005, p. 141). As Witt (2008) states, "The entire landscape of international education in the US shifted dramatically from a posture of recruitment to one of determent, from receptive to suspicious, from hospitable to hostile" (p. 6). "The global war on terrorism replaced the cold war as the national security meta narrative" (Campbell, 2005, p.139). This was a time of crisis with the United States experiencing its first substantial drop of international students in thirty years. IE came to be viewed by the U.S. federal government as a risk to national security.

This major shift in attitude toward IE translated into a growing distrust of higher education. Area and international studies faculty, courses, and programs were accused of promoting anti-Americanism with Congress proposing highly invasive legislation to regulate and monitor international academic programs and their curriculums within universities. For example, the International Advisory Board was created, whose mission was to strip federal funding from those Title VI programs that do not serve national interests. Added to this was the growth of groups like the American Council of Trustees and Alumni, Campus Watch, NoIndoctrination.org, and Students for Academic Freedom, which managed to set a legislative agenda to support the most extreme government oversight of education in U.S. history (McClennen, 2006).[3] Further, restrictive immigration and visa policies diminished the attractiveness and accessibility of U.S. higher education. With both national security and global economic competition identified as important rationales, the "secure borders, open doors" campaign came to dominate the IE policy discourse (Campbell, 2005, p. 140).

Once again, IE faced "a uniquely challenging and paradoxical environment" (Campbell, 2005, p. 127) as the federal government under Bush Jr. announced legislation to significantly increase funding for exchange programs (Nye, 2017). The Cultural Bridges Act of 2002 authorized $95 million/year from 2003 to 2007 for new and expanded IE programs with the Islamic world. As Campbell (2005) cogently states, "Mutual understanding ha[d] come back into the [federal] frame but with a harder edge, lined primarily with the notion of global competence and America's need to communicate and relate in a multi-cultural globalized, political and economic environment" (p. 148). Capitalizing on the "why do they hate us?" sentiment (as cited in Campbell, 2005, p. 142), a spotlight was created on the need for and role of public diplomacy in fighting terrorism. Karen Hughes as the new undersecretary of state for public diplomacy became one of the most "visible advocate[s] for exchanges," supporting a budget of $430 million (from $74 million) in 2006 for the DOS public diplomacy initiatives. Powerful dignitaries such as Secretaries of State Colin Powell and Condoleezza Rice spoke of IE as the government's soft power tool. Several new initiatives and policy priorities were introduced, including an investment in academic exchanges, particularly with the Islamic world; investment in study abroad for American students (2005 Commission on Abraham Lincoln Study Abroad Fellowship Program and the Senator Paul Simon Study Abroad Foundation Act); and concern with improving the market share of international students (Government Accountability Office [GAO, 2009] study on challenges and best practices in attracting international students to the United States).

2009–2017

A return to the founding principles of IE? With the election of President Obama (2009–17), there was a revival of the original values of IE as an instrument to build ties of peace and partnership among countries. Obama spoke about finding "new ways to connect young Americans to young people all around the world, by supporting opportunities to learn new languages, and serve and study, welcoming students from other countries to our shores. That's always been a critical part of how America engages the world" (B. Obama, 2009, para. 17). Study abroad was promoted as a "vital part of our foreign policy" (M. Obama, 2014, para. 6) with the announcement of the 100,000 Strong initiative, an effort to dramatically increase the number and composition of American students studying in China, followed by the 100,000 Strong in the Americas, to increase international study in Latin America and the Caribbean (Fischer, 2019). In his famous speech in Cairo, Obama (2009) called for a new beginning in relations between the United States and Muslim-majority countries and committed to U.S. cooperation in international science as a core component of his foreign policy.

At the same time, Obama also embraced globalization and the rhetoric of national economic competitiveness. "Are we a nation that educates the world's best and brightest in our universities, only to send them home to create businesses in countries that compete against us?" he asked. "Or are we a nation that encourages them to stay and create jobs here, create businesses here, create industries right here in America?" (Duncan, 2014, paras. 3–4). He expanded and extended the federal Optional Practical Training (OPT) program, which allows international students to work in the United States while studying. Thus, in tandem with old values were new values of the growing economic rationale for IE. Altbach therefore speaks of this as a time for new directions in internationalization and a growing interest in its "commercialization" (as cited in Fischer, 2019, p. 26). The U.S. Department of Commerce became increasingly interested in international students as "big business." Per the 2009–2010 estimates, the U.S. economy earned $19 billion from international students, a promising figure that prompted the department's first overseas trade mission on higher education, setting the stage for its future role in IE of promoting American education abroad. Several American universities opened campuses abroad and hired senior administrators to manage their burgeoning overseas portfolios, including student exchanges, faculty research, and joint degrees. At home, the government was urged to do away with antiquated and "outmoded" policies (Douglass and Edelstein, 2009, p. 6) such as requiring international students to speak of their intent to return home "before they even start their studies" (as cited in Smith, 2014, para. 5). Attention was drawn to the fact that "educated [international] students are exactly the kinds of immigrants we should encourage to stay in the US" (NAFSA, as cited in Smith, 2014, para. 5). IE was now being recognized as a global talent acquisition strategy (Douglass and Edelstein, 2009).

In November 2012, the U.S. DoED established its first-ever IE strategy, published as the report *Succeeding Globally Through International Education and Engagement*, which addressed several components of IE, including the objectives of increasing global competencies of U.S. students and establishing best IE practices (Thomas, 2013). Several scholars suggest that this era was once again "golden" even though it was "born out of the grimmest of events: the September 11 terrorist attacks and the conviction that the violence—whose perpetrators were erroneously said to have been in the United States on student visas—called for greater engagement with the world, not less. Its end date came a decade and a half later, signaled by the election of Donald J. Trump, on a platform of "America First" (Fischer, 2019, pp. 6–7).

2017–present

IE as harmful to America First interests. Altbach describes the current period as one where "the era of internationalization might be over, or on life support" (as cited in Fischer, 2019, p. 9). Among the first policy shifts that the Trump administration introduced was the ban on all immigration from seven Muslim nations, including stopping the entry of students/scholars with valid study and work visas from those countries (Lane, 2017). The Trump administration singlehandedly created a chilly and unwelcoming climate for international students on U.S. campuses. The Department of Homeland Security was accused of screening and policing international students in unlawful ways to legitimize its restrictive immigration policies (J. Hall, 2019). A national survey of college enrollment managers cites Trump's rhetoric and anti-immigration policies as reasons for a sudden slump in the number of international students (Dennis, 2019; Fischer, 2019). Since Trump was elected, applications from around the world to American institutions have plummeted nearly 40 percent (McClory, 2017).

Linked to the dramatic shift in immigration policies has been Trump's radical shift in U.S. foreign policy. Trump's America First doctrine has completely altered America's role in the world from a globally engaged superpower to one that heavily subscribes to an isolationist doctrine (Fischer, 2019; McClory, 2017; Knowledge Network, 2018). Trump has withdrawn U.S. global leadership, at times undermining international norms, established conventions, and long-standing commitments. His populist-nationalist mind-set has promoted anger against the "unfulfilled promises of globalization" (Lee, as quoted in Fischer, 2019, p. 20) and turned America "in on itself" (McClory, 2017, p. 17). IE has no rationale or relevance when both foreign and domestic policies perceive no role for America in the world and question whether the country should even have one.

Additionally, recent geopolitical conflicts between the United States and China are spilling into IE, influencing its very ability to be used as a soft power tool (Dennis, 2019). U.S. cybersecurity concerns over China have resulted in visa restrictions for Chinese students/scholars. Since 2018, nearly 300 Chinese scholars have had their visas either canceled or delayed. The Trump administration announced a new policy limiting visas to one year for Chinese graduate students studying robotics, aviation, or high-tech manufacturing (Dennis, 2019). Chinese students/scholars are viewed as security threats, and the government cautions university administrators not to be naive about Chinese students/scholars studying on their campuses. The U.S. government has even pressured universities including MIT and the University of California at Berkeley, among others, to reject research funding from Huawei, China's premier technology company (Postiglione, 2019, para. 10). The president of MIT has therefore accused the U.S. government of "creating a toxic atmosphere of unfounded suspicion and fear" (Postiglione, 2019, para. 8), with FBI agents making ethnic Chinese academics feel unsafe and uncomfortable on U.S. campuses (Fischer, 2019). Universities are reporting changes in student application rates, educational exchanges, scholar visa approvals, revenue streams, and international research cooperation (Postiglione, 2019). In the decade leading up to Trump's election, American institutions opened thirty-four campuses overseas. Since then, they've opened five (Savin, 2018). What have these dramatic shifts in foreign policy and immigration regulations meant for IE? Have they in effect undermined the use of IE as a soft power tool for the United States (Lane, 2017)?

DISCUSSION

As mentioned above, the story of the U.S. federal government's investment in IE has largely been one of ebbs and flows, depending no doubt on global geopolitics but mostly on the changing foreign policy ideologies of its own government and its vision of the role of America in the world. The early beginnings of IE were entrenched in a post–World War II ideology where America's role in mutual understanding and world peace was prioritized. In tandem were U.S. interests in ensuring national security in the wake of the Cold War (I. Hall, 2018). In fact, the Cold War provided a central raison d'être for the federal investment in IE. Therefore, after the Cold War, there was hesitancy on the part of the government to invest in IE. However, U.S. foreign policy soon found its bearings in a post–Cold War period investing in IE once again, this time in several post-Soviet countries in the form of academic exchanges (Cull, 2010; Savin, 2018). The events of 9/11 reshaped the U.S. approach to IE. However, even after 9/11, the focus on the war on terrorism resulted in the federal government's surprising investment in IE to strengthen and enhance American knowledge of international relations, world regions, and foreign languages, and vice versa, especially with Islamic countries, to better promote "homeland security."

Thus, while the original principle of mutual understanding and world peace has had wavering resonance, and the economic rationale good traction, the prime rationale for government investment in IE has remained constant, securing America's national security and geopolitical interests. Whether it be international development aid, academic partnerships and exchanges, Title VI language and area studies programs, or the tinkering of foreign student immigration regimes, the United States, as Savin (2018) suggests, has always kept the geopolitical context of IE alive and well. This consistency in policy rationale has shifted dramatically under Trump. With Trump's America First policy, the United States has dropped three places according to the annual global ranking of nations' soft power by London-based Portland Communications and USC's Center on Public Diplomacy (McClory, 2017; Nye 2019). Reports suggest that "only 30% of people recently polled by Gallup in 134 countries held a favorable view of the United States under Trump's leadership, a drop of almost 20 points since Barack Obama's presidency" (Nye, 2018, para. 1). The reason for this is Trump's defenders "believe that soft power—what happens in the minds of others—is irrelevant," with Trump's then budget director, Mick Mulvaney, therefore wanting to slash funding for the State Department and USAID in 2017 by nearly 30 percent (Mohammed, 2017; Nye, 2018, para. 2). This current period is therefore an anomaly in the history of the U.S. federal government's use of soft power as an aspect of its foreign policy and will undoubtedly have effects on investments in IE and the global engagement of American universities. The first lesson one can draw from U.S. history is that IE as a soft power tool is used by governments to strengthen their images only when their foreign policies are both outward looking and globally engaged. Without a vision of national global engagement as a core aspect of its foreign policy, a federal government has little reason to invest in IE and link it with its foreign policy.

Immigration is another theme that closely relates IE with a country's soft power interests. The United States has in the past viewed itself as a country of immigrants, it has been open to international students, and it has recognized their contributions to U.S. education and society, as well as to the economy. However, this view has been shrinking over time, reaching its low after 9/11 and its bottom under Trump. The environment toward international students in the United States has become one of suspicion and hostility, influencing the country's attractiveness as a study abroad destination (Lane, 2017). Hence, the second lesson is that in order for IE to serve as a soft power tool for a government, a nation needs to keep its doors open to allow mobility both in and out of its academic institutions, and it needs to recognize the contributions of international students and scholars to its institutions and encourage the same from institutions abroad.

Even though the federal role in higher education is fairly circumscribed, it has carved a niche for itself given IE's rationale as a soft power foreign policy tool. Before the NDEA, there had been strong opposition to any federal involvement in higher education, but Sputnik had launched a national emergency. Title VI of the NDEA was dedicated to fostering foreign language and area studies for use in national defense. Such direct investment in academic programs by the federal government would not be so easily accepted in other jurisdictions (Trilokekar, 2007). Yet, there was acceptance of a partnership between the federal government and higher educational institutions, which was severely damaged first under the Bush Jr. administration and now under Trump. With a mood of suspicion and mistrust, with "academic staff, postdoctoral fellows and students feeling scrutinised, stigmatised and on edge because of their ethnicity or nationality," and with "the restricted flow of information and unnecessary secrecy" (Postiglione, 2019, para. 20) IE cannot serve as a soft power tool. The third lesson is that for IE to function as a soft power tool, governments need to have minimum oversight and control of IE programs. Instead, they should enable university autonomy and academic freedom to contribute to what higher education does best: promote free flow of ideas, collaboration, and partnership within and across people and borders.

Unfortunately, as Pomerantz (2020) states, "the United States' prominence in international education is likely to be COVID-19's latest fatality" (para. 1). As it is, Trump's America First foreign policy of protectionism and nationalism resulted in restricted immigration regulations. With COVID-19, IE in the United States will be even more severely challenged. Air travel restrictions aside, global student mobility to the United States will be greatly influenced for a few reasons.

First, the United States is identified as the global epicenter of this pandemic. Second, the U.S. government's continued and systematic dismantling of immigration policies is an attempt to call for an end to IE as we know it. The U.S. Department of Homeland Security recently issued a rule prohibiting international students from returning to or remaining in the United States this fall if the colleges they attend adopt online-only instruction models amid the pandemic (Whitford, 2020)—this after the government had earlier suspended the OPT program accessed by international students (Schulmann and Trines, 2020). The U.S. government is intentionally working against IE and the interests of its own higher educational institutions, calling for, as Pomerantz (2020) suggests, a "loss of [the] country's major tools of soft diplomacy: international students" (para. 6). Third, a rising sentiment against foreigners who take jobs away from Americans (Schulmann and Trines, 2020), amid Trump's political tensions and polarity with China (Jones, 2017), is feeding into anti-Asian sentiments. Asian students (both American and international) are facing increased racism (Yao, 2020). U.S. institutions are host to 1.1 million foreign students (as of 2018)—34 percent of them came from China alone—representing USD 11 billion in fees (Symonds, 2020). The loss of revenue from international students will be devastating to the U.S. higher education sector, especially considering what Marginson (2020) describes as a "buyers' market where incoming students are scarce and competition to recruit them is more intense" during and also anticipated after COVID-19. He suggests that "East-to-West student traffic will shift into East Asian mobility traffic and some of that change will become permanent" (para. 19). "East Asia . . . will now rise further in international education because of strong health and governance regimes and the bounce back factor" (para. 18). Meanwhile the U.S. government's unilateral, self-interested, and blame-game approach to diplomacy will result in a shortsighted approach to IE in this new era of geopolitics (Schake, 2020). Indeed, this period might represent the end of IE, a far cry from the beginnings of IE in the United States during its golden years.

CONCLUSION

The United States still retains the largest global market share of international students and is number one in terms of a high degree of soft power in education (Knowledge Network, 2018). This is because it takes generations to build soft power, and when one looks at the U.S. history, its federal government invested in IE with a long-term perspective in mind. These efforts and investments have given the United States considerable dividends when it comes to building goodwill around the world (Lane, 2017; McClory, 2017; Nye, 2004b). However, Nye (2005) reminds us that while government policies can strengthen and reinforce soft power, they can also squander it. "Domestic or foreign policies that appear to be hypocritical, arrogant, indifferent to the opinion of others, or based on a narrow approach to national interests can undermine soft power" (para. 10). Under the current regime, it is unlikely that the United States will continue to reap benefits from its earlier investments. This was particularly salient during the COVID-19 period and soon after that given the current geopolitics where power is said to be shifting from the West to the East, with Asia's soft power steadily rising (Falk, 2012; Jones, 2017). This is particularly evident in the case of China, as it takes on a larger global leadership role at the same time that the United States has entered a period of retreat from the world (McClory, 2017). Gunn and Mintrom (2017) go so far as to state that the epicenter of global higher education is shifting to Asia. Whether this is the future or not, and whether more nonstate actors leverage international soft power influence (McClory, 2017), governments still remain the primary actors when it comes to promoting their soft power. This brief review of U.S. federal government's investment in IE as a soft power tool, beginning after World War II, suggests that these investments have, to date, made a unique and lasting contribution, broadly to U.S. foreign policy, but perhaps more specifically to America's image as an important center for international higher education. While I do not argue for or against the use of IE as a soft power tool, I do argue that governments actively leverage IE as a soft power foreign policy tool. Governments that embed IE in a foreign policy that is global, an immigration regime that is open, and a higher education environment that thrives under the principles of institutional autonomy and academic freedom reap its positive benefits. The United States does provide an exemplary case of the close intersection of IE and geopolitics but also the potential use and misuse of IE as a soft power tool, its misuse particularly evident in America's response during the COVID-19 pandemic. Thus, while I agree with Knight (2014) that soft power has its limitations and that knowledge diplomacy might be more promising to work mutually, reciprocally, and cooperatively across countries, this perspective varies greatly depending on the actors being examined. This chapter examined the role of the federal government, and as far as national governments go, their investments in IE are more often than not based on the notion of soft power, given the link between IE and foreign policy. What the U.S history of federal government engagement in IE serves to illustrate is that through the use of IE as soft power, governments can support and enhance the global engagement of higher education and even pursue a mutuality of interests and enhance cooperation among nations. However, this is only feasible when national governments invest in a geopolitical ideology, which is first and foremost global and international in orientation, an approach hugely missing under the Trump administration, which is likely to do much more damage both during the COVID-19 pandemic and after, when international cooperation, solidarity, and global goodwill are a necessity (Schake, 2020).

NOTES

1. The Soviet Union launched the first artificial Earth satellite in 1957, initiating a period of public fear and anxiety in Western nations about the perceived technological gap between the United States and the Soviet Union.
2. For a detailed outline, see Read, 1966.
3. For further details, see McClennen, 2006.

REFERENCES

Altbach, P. G., and Peterson, P. M. (2015). Higher education as a projection of America's soft power. In W. Yasushi and D. L. McConnell (Eds.), *Soft power superpowers: Cultural and national assets of Japan and the United States* (pp. 37–53). New York, NY: Routledge.

Bertelsen, R. G. (2014). The university as a transnational actor with transnational power: American missionary universities in the Middle East and China. *P.S. Political Science & Politics*, 47(3), 624–627.

Bureau of Educational and Cultural Affairs. (n.d.). An informal history of Fulbright. Retrieved from http://eca.state.gov/fulbright/about-fulbright/history/early-years

Byrne, C., and Hall, R. (2014). International education as public diplomacy. *Research Digest*, 3, 1–10. Australia: International Educational Association of Australia (IEAA) and International Education Research Network (IERN). Retrieved from https://www.ieaa.org.au/documents/item/258.

Campbell, D. (2005). International education and the impact of the 'war on terrorism.' *Irish Studies in International Affairs*, 16, 127–154.

Clinton, W. (2000). Memorandum on international education policy. *The American Presidency Project*. Retrieved from https://www.govinfo.gov/content/pkg/WCPD-2000-04-24/pdf/WCPD-2000-04-24-Pg878.pdf

Cull, N. J. (2010). Speeding the strange death of American public diplomacy: The George H. W. Bush administration and the U.S. Information Agency. *The Journal of the Society for Historians of American Foreign Relations. Diplomatic History*, 34(1), 47–69.

Davis, J. M. (1970). The US government and international education: A doomed program? The Phi Delta Kappan. *International Education*, 51(5), 235–238.

Dennis, M. (2019, 11 May). Fewer Chinese students in the US may not be a bad thing. *University World News*. Retrieved from https://www.universityworldnews.com/post.php?story=20190507111155578

Douglass, J. A., and Edelstein, R. (2009). *The global competition for talent: The rapidly changing market for international students and the need for a strategic approach in the US* (CSHE Research and Occasional Paper Series), University of California, Berkeley.

Duncan, K. (2014, November 25). Obama's immigration overhaul to benefit some international students. *The Pie News*. Retrieved from https://thepienews.com/news/obamas-immigration-action-benefit-international-students/

Falk, R. (2012, August 13). Is there a new geopolitics? A new form of geopolitics is threatening to dethrone the old paradigm of a hard power, West-centric world. *AlJazeera*. Retrieved from https://www.aljazeera.com/indepth/opinion/2012/08/201281123554276263.html

Fischer, K. (2019, March 28). How international education's golden age lost its sheen. *The Chronicle of Higher Education*. Retrieved from https://www.chronicle.com/interactives/2019-03-28-golden-age

Government Accountability Office. (2009, April). *Higher education approaches to attract and fund international students in the US and abroad.* Retrieved from http://www.gao.gov/products/GAO-09-379

Gunn, A., and Mintrom, M. (2017, June 2). The changing shape of global higher education geopolitics. *University World News.* Retrieved from https://www.universityworldnews.com/post.php?story=20170529151430202

Hall, I. (2018, April 3). Confucius Institutes and U.S. exchange programs: Public diplomacy through education. *World Education News and Reviews (WENR).* Retrieved from https://wenr.wes.org/2018/04/confucius-institutes-and-u-s-exchange-programs-public-diplomacy-through-education

Hall, J. (2019, May 9). US: Student visa crackdown questioned by stakeholders and courts. *The PIE News.* Retrieved from https://thepienews.com/news/us-student-visa-crackdown-questioned-in-the-courts/

Jones, B. (2017, November 28). The new geopolitics. *Brookings Institution.* Retrieved from https://www.brookings.edu/blog/order-from-chaos/2017/11/28/the-new-geopolitics/

Knight, J. (2014, January 31). The limits of soft power in higher education. *University World News.* Retrieved from http://www.universityworldnews.com/article.php?story=20140129134636725

Knowledge Network. (2018, December 19). America's soft power slips in global rankings. *Thunderbird School of Management.* Retrieved from https://thunderbird.asu.edu/knowledge-network/americas-soft-power-slips-in-global-rankings

Lane, J. (2017, January 30). Trump's immigration ban: Will it undercut American soft power? *The Conversation.* Retrieved from https://theconversation.com/trumps-immigration-ban-will-it-undercut-american-soft-power-72156

Mai, D. (2015, April 2). Education drives America's strongest soft power resource. *The HOYA.* Retrieved from https://www.thehoya.com/education-drives-americas-strongest-soft-power-resource/

Marginson, S. (2020, March 26). Global HE as we know it has forever changed. *Times Higher Education.* Retrieved from https://www.timeshighereducation.com/blog/global-he-we-know-it-has-forever-changed

McAllister-Grande, B. (2008). *The historical roots of internationalization in U.S. higher education: Mapping theories and rationales of international education and cultural diplomacy in the post World War II Period (1945–1970).* Unpublished paper. Retrieved from http://www.nafsa.org/_/File/_/ac08sessions/GS089.pdf

McClennen, S. A. (2006). The geopolitical war on U.S. higher education. *College Literature, 33*(4), 43–75.

McClory, J. (2017). *The Soft Power 30: A global ranking of soft power.* Portland, USC Center for Public Diplomacy. Retrieved from https://softpower30.com/wp-content/uploads/2018/07/The-Soft-Power-30-Report-2018.pdf

Miyokawa, N. (2009). *International student access to US higher education since World War II: How NAFSA (Association of International Educators) has influenced federal policy* (PhD dissertation, Pennsylvania State University). Retrieved from https://etda.libraries.psu.edu/paper/10183/

Mohammed, A. (2017). Trump plans 28 percent cut in budget for diplomacy, foreign aid. *Reuters.* Retrieved from https://www.reuters.com/article/us-usa-trump-budget-state-idUSKBN16N0DQ

Newell, B. W. (1987). Education with a world perspective—A necessity for America's political and economic defense. *Annals of the American Academy of Political and Social Science, 491,* 134–139.

Nye, J. (2004a). *Soft power: The means to success in world politics.* New York, NY: Public Affairs.
———. (2004b, May/June). The decline of America's soft power. *Foreign Affairs.* Retrieved from https://www.foreignaffairs.com/articles/2004-05-01/decline-americas-soft-power
———. (2005). Soft power and higher education. *Forum for the Future of Higher Education.* Retrieved from http://www.educause.edu/ir/library/pdf/FFP0502S.pdf
———. (2007). Squandering the U.S. 'soft power' edge. *International Educator, 1*(16), 4–6. Retrieved from https://www.nafsa.org/sites/default/files/ektron/files/underscore/frontlines_jan_feb.pdf
———. (2018). Donald Trump and the decline of US soft power. *Confidencial.* Retrieved from https://confidencial.com.ni/donald-trump-and-the-decline-of-us-soft-power/
———. (2019). American soft power in the age of Trump. *The Strategist.* Australian Strategic Policy Institute. Retrieved from https://www.aspistrategist.org.au/american-soft-power-in-the-age-of-trump/
Obama, B. (2009, April 7). President Obama's remarks at a student roundtable in Turkey. *The New York Times.* Retrieved from https://www.nytimes.com/2009/04/07/us/politics/07obama-turkey-transcript.html
Obama, M. (2014, March 22). Remarks by the First Lady at Stanford Center at Peking University. *The White House.* Retrieved from https://obamawhitehouse.archives.gov/the-press-office/2014/03/22/remarks-first-lady-stanford-center-peking-university
Peterson, P. M. (2014). Diplomacy and education: A changing global landscape. *International Higher Education, 75,* 2–3.
Pomerantz, P. (2020, June 22). Another COVID-19 victim: International education. *The Hill.* Retrieved from https://thehill.com/opinion/education/503954-another-covid-19-victim-international-education
Postiglione, G. (2019, July 30). No US or China higher education winners in trade wars. *University World News.* Retrieved from https://www.universityworldnews.com/post.php?story=20190730145049433
Read, G. (1966). The International Educational Act of 1966. *The Phi Delta Kappan, 47*(8), 406–409.
Ruther, N. (2002). *Barely there, powerfully present: Thirty years of U.S. policy on international higher education.* New York, NY: Routledge Falmer.
Savin, L. (2018). The changing shape of global higher education geopolitics. *KATEHON.* Retrieved from https://katehon.com/article/education-tool-us-geopolitics
Schake, K. (2020, March 20). The damage that 'America First' has done. A self-interested strategy will not help the U.S. fight the coronavirus outbreak. *The Atlantic.* Retrieved from https://www.theatlantic.com/ideas/archive/2020/03/america-first-is-making-the-pandemic-worse/608401/
Schulmann, P., and Trines, S. (2020, May 26). Perfect storm: The impact of the coronavirus crisis on international student mobility to the United States. *World Education Trends News & Reviews. Mobility Trends.* Retrieved from https://wenr.wes.org/wp-content/uploads/2020/05/iStock-1214322536-740x440-1.jpg
Smith, B. (2014). US immigration educators lobby democrats push for vote. *The Pie News.* Retrieved from http://thepienews.com/news/us-immigration-educators-lobby-democrats-push-for-vote/
Snow, N. (2008). International exchanges and the U.S. image. *Annals of the American Academy of Political and Social Science, 616,* 198–222.
Symonds, M. (2020, June 22). Can international higher education survive Covid-19? *Forbes.* Retrieved from https://www.forbes.com/sites/mattsymonds/2020/06/22/can-international-higher-education-survive-covid-19/#643fea8a6a6d

Thomas, D. (2013, January 8). US international strategy short on detail. *The PIE News*. Retrieved from http://thepienews.com/news/us-international-education-strategy-short-on-detail/

Trilokekar, R. D. (2007). *Federalism, foreign policy and the internationalization of higher education: A case study of the Department of Foreign Affairs (FAC), Canada* (Unpublished doctoral dissertation). University of Toronto, Toronto, Ontario, Canada.

———. (2015). *From soft power to economic diplomacy? A comparison of the changing rationales and roles of the U.S. and Canadian federal governments* (CSHE Research & Occasional Paper Series). Retrieved from https://cshe.berkeley.edu/sites/default/files/publications/rops.cshe_.2.15.desaitrilokekar.softpowerecondeplomacy.2.9.2015.pdf

U.S. Department of Education. (2012). *Succeeding globally through international education and engagement* (International Strategy 2012–16). Retrieved from http://www2.ed.gov/about/inits/ed/internationaled/international-strategy-2012-16.html

Whitford, E. (2020, July 7). International students banned from online-only instruction. *Inside Higher Education*. Retrieved from https://www.insidehighered.com/news/2020/07/07/department-homeland-security-rule-bans-international-students-online-only#:~:text=The%20new%20Department%20of%20Homeland%20Security%20rule%20prohibits,adopt%20an%20online-only%20instruction%20model%20for%20the%20fall.

Witt, A. M. (2008). Closed borders and closed minds: Immigration policy changes after 9/11 and U.S. Higher Education. *Journal of Educational Controversy*, 3(1), 1–11. Retrieved from https://cedar.wwu.edu/jec/vol3/iss1/5

Wojciuk, A. (2018). Higher education as a soft power in international relations. In Y. Watanabe (Ed.), *Handbook of cultural security*. Northampton, MA: Edward Elgar.

Yao, C. (2020, June 26–27). Internationalization, race and racism in U.S. higher education. Presentation at Critical Internationalization Studies Virtual Conference Session. Retrieved from https://criticalinternationalization.net/events/internationalization-for-an-uncertain-future/

3 • WHAT DO GLOBAL UNIVERSITY RANKINGS TELL US ABOUT U.S. GEOPOLITICS IN HIGHER EDUCATION?

ELLEN HAZELKORN

Over the past decades, globalization, massification, and internationalization have transformed the higher education landscape. The escalation and intensification of the movement and integration of trade, capital, and people across borders have created many new goods and services, cross-border supply chains, and markets and opportunities, further integrating nations into an increasingly competitive yet interdependent world—a contemporary version of Marx's "heavy artillery... batter[ing] down all Chinese walls" (Marx and Engels, 1948, p. 125). These changes have, in turn, driven and been driven by social, demographic, and technological changes affecting the way we think about issues, identify ourselves, and perceive and pursue our interests.

Education has not been immune from these trends. As the world has become more integrated, higher education has become a global enterprise. Colleges and universities have deep historical roots in their towns and cities, and nation-states are likely to remain the largest investors in public R&D, but higher education research and development (HERD) is an open system. In fact, the transformation of higher education from being a local institution with strong links to its city or regional benefactors to one of geopolitical significance for individuals and nations has been one of the most noteworthy features of the past decades. Universities are global actors, supported by an expanding global infrastructure, wherein geopolitical factors are prominent.

These developments have coincided with, and been driven by, demographic growth, resulting in growing demand for higher education everywhere. The world's population is now expected to reach 9.8 billion by 2050, and 11.2 billion by 2100 (United Nations [U.N.], Department of Economic and Social Affairs, Population Division, 2017, p. 2). As a consequence, the number of students enrolled in higher education is estimated to reach 660 million by 2040, rising from 28.6 million students in 1970; this represents 10 percent of the world's population (aged fifteen to seventy-nine years old), compared with 4 percent in 2012 (Calderon, 2018, p. 187). Most of this growth is anticipated to occur in Africa, while the population of the more developed regions is expected to remain largely unchanged (U.N. Department of Economic and Social Affairs, Population Division, 2017).

This growth is reflected in the number of universities, rising from around 12,000 in 1997 to 19,400 in 2020, according to the International Association of Universities (IAU), although the number is almost certainly higher because countries differ with regard to name and status of a "university" in national law (IAU WHED Portal). It has changed the public-private mix. Whereas private, and especially not-for-profit, higher education has been a long-standing feature of the U.S. landscape, its steady growth elsewhere has been due to demographic and ongoing massification pressures, the continuing transition to knowledge-intensive economies and services and changes to the labor market, the expansion in lifelong learning, and the contraction in public budgets and, conversely, the investment by private providers (Douglas-Gabriel, 2017; Teixeira, Kim, Landoni, and Gilani, 2017). Over 13 million students pursue cross-border education online (Organisation for Economic Co-operation and Development [OECD], 2016), and the number of branch campuses has increased from around 84 in 2000 to more than 300 today (Verbik, 2015).

The United States was one of the first countries to experience massification, followed by Europe. According to the OECD (2019c), 49 percent of Americans, compared with 44 percent of twenty-five-to-thirty-four-year-olds in other advanced countries, had a tertiary degree in 2017, up from 26 percent in 2000; yet only 11 percent had a master's or doctorate, compared with 15 percent of non-Americans (p. 2). Demographic change is another critical factor. The U.S. population is growing, but the fertility rate is declining, owing to millennials having fewer children, and later in life (Hamilton, Martin, Osterman, Driscoll, and Rossen, 2018). This decline, similar to that in other advanced countries, is occurring at the same time the population is graying. In other words, the proportion of those over age sixty-five is likely to reach about 20 percent by 2050, up from 13 percent today.

Yet, despite spending more than other countries on education, the U.S. domestic population is falling behind. It is anticipated that only 50 percent of U.S. young adults, excluding international students, will enter tertiary education for the first time, compared with 58 percent on average across OECD countries (OECD, 2018b, p. 2); in other words, fewer young people will have "attained degrees at higher rates than did their parents" (Cantwell, 2018, p. 229). Furthermore, as older, better-educated people retire, the domestic talent pool will have, on average, lower literacy and numeracy skills (Rothwell, 2016; Rushe, 2018). Evidence from both Programme for International Student Assessment (PISA) (OECD, 2019a) and PIACC (OECD, 2013a) shows that U.S. students and adults have poorer literacy, numeracy, and problem-solving skills than their counterparts in other countries (Barshay, 2019; OECD, 2013b, 2019a). Given that education is a human capital pipeline, these trends are occurring parallel to a decline in manufacturing and a shift to service sector employment when more jobs require a minimum of two years post-secondary education (Carnevale, Ridley, Strohl, and Campbell, 2019; Carnevale, Strohl, Cheah, and Ridley, 2017).

These developments are occurring alongside a dramatic transformation in the balance of the global economy and talent pool. OECD countries are experiencing a decline in their shares of global gross domestic product (GDP), from 60 percent in 2000 to a projected 44 percent by 2032 (OECD, 2018a). The United States will remain the dominant power, with "global economic, military, technological and financial reach, a global currency and an unrivalled system of global alliances" (European Strategy and Policy Analysis System, 2015, p. 27), but other countries, especially China and India, are quickly catching up. China's GDP in purchasing power terms has already outstripped that of the United States, and India is expected to overtake the United Kingdom (UK) and France to become the fifth-largest economy (in nominal GDP terms); Indonesia will figure in the top ten by 2032 (OECD, 2018a, pp. 58–59).

As economic growth advances, it accelerates rates of tertiary education participation, which in turn impacts on the overall size and geographic balance of the global talent pool. (See figure 3.1 and also note that the United States is not present in the chart.) By 2030, a majority of the global population will be middle class, two-thirds of whom will reside in Asia (Barton, Chen, and Jin, 2013; Kharas, 2017). By then, China and India could account for more than 60 percent of STEM (science, technology, engineering, and mathematics) graduates in the G20 area, with Europe and the United States providing only 8 percent and 4 percent, respectively (OECD, 2013a, p. 3; Schleicher, 2016).

As knowledge and innovation processes become more dispersed and openly accessible, the cross-border movement of people and ideas becomes indispensable for growing economies with declining populations. The number of internationally mobile students is estimated to reach around 8 million by 2025, compared with 0.8 million in 1975. For decades the United States and the UK have had the highest international student enrollments; international students make up the overwhelming majority of full-time students in U.S. graduate science and engineering programs (National Foundation for American Policy, 2017). But other regional education hubs and markets, especially in east Asia, have been expanding provision and are becoming more attractive and affordable to students, especially as their universities climb in the rankings (ICEF Monitor, 2018; OECD,

Projections of the share of the population aged 15+ educated to degree level by country

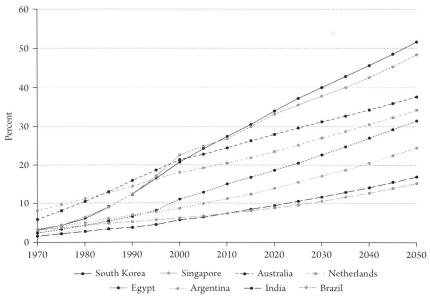

FIGURE 3.1. Projections of the share of the population aged fifteen and older educated to degree level by country. (*Source*: "Tertiary Education," by M. Roser and E. Ortiz-Ospina, 2019, *Our World in Data*, retrieved from https://ourworldindata.org/tertiary-education.)

2018b, p. 3). Attracting mobile students and academic professionals, especially if they stay permanently, is an important way to tap into the global talent pool. They can help compensate for weaker domestic educational capacity, support the development of innovation and production systems, and mitigate the impact of an aging population on the supply of future skills as the economy and labor market change (NAFSA, 2019; OECD, 2015). These trends are likely to be affected by student and political responses to COVID-19 (Altbach and de Wit, 2020).

These shifts are also reflected in research, development, and innovation (RDI), and specifically in scientific performance and achievement, which are an expression of global progress (Roser, 2019). While university-based research is still dominated by research-intensive U.S. and (Western) European universities, many more nations and their universities are now highly active in research. This is shifting the geopolitical "center of gravity" eastward and southward (Levin, 2010). According to Leydesdorff, Wagner, Park, and Adams (2013), the leading group of scientific nations now includes more than forty nations. The picture emerging is of a multipolar world in which more countries participate

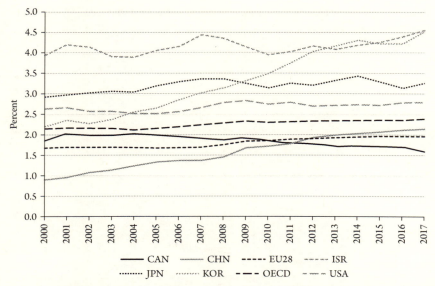

FIGURE 3.2. R&D intensity: Gross domestic expenditure on R&D as a percentage of GDP, 2000–2017. (*Source: OECD Main Science and Technology Indicators R&D: Highlights 2019*, by OECD, March 2019, Directorate for Science, Technology and Innovation, retrieved from https://www.oecd.org/sti/msti2019.pdf.)

in higher education and science rather than a world dominated by a few big powers.

Previous decades saw the European Union (EU), Japan, and the United States dominate science and technology research. Recent years have seen the rapid expansion of R&D performance in the East/Southeast and South Asia (see figure 3.2). China now accounts for 20 percent of total world R&D and is forecast to be a global leader in science and innovation by 2050 (Veugelers, 2017). This trend is especially manifest in the significant increase in published science papers (especially those in the physical sciences and STEM disciplines) since 2003 (Marginson, 2018, pp. 7–9), and notably China's ascendancy in new technologies, such as artificial intelligence (AI). Japan, Korea, and the United States together contributed 62 percent of all AI patents between 2010 and 2015, but today China is about to overtake the United States (Duranton, Erlebach, and Pauly, 2018; Khan and Gawalt, 2018, p. 36; OECD, 2019b, p. 29). Some commentators suggest that these developments, rather than representing a "sudden break," simply constitute "the reversal of a historical anomaly"; in other words, the "shrinking gap between the industrialized [Western] world and the emerging countries marks the end of developed countries' monopoly of advanced high-end manufactured production and high added-value services" and a return to the situation in the eighteenth century when Asia dominated the world economy (European Strategy and Policy Analysis System, 2015, p. 24).

Significantly, in the context of accelerating competition, "research collaboration is flourishing" (Marginson, 2018, p. 19). According to Adams (2013), international collaborative research is increasingly synonymous with excellent research and heightened citation impact, indicators that are vital for rankings. Co-authored papers, as a percentage of all scientific papers, have more than doubled in number over the past twenty years, and today account for all the output growth by scientifically advanced countries (Adams and Loach, 2015). While geographic, linguistic, and historical ties remain strong, international collaboration has become the defining feature of a new global geography of science (Kwiek, 2020). The trend is most explicit in developed countries, but everywhere international collaboration is beginning to outpace single authorship and institutional collaboration. The transformation of science into a global enterprise is driven by several factors, including government funding as well as the search for national and researcher prestige and resources.

There is also a realization that solving societal challenges requires collaborative action, as exemplified by the human genome project, which involved twenty universities and research centers in the United States, the UK, Japan, France, Germany, and China, and adoption of the U.N. 2030 Agenda for Sustainable Development (2015) with seventeen Sustainable Development Goals (SDGs) (United Nations, 2015). The technological and digital revolution and embrace of open science, open access publishing, and shared data platforms is facilitating and intensifying transnational collaborations and networks. Recent global efforts to find a vaccine for COVID-19 (Casey, 2020; Xu, 2020) have publicly highlighted the value of research as well as the fact that no country has the knowledge or research infrastructure to solve such problems on its own.

University networks, with membership stretching around the world, are a feature of this interconnectedness and of the university's desire to enhance its global footprint (Calderon, 2018, pp. 198–205). The past decades have seen an evolution from nationally oriented to cross-border/transnational associations linked to geographic regions to international/globally focused associations (Brankovic, 2018). Increasingly, universities have formed groups with university peers with the objective of maximizing access to talent and resources, and boosting their reputation on the global stage. Membership in such "clubs" is often determined and shaped by criteria of excellence and occasionally rankings.[1] Yet, even here, there is evidence of the world order shifting. Traditionally these networks have been dominated/led by top universities of developed countries. Formation of the Asian Universities Alliance in 2017, bringing together fifteen universities from fourteen Asian countries (including mainland China and Hong Kong), conspicuously excluded Australia (Sharma, 2017).[2] Its establishment marked an ambitious Asian regionalism, challenging the hegemony of the United States and Europe (Blue Ribbon Panel on Global Engagement, 2011; Chao, 2017; Hazelkorn, 2018).

GLOBALIZATION, ACCOUNTABILITY AGENDA, AND RANKINGS

These changes at the global level reveal a dynamic, complex, and competitive world economy. For higher education and research, the global order of the twenty-first century involves cross-border flows of students, researchers, academics, and other professionals; a myriad of universities and educational models; transnational and branch-campus and e-learning providers; and transnational knowledge networks and open science platforms, research collaborations, large-scale infrastructure and multiparty spin-offs, and other corporate ventures. Universities are increasingly networked, collaborating both locally and cross-border, initially on the basis of bilateral agreements but increasingly as members of recognized networks and associations. Use of English as the lingua franca for scientific communication and for teaching, especially when combined with the internet, makes communication easier and quicker.

At the same time, many of the sureties of previous decades are fading. For people of my generation across developed/OECD countries, the underlying belief was that each generation would be better off than the previous one; progress was seen as a birthright. Despite the fact that the demand for higher education is growing, more people feel left behind. Globalization has brought benefits, but it has also increased economic insecurity (felt by individuals, their families, and communities), widening disparities of political views, wealth, and opportunities according to educational attainment, institutional status, and place. Gaps within countries are often greater than those between countries. These disparities are leading to questions about student learning outcomes and employability, and more generally about higher education's commitment to enrolling and meeting the needs of a more diverse student population as it chases global status and reputation.

These different issues and experiences converge around the accountability agenda, a term used to refer to the public and political desire for greater transparency and external oversight of public services, including higher education, and more widely issues of public trust. Quality is a concern for everyone. Quality assurance and accreditation, recognition of new credentials and providers, transnational recognition of qualifications, and regulation of transnational providers are all required to underpin and facilitate knowledge, talent, skills, and resource transfer across borders. New communities of practice, guidelines, regulations, and codes of practice are necessary to make the system work smoothly and efficiently. Students, graduates, and employers, and society overall, require confidence in the quality of higher education and research provision whether in their neighborhood, their country, or around the world (Hazelkorn, Coates, and McCormick, 2018).

Global university rankings emerged in the early years of the millennium. They were promoted as an accountability and transparency instrument, filling an information gap. They were a logical development in a world in which massification and the demand for higher education participation were rocketing everywhere, and where talent and knowledge were becoming the premium indicator of personal and economic success (Hazelkorn, 2015, 2016; Locke, Verbik, Richardson, and King, 2008; Yudevich, Altbach, and Rumbley, 2016). They have succeeded in highlighting higher education quality and placing it within a comparative and international framework. In so doing, rankings took the debate about quality and performance beyond higher education and placed it firmly on the public and policy agenda around the world. Moreover, by operating outside of traditional structures, they have come to fill a gap in the global knowledge intelligence ecosystem, becoming one of the "missing institutions" of globalization (Nayyar, 2002).

Despite criticism of rankings—their unsuitable methodology, insufficiently meaningful indicators, unreliable data, and disproportionate focus on research and reputation—they are widely used by governments, universities and students, other stakeholders, and the media because they tell a complex story simply. Essentially, rankings measure the outcomes of historical competitive advantage. Elite universities and nations benefit from accumulated public and/or private wealth and investment and intellectual capital over decades, if not centuries. In many cases these universities have profited from their government's colonial expansion. They also benefit from attracting high-achieving and high-socioeconomic-status students who graduate on time and go on to have successful careers. All these factors are reproduced in the indicators that rankings use and popularize. Hence, rankings reflect the structure of society, the world economy, and global science. They are, as Cantwell (2016) argues, a "report card" on disparities in resources and the unevenness in the global production of knowledge, the effect of which is to legitimize such inequities. Imbalances may have shifted and collaboration may be the name of the game, but pursuit of world-class excellence puts research universities, and high-performing science systems, at the top of the competitive hierarchy—and drives student choice.

Accordingly, rankings display an underlying "epiphenomenon" about scientific and academic prowess—telling us "something" about the competitive advantages of our institutions, and our nations. The ability *versus* the inability to compete at this level reveals global divisions between economic regions, and between universities, and is shaping institutional strategies. The exact nature of the relationship among global rankings, policymaking, and strategic decision-making can be difficult to pin down, but there is good evidence to show that rankings have been a significant influence at all levels of government and institutional governance.

University leaders use rankings to drive strategy, to set priorities, and to applaud achievements. They use rankings to publicize their attractiveness to top/international talent. Many U.S. universities have been exposed for providing false or dubious information about student enrollment and performance to enhance their ranked positions (e.g., Jaschik, 2018; Schwartz, 2019). The UK consumers association recently chastised universities for misrepresenting their positions in the rankings in an effort to attract students (Busby, 2018). Students use rankings to help choose a university, in some cases deciding on the basis of a few statistically insignificant percentage points. A recent controversy in the United States about back-door routes into high-ranked elite universities is symptomatic of how the pursuit of elite status drives behavior even among the elite (Medina, Benner, and Taylor, 2019).

Governments and politicians are also sensitive to rankings. Almost everywhere, governments have either embedded rankings within their own processes or developed alternative instruments and processes by which to evaluate, assess, and often fund higher education institutions. Doing well sends out messages to employers, mobile capital, and talented professionals. This is why the performance and reputation of higher education now sit at the fulcrum of a geopolitical struggle for a greater share of the global market and the emerging new world order (Hazelkorn, 2015, pp. 91–166).

WHAT UNIVERSITY RANKINGS TELL US

The changing geopolitical dynamics discussed above are evidenced in the shifting pattern of global rankings. Change may be slow owing to limits on what can be achieved without significant and sustained investment, and systemic change to governance, organizational structures, academic culture, and research capability. Rankings lack sufficient granularity, and therefore they should not be used for policy and strategy; but they do display an overall pattern or trend. The shift from a U.S.-dominated unipolar world to a multipolar one is signaled by both the growing economic and political strength of China and intellectual voracity as expressed in global university rankings, which increasingly feature Chinese universities among the top 200 and 500 (Europa, 2012; Fabbrini and Marchetti, 2017); however, China's remarkable rise masks less spectacular changes elsewhere among Brazil, Russia, India, China, and South Africa (BRICS) (Bishop, 2016). Nonetheless, once one looks beyond the top group, the growing multipolarity of higher education and scientific knowledge becomes apparent, suggesting "features more similar to an open system with some regional differentiation" (Leydesdorff et al., 2013, p. 16), which is very different from the traditional core-periphery model that has characterized previous thinking about the global system (Cibilis, 2016).

In 2004, a year after the *Academic Ranking of World Universities* (ARWU) first emerged on the world stage, the Americas and Europe dominated, with 180 universities in the top 200; by 2020, they held only 152 places. In contrast, 18 countries appeared in the top 100 in 2020, compared with 17 in 2004; the biggest change however is among the top 500 cohort, with 42 countries in 2020 compared with 37 in 2004. These figures controversially group together mainland China, Taiwan, and Hong Kong SA. Most notable is China's ascent. China had 1 university in the top 200, compared with 90 for the United States and 18 for the UK in 2004. By 2020, China inclusively had 24 universities in the top 200, compared with the United States' 65 and the UK's 20. China inclusively had a whopping 81 among the top 500 in 2020, compared with only 16 in 2004 (see tables 3.1 and 3.2). The rate of growth, an increase of 406.25 percent, is staggering—which tells us almost everything we need to know about geopolitics today.

Equally noteworthy is the university and country shift evident in the latest QS World University Rankings for 2021. The United States recorded its lowest performance with only 27 universities among the top 100, compared with 33 in 2018, while China (including Hong Kong SAR) has 11 among the top 100 ("Asia rises," 2020; Calderon, 2020). QS is unique in assigning 50 percent of its total weighting to reputational indicators; these are hugely problematic measures of quality (Lawrence and Green, 1980), but they do provide a litmus test as to how institutions are perceived by peers.

The position of individual universities and countries can change depending on the methodology used to determine the rankings. However, the message is consistent: there is a more diverse set of players, universities, and countries among the top rankings. And more importantly, there is a pipeline of universities and scholars coming from a more diverse set of countries, which points to an increasingly multipolar world.

Another way of looking at this global complexity is suggested by changes in the rankings themselves (Hazelkorn, 2015, pp. 26–38). When rankings first emerged in the early twentieth century, they were individual efforts to identify so-called geniuses drawing on eugenics. The first institutional attempt was in 1910 when a classification of undergraduate training at colleges was published on behalf of the American Association of Universities (Myers and Robe, 2009, p. 9; Usher, 2017, pp. 25–27; Webster, 1986, pp. 4, 107–119).

The historical turning point came in 1959 when rankings emphasizing reputation factors began to dominate over those focused on "academic origins." The *Science Citation Index* (1961) and the *Social Sciences Citation Index* (1966) then enabled access to scholarly/scientific data and thus transformed the reliability of the data. In 1983, *U.S. News and World Report* (USNWR) Best College Rankings

TABLE 3.1   ARWU distribution of universities in top 20–top 500 by world region, 2004 and 2020

	Top 20		Top 100		Top 200		Top 500	
Region	2004	2020	2004	2020	2004	2020	2004	2020
Americas	17	15	55	45	101	75	200	161
Europe	2	5	37	36	79	77	209	185
Asia/Oceania	1	—	8	19	21	48	89	149
Africa	—	—	—	—	—	—	4	5

SOURCES: *Academic Ranking of World Universities*, 2004 and 2020. Retrieved December 28, 2020, from http://www.shanghairanking.com/ARWU-Statistics-2004.html; http://www.shanghairanking.com/ARWU-Statistics-2020.html

TABLE 3.2   ARWU distribution of select universities in top 20–top 500 by country, 2004 and 2020

	Top 20		Top 100		Top 200		Top 500	
Country	2004	2020	2004	2020	2004	2020	2004	2020
United States	17	15	51	41	90	65	170	133
United Kingdom	2	3	11	8	18	20	42	36
Japan	1	—	5	3	9	7	36	14
Germany	—	—	7	4	17	10	43	30
Canada	—	—	4	4	9	9	23	19
France	—	1	4	5	8	8	22	17
Australia	—	—	2	7	6	8	14	23
Israel	—	—	1	1	3	4	7	6
Russia	—	—	1	1	1	1	2	3
Singapore	—	—	—	2	1	2	2	2
China	—	—	—	6	1	24	15	81
• Mainland	—	—	—	6	—	22	8	71
• Taiwan	—	—	—	—	1	—	2	5
• Hong Kong	—	—	—	—	—	2	5	5
South Korea	—	—	—	—	1	1	8	11
South Africa	—	—	—	—	—	—	4	4
India	—	—	—	—	—	—	3	—

SOURCES: *Academic Ranking of World Universities*, 2004 and 2020. Retrieved December 28, 2020, from http://www.shanghairanking.com/ARWU-Statistics-2004.html; http://www.shanghairanking.com/ARWU-Statistics-2020.html

created a national league table of undergraduate and graduate programs that became nationally and ultimately internationally influential. In Canada, *Maclean's*, a national newsmagazine, began producing a *USNWR*-style ranking in late 1991, followed by the *Times Higher Education Supplement* in the UK in 1996. Since then there has been a proliferation of different types of rankings, primarily produced by media or other commercial organizations, using multi-indicators and summative scores per university. The defining characteristic is their national orientation.

Global rankings were the next transformative intervention. *Asiaweek* produced only three editions in the late 1990s before it folded. The Shanghai Jiao Tong *Academic Ranking of World Universities* (*ARWU*) launched in 2003 and quickly gained "first mover" advantage. It pioneered international comparisons of university performance using a combination of reputational factors and bibliometric indicators and citations drawn from Thomson Reuters's *Web of Science* or Elsevier's *Scopus* databases, from which ARWU has barely deviated since enabling good trend comparisons. It was followed by *Webometrics* (produced by the Spanish National Research Council) and *THE-QS World University Ranking* (*THE-QS*) in 2004. THE and QS split in 2009, each subsequently developing its own ranking, both of which have gone on to be global leaders alongside ARWU.

There have also been important interventions by international organizations such as the OECD and the European Commission. However, the former's AHELO (Assessment of Higher Education Learning Outcomes) initiative did not progress beyond the testing phase because of university opposition, and U-Multirank is operating below its ambition level. Over the decades, different types of rankings have been produced by a growing list of private and public organizations. Indicators have sought, inter alia, to measure community engagement, added value to students and society, and commitment to the environment or the U.N. SDGs (Hazelkorn, 2020). There have also been world-region rankings, most notably focusing on the BRICS, Asia, and the Middle East and North Africa (MENA) region. Today there are around twenty global rankings, and, at a rough guestimate, upward of several hundred other rankings (Hazelkorn, 2015, pp. 43–48; IREG Observatory, 2018).

Amazingly, the (multi)annual release of ranking results continues to send shockwaves around the world. Both universities and policymakers respond to the grading of their institutions with delight or grave disappointment. The United States has remained largely outside this international hubbub in contrast to the frenzy that accompanies the release of *USNWR* rankings (Hazelkorn, 2015, pp. 91–132). U.S. (non)reaction to global rankings is understandable given the size of the national system and the fact that U.S. universities continue to dominate the top echelons of rankings worldwide.

The launch of *USNWR Best Global Rankings* (2014) and the *Wall Street Journal/Times Higher Education College Rankings* (*WSJ/THE*) suggests different factors may be coming into play. THE's partnership with WSJ is notable for the involvement of a non-U.S. organization in the U.S. market. Basing its indicators around an annual U.S. student survey, the WSJ/THE ranking confirms that rankings are good business and that the United States is an untapped market. USNWR's global venture sends a different message. It again recognizes the commercial opportunities, but more significantly, it begins to bring the United States more directly into a conversation around global competitiveness. Because it's the USNWR, it can probably more easily gain a foothold among U.S. readers and opinion formers. As tables 3.1 and 3.2 above suggest, timing is noteworthy. U.S. elite private universities continue to dominate the top 20 worldwide, but the performance of other U.S. universities—where the majority of domestic students attend—is beginning to slump, relatively speaking.

DOES ANY OF THIS REALLY MATTER?

Universities are predominantly national entities. But in a global world, everything is interconnected; as graduates, students will work in an environment that is interconnected with everything they do, regardless of whether they leave their hometown. Recent politico-religious movements (e.g., jihadi extremism), health issues (e.g., coronavirus, Ebola), and migration issues (e.g., Mediterranean migration) illustrate the extent to which local or regional issues easily and quickly acquire global implications, while climate change shows, conversely, how global issues have significant knock-on effects on our food, health, water, and the ecosystem. The same universities that compete against each other for world-class status—defined as being in the top 100—collaborate on research, education programs, and student and faculty mobility.

Universities have generally felt relatively safe within national boundaries and national legislation. Indeed, many of the fundamental structures for higher education remain unchanged at the national level. Yet, despite being a very imperfect measure, rankings expose a globally competitive environment. Being able to participate in global science has transformed measurements of quality and excellence into the oil of the twenty-first century—a symbol of knowledge power and economic authority boosting the position of elites. In response, some universities have worked hard to retain and/or maximize their status and reputation, while others have simply been content to be included somewhere on the list. Rankings draw our attention to these changing dynamics.

At this juncture (July 2020) it is difficult to judge the longer-term effects of COVID-19 on international higher education and global science. However, it is likely to accelerate existing trends and expose underlying weaknesses rather than produce a big bang effect. Populist reactions by and within particular countries reflect ongoing concerns that many traditional assumptions of personal and national status are under challenge (Inglehart and Norris, 2016). Geopolitical shifts in the world order highlight involvement of a greater number of countries and people at a time when the United States appears to be exiting the world stage with a widespread conviction of its own exceptionalism and isolationism. If the data are to be believed, the world is moving in a different direction.

NOTES

1. Examples include high-level initiatives such as the UK/U.S. Study Group on Higher Education and Collaboration in Global Context (2009), and university networks such as the League of European Research Universities (LERU), Coimbra Group, Universitas 21, World University Network (WUN), Compostela Group of Universities (CGU), World Cities or the WC2 University Network, and the Association of Southeast Asian Nations (ASEAN) University Network.
2. Asia University Alliance. Retrieved 28 December, 2020 from http://www.asianuniversities.org

REFERENCES

Adams, J. (2013). The fourth age of research. *Nature, 497*, 7–10. Retrieved from https://www.nature.com/articles/497557a.pdf

Adams, J., and Loach, T. (2015). Comment: A well-connected world. *Nature, 527*(7577), S58–S59. https://doi.org/10.1038/527S58a

Altbach, P. G., and de Wit, H. (2020, April 4). Post pandemic outlook for HE is bleakest for the poorest. *University World News.* Retrieved from https://www.universityworldnews.com/post.php?story=20200402152914362

Asia rises, US, UK, Europe decline in new QS rankings. (2020, June 10). *University World News.* Retrieved from https://www.universityworldnews.com/post.php?story=20200610154557289

Barshay, J. (2019, December 19). What PISA rankings 2018 tell us about U.S. schools. *The Hechinger Report.* Retrieved from https://hechingerreport.org/what-2018-pisa-international-rankings-tell-us-about-u-s-schools/

Barton, D., Chen, Y., and Jin, A. (2013, June). Mapping China's middle class. *McKinsey Quarterly,* 1–9. Retrieved from http://www.mckinsey.com/insights/consumer_and_retail/mapping_chinas_middle_class

Bishop, M. (2016). Rethinking the political economy of development beyond "The Rise of the BRICS." In *SPERI Paper No. 30* (No. 30). Retrieved from http://speri.dept.shef.ac.uk/wp-content/uploads/2018/11/Beyond-the-Rise-of-the-BRICS.pdf

Blue Ribbon Panel on Global Engagement. (2011). *Strength through global leadership and engagement: U.S. higher education in the 21st century.* Retrieved from https://www.acenet.edu/news-room/Documents/2011-CIGE-BRPReport.pdf

Brankovic, J. (2018). How do meta-organizations affect extra-organizational boundaries? The case of university associations. In L. Ringel, P. Hiller, and C. Zietsma (Eds.), *Towards permeable boundaries of organizations?* (Book series, Vol. 57, pp. 259–281). https://doi.org/10.1108/S0733-558X20180000057010

Busby, E. (2018, September 21). Universities make "misleading" marketing claims to students, report suggests. *The Independent.* Retrieved from https://www.independent.co.uk/news/education/education-news/marketing-claims-students-which-university-rankings-advertising-standards-authority-a8547416.html

Calderon, A. (2018). The geopolitics of higher education: Pursuing success in an uncertain global environment. In B. Cantwell, H. Coates, and R. King (Eds.), *Handbook on the politics of higher education* (pp. 187–208). Cheltenham, UK: Edward Elgar Publishing.

———. (2020, June 12). New rankings results show how some are gaming the system. *University World News*. Retrieved from https://www.universityworldnews.com/post.php?story=20200612104427336

Cantwell, B. (2016). The geopolitics of the education market. In Hazelkorn, E. (Ed.). *Global rankings and the geopolitics of higher education: Understanding the influence and impact of rankings on higher education, policy and society*. https://doi.org/10.4324/9781315738550

———. (2018). Broad Access and Steep Stratification in the First Mass System: High Participation in the United States of America. In B. Cantwell, S. Marginson, and A. Smolentsiva. (Eds.), *High Participation Systems of Higher Education* (pp. 227–265). New York: Oxford University Press.

Carnevale, A. P., Ridley, N., Strohl, J., and Campbell, K. P. (2019). *Upskilling and downsizing in American manufacturing*. Retrieved from https://1gyhoq479ufd3yna29x7ubjn-wpengine.netdna-ssl.com/wp-content/uploads/Manufacturing_FR.pdf

Carnevale, A. P., Strohl, J., Cheah, B., and Ridley, N. (2017). *Good jobs that pay without a BA*. Retrieved from https://goodjobsdata.org/wp-content/uploads/Good-Jobs-States.pdf

Casey, R. (2020, February 6). Researchers ramp up efforts to develop coronavirus vaccine. *Al Jazeera*. Retrieved from https://www.aljazeera.com/news/2020/02/researchers-ramp-efforts-develop-coronavirus-vaccine-200206120657215.html

Chao, R., Jr. (2017). A new dawn for Asian higher education regionalisation? *University World News*. Retrieved from http://www.universityworldnews.com/article.php?story=2017050822311447

Cibilis, A. B. (2016). The resurgence of dependency analysis: Nostalgia or renewed relevance? In C. Sunna and D. Gualerzi (Eds.), *Development economics in the twenty-first century* (pp. 104–121). Cheltenham, UK: Routledge.

Douglas-Gabriel, D. (2017, November 9). Private universities to surpass their public counterparts in tuition revenue growth. *Washington Post*. Retrieved from https://www.washingtonpost.com/news/grade-point/wp/2017/11/09/private-universities-to-surpass-their-public-counterparts-in-tuition-revenue-growth/?utm_term=.9a10d9aba57d

Duranton, S., Erlebach, J., and Pauly, M. (2018). *Mind the (AI) gap: Leadership makes the difference*. Retrieved from http://image-src.bcg.com/Images/Mind_the%28AI%29Gap-Focus_tcm108-208965.pdf

Europa. (2012). *Global Europe 2050*. https://doi.org/10.1016/j.jmig.2016.01.018

European Strategy and Policy Analysis System. (2015). *Global trends to 2030: Can the EU meet the challenges ahead?*. Retrieved from https://ec.europa.eu/epsc/sites/epsc/files/espas-report-2015.pdf

Fabbrini, S., and Marchetti, R. (Eds.). (2017). *Still a Western world? Continuity and change in global order*. Abingdon, United Kingdom: Routledge.

Hamilton, B. E., Martin, J. A., Osterman, M.J.K.S., Driscoll, A. K., and Rossen, L. M. (2018). Vital statistics rapid release births: Provisional data for 2018. *Vital Statistics Rapid Release* (007). Retrieved from https://www.cdc.gov/nchs/products/index.htm.%0Ahttps://www.cdc.gov/nchs/data/vsrr/report002.pdf

Hazelkorn, E. (2015). *Rankings and the reshaping of higher education: The battle for world-class excellence* (2nd ed.). https://doi.org/10.1057/9781137446671

———. (2016). *Global rankings and the geopolitics of higher education: Understanding the influence and impact of rankings on higher education, policy and society*. https://doi.org/10.4324/9781315738550

———. (2018). Reshaping the world order of higher education: The role and impact of rankings on national and global systems. *Policy Reviews in Higher Education*, 2(1), 4–31. https://doi.org/10.1080/23322969.2018.1424562

———. (2020, March 21). Should universities be ranked for their SDG performance? *University World News*. Retrieved from https://www.universityworldnews.com/post.php?story=20200317145134326

Hazelkorn, E., Coates, H., and McCormick, A. C. (2018). Quality, performance and accountability: Emergent challenges in the global era. In E. Hazelkorn, H. Coates, and A. C. McCormick (Eds.), *Research handbook on quality, performance and accountability* (pp. 3–12). Cheltenham, UK: Edward Elgar Publishing.

Human Genome Project. Retrieved 27 December 2020 from https://en.wikipedia.org/wiki/Human_Genome_Project

IAU WHED Portal (World Higher Education Database Portal), International Association of Universities, Paris. Retrieved 27 December 2020 from https://whed.net/home.php

ICEF Monitor. (2018). Up and down the table: Growth trends across major international study destinations - ICEF Monitor - Market intelligence for international student recruitment. *ICEF Monitor*. Retrieved from http://monitor.icef.com/2018/08/up-and-down-the-table-growth-trends-across-major-international-study-destinations/

Inglehart, R. F., and Norris, P. (2016). *Trump, Brexit, and the rise of populism: Economic have-nots and cultural backlash*. Cambridge, MA: Harvard Kennedy School.

IREG Observatory. (2018). *IREG inventory of international university rankings, 2014–2017*. Retrieved from http://ireg-observatory.org/en/pdfy/IREG-Inventory-of-International-University-Rankings.pdf

Jaschik, S. (2018, July 10). Lies, damned lies and rankings. *Inside Higher Ed*.

Khan, B., and Gawalt, J. R. (2018). *Science & engineering indicators: 2018*. https://doi.org/10.1016/0040-1625(91)90008-4

Kharas, H. (2017). *The unprecedented expansion of the global middle class: An update* (No. 100). Retrieved from Brookings Institute website: https://www.brookings.edu/wp-content/uploads/2017/02/global_20170228_global-middle-class.pdf

Kwiek, M. (2020). What large-scale publication and citation data tell us about international research collaboration in Europe: Changing national patterns in global contexts. *Studies in Higher Education*, (January). https://doi.org/10.1080/03075079.2020.1749254

Lawrence, J. K., and Green, K. C. (1980). *A question of quality: The higher education ratings game*. AAHE-ERIC/Higher Education Research Report No. 5. Retrieved from https://eric.ed.gov/?id=ED192667

Levin, R. C. (2010, April 20). The rise of Asia's universities. *The New York Times*. Retrieved from http://www.nytimes.com/2010/04/21/opinion/21iht-edlevin.html

Leydesdorff, L., Wagner, C. S., Park, H. W., and Adams, J. (2013). International collaboration in science: The global map and the network. *El Professional de La Informacion*, 22, 87–96. https://doi.org/http://dx.doi.org/10.3145/epi.2013.ene.12

Locke, W., Verbik, L., Richardson, J.T.E., and King, R. (2008). *Counting what is measured or measuring what counts? League tables and their impact on higher education institutions in England*. https://doi.org/10.1080/03797720701618906.Berry

Marginson, S. (2018). *World higher education under conditions of national/global disequilibria* (No. 42). Retrieved from https://www.researchcghe.org/perch/resources/publications/wp422.pdf

Marx, K., and Engels, F. (1948). *The Communist manifesto*. London, England: George Allen and Unwin.

Medina, B. J., Benner, K., and Taylor, K. (2019, March 12). Other wealthy parents charged in U.S. college entry fraud. *The New York Times*. Retrieved from https://www.nytimes.com/2019/03/12/us/college-admissions-cheating-scandal.html

Myers, L., and Robe, J. (2009). *College rankings: History, criticism and reform*. Retrieved from Center for College Affordability and Productivity website: http://www.centerforcollegeaffordability.org/uploads/College_Rankings_History.pdf

NAFSA. (2019). *Losing talent: An economic and foreign policy risk America can't ignore*. Retrieved from https://www.nafsa.org/sites/default/files/media/document/nafsa-losing-talent.pdf

National Foundation for American Policy. (2017). The importance of international students to American science and engineering. In *NFAP Policy Brief*. Retrieved from http://nfap.com/wp-content/uploads/2017/10/The-Importance-of-International-Students.NFAP-Policy-Brief.October-20171.pdf

Nayyar, D. (2002). The existing system and the missing institutions. In D. Nayyar (Ed.), *Governing globalization: Issues and institutions* (pp. 356–384). Oxford, UK: Oxford University Press.

Organisation for Economic Co-operation and Development. (2013a). PIACC country note. United States. In *Survey of Adult Skills First Results* (pp. 1–15). https://doi.org/10.1787/9789264204904-en

———. (2013b). *Time for the U.S. to Reskill? What the Survey of Adult Skills says*. https://doi.org/10.1787/9789264204904-en

———. (2015). Education indicators in focus: How is the global talent pool changing (2013, 2030)? In *Education Indicators in Focus*, pp. 1–4. https://doi.org/http://dx.doi.org/10.1787/5js33lf9jk41-en

———. (2016). Megatrends affecting science, technology and innovation. In *OECD Science, Technology and Innovation Outlook 2016*, p. 18. Retrieved from https://www.oecd.org/sti/Megatrends affecting science, technology and innovation.pdf

———. (2018a). *Meeting of the OECD Council at ministerial level. Key issues paper*. Retrieved from http://www.oecd.org/mcm-2018/documents/C-MIN-2018-2-EN.pdf

———. (2018b). People's Republic of China. *Education at a Glance. Country Note*. Retrieved from http://gpseducation.oecd.org/Content/EAGCountryNotes/CHN.pdf

———. (2019a). *PISA 2018 results. Combined executive summaries. Vol. I, II, III*. https://doi.org/10.1017/CBO9781107415324.004

———. (2019b). *Trends shaping education 2019*. Retrieved from https://read.oecd-ilibrary.org/education/trends-shaping-education-2019_trends_edu-2019-en#page8

———. (2019c). *United States. Education at a Glance. Country Note* (pp. 1–20). https://doi.org/10.1787/78de0586-en

Roser, M. (2019). The short history of global living conditions and why it matters that we know it. Retrieved from Our World in Data website: https://ourworldindata.org/a-history-of-global-living-conditions-in-5-charts

Rothwell, J. (2016). *The declining productivity of education*. Retrieved from https://www.brookings.edu/blog/social-mobility-memos/2016/12/23/the-declining-productivity-of-education/

Rushe, D. (2018, September 7). The US spends more on education than other countries. Why is it falling behind? *The Guardian*, p. 1. Retrieved from https://www.theguardian.com/us-news/2018/sep/07/us-education-spending-finland-south-korea

Schleicher, A. (2016). *Opening remarks: Higher Education Stakeholder Forum 2016*. Retrieved from http://www.oecd.org/edu/skills-beyond-school/andreasschleicher-highereducationstakeholderforum2016-opening.htm

Schwartz, N. (2019, July 29). U.S. News removes UC Berkeley, 4 other schools from ranking. *Education Dive*.

Sharma, Y. (2017). New Asian universities' alliance to increase mobility. *University World News* (458). Retrieved from http://www.universityworldnews.com/article.php?story=20170504205518718

Teixeira, P., Kim, S., Landoni, P., and Gilani, Z. (Eds.). (2017). *Rethinking the public-private mix in higher education: Global trends and national policy challenges*. Rotterdam, Netherlands: Sense Publishers.

United Nations (2015). "Sustainable Development Goals." Retrieved 27 December 2020 from https://sustainabledevelopment.un.org/?menu=1300

Usher, A. (2017). A short global history of rankings. In E. Hazelkorn (Ed.), *Global rankings and the geopolitics of higher education: Understanding the influence and impact of rankings on higher education, policy and society* (pp. 23–53). London, England: Routledge.

Verbik, L. (2015). The international branch campus: Models and trends. *International Higher Education* (46), 14–15. https://doi.org/10.6017/ihe.2007.46.7943

Veugelers, R. (2017). The challenge of China's rise as a science and technology powerhouse. In *Policy Contribution*. Retrieved from http://bruegel.org/wp-content/uploads/2017/07/PC-19-2017.pdf

Webster, D. S. (1986). *Academic quality rankings of American colleges and universities*. Retrieved from http://www.eric.ed.gov/ERICWebPortal/custom/portlets/recordDetails/detailmini.jsp?_nfpb=true&_&ERICExtSearch_SearchValue_0=ED270066&ERICExtSearch_SearchType_0=no&accno=ED270066

Yudevich, M., Altbach, P. G., and Rumbley, L. E. (Eds.). (2016). *The global academic rankings game: Changing institutional policy, practice and academic life*. New York, NY: Routledge.

4 • INTERNATIONAL ACCREDITATION AS GEOPOLITICAL SPACE

U.S. Practices as "Global Standards" for Quality Assurance in Higher Education

GERARDO L. BLANCO

U.S.-based accreditation continues to enjoy a strong international reputation. Many countries aspire to develop American-style quality assurance procedures and standards, and many universities around the world pursue the coveted seal of approval from U.S. regional accrediting agencies (Blanco Ramírez, 2015b). This trend is made evident by the visits that ministries of higher education from around the world pay to U.S. regional accreditors, and by the rapid growth of the International Quality Group (IQG) of the Council for Higher Education Accreditation (CHEA). On the program accreditation front, U.S.-based accreditors in business and engineering occupy a dominant position as global providers of accreditation in these important fields (Patil and Codner, 2007; Romero, 2008).

This chapter explores institutional and programmatic accreditation from an international perspective and analyzes the privileged role that U.S.-based quality assurance providers, practices, and assumptions play in the global higher education landscape. To be precise, international accreditation is a somewhat misleading label as it implies a type of accreditation that emerges from multilateral engagement and joint development of standards from more than one country. This is not the case; while too convoluted to make the title of this chapter, my focus is on the internationalization of U.S. accreditation and its legitimizing processes. By casting U.S. accreditation as the world's "gold standard" of quality assurance in higher education (Jackson, Davis, and Jackson, 2010, p. 9), the

American higher education system simultaneously participates in a system of global competition for legitimacy and recognition, and influences the norms of such competition.

Previous research has illustrated the influential role that U.S. accreditors have beyond their national boundaries. A single country case, Mexico, provides multiple accounts of research studies documenting the motivations for universities outside the United States to adopt American accreditation, both institutional (Barrett, Fernandez, and Gonzalez, 2019; Blanco Ramírez, 2015b) and programmatic (Prasad, Segarra, and Villanueva, 2019). Taken together, these studies make evident the strong influence that American accreditors exert on the competitive global higher education system. To further illustrate the global scope of U.S. accreditation, American accreditation agencies recognize, as of 2019, programs and institutions in more than eighty countries (CHEA, 2019). The largest organization of U.S. accreditors, CHEA, has a group focused on international accreditation issues. In less than five years, this group has attracted members in over thirty countries and five continents (CHEA-IQG, 2019).

A central argument developed in this chapter is that the dual role of U.S. higher education as player and referee, to use a sports analogy, is primarily a geopolitical issue. At its core, geopolitics is about analyzing the "relationship between territory and people in time contexts" (O'Reilly, 2019, p. 11). Accordingly, in this chapter I seek to trace the relationship between U.S. geopolitical centrality, the position that American research universities occupy as international reputational leaders, and the role that U.S. accreditors play in setting international practices and standards.

In this chapter, I rely on postcolonial theory as the conceptual lens to analyze how international accreditation reinforces global hierarchies that legitimize not only U.S. higher education institutions (HEIs) and programs but also the role of U.S. organizations as evaluators of global standards and best practices (Blanco Ramírez, 2014, 2015a). Postcolonial theory focuses on direct forms of domination and, even more importantly, on complex systems of representation that justify and perpetuate Anglo-European supremacy (Said, 1978). To illustrate this argument, I present an analysis of the global activities that U.S. program accreditors for business and engineering have undertaken in recent years and the discourses they employ to legitimize such activities.

DEFINING ACCREDITATION

Accreditation is rooted in the peer-review process that permeates much of academic culture. The purpose of accreditation is to determine whether an institution or program meets minimum standards of quality. However, it is very important to note that the concept of quality is subjective and heavily contested (Harvey and Newton, 2007). Providing evidence of being accredited enables programs and institutions to demonstrate their quality to their peers and to the public, thus making them more visible and competitive. Accreditation also serves as an accountability mechanism given that governments can tie funding or degree recognition to accreditation. In the United States, for example, institutional accreditation is required for students to take their federal financial aid to a specific institution. In other national contexts, the stakes are even higher because accreditation is tied to a university's ability to award degrees or to operate altogether.

Accreditation translates ideas and assumptions about quality in higher education into a context-specific set of agreed-upon standards of quality and accepted processes to ensure compliance with such standards. The idea of being context-specific here is crucial, because it denotes that standards—and the notions of quality that legitimize these standards—can change over time and from one national context to another. In contrast to rankings or league tables, which have become very influential in recent years, accreditation compares programs and institutions against a set of standards, rather than against each other.

Institutional and Program Accreditation

There are two main types of accreditation. Institutional accreditation refers to the process intended to ensure the quality of an HEI as a whole. Institutions are evaluated against a set of standards related to student characteristics and outcomes, the qualifications of their faculty and instructors, their facilities and educational resources, their curricular offerings, their governance and administration structures, and their financial viability. Even though the same set of standards is applied to all the institutions in the same region, each institution is evaluated in the context of its mission and stated purpose. On the other hand, program accreditation—also known as specialized accreditation—focuses on specific programs of study. Sometimes program accreditation is tied to professional licensure.

The literature on accreditation tends to emphasize self-regulation and the convergence of institutional peers in establishing agreed-upon standards (Brittingham, 2009). While accreditation bodies coordinate processes and communicate outcomes, decisions about accreditation are based on recommendations issued by peers with expertise in the areas they are responsible for evaluating. While the procedures are different for institutional and programmatic accreditation, and while different countries and regions establish different steps, it is possible to identify several common features across all accreditation processes. U.S. accreditors often emphasize voluntary participation as a core feature of accreditation (Eaton, 2009). Voluntary participation in accreditation has deep historical roots because in the United Sates, where higher education accreditation has a long tradition, the evaluation of HEIs by their peers predates the creation of any government-mandated review process. The traditions and cultural context that shaped the American accreditation system, such as voluntary participation, make it idiosyncratic when placed in a global context. For instance, general education can be a sticking point when U.S. accreditors review institutions abroad. General education is a significant feature of the American university curriculum. U.S. accreditors set expectations and standards for general education, but in many national contexts the notion of general education is alien. In large parts of Europe and Latin America, candidates select a major when applying to a university and are admitted to a specific major from the beginning. When evaluating institutions outside of their traditional jurisdiction, accreditors may fail to understand that the differences result from fundamentally different expectations rather than from a shortcoming on the part of the institution they are reviewing.

ACCREDITATION IN A GLOBAL CONTEXT

Globalization has transformed many aspects of higher education and introduced new dynamics of competition. As part of their response to this new environment, HEIs seek recognition from international accrediting bodies or from accreditation agencies situated in prestigious higher education systems. This internationalization of accreditation can be observed within both institutional and program accreditation. The internationalization of accreditation involves many interrelated processes, including (a) programs or institutions seeking accreditation from accreditors in other countries, (b) emergent higher education systems seeking assistance from more established ones to develop their own accreditation procedures and standards, (c) national accreditation systems harmonizing their standards and pursuing mutual recognition of credentials, and (d) online or dual degree programs and branch campuses navigating different national accreditation systems and regulators. Students, especially those who have the potential to pursue degrees in different countries, are sensitive to prestige, reputation, and the importance of obtaining credentials that will be recognized in a global labor market.

Institutional accreditation agencies in the United States have extended their recognition to non-U.S. institutions for decades. Nevertheless, what used to be a phenomenon limited to American-style HEIs in a handful of countries has grown rapidly, and U.S. accreditors as of 2019 recognize programs and institutions in more than eighty countries (CHEA, 2019). Nearly all U.S. regional accrediting agencies have engaged in the recognition of international universities either regularly or on a pilot-program basis (Blanco Ramírez, 2015a), and accreditors based in the United States often assist or consult with governments in other countries that seek to develop their accreditation systems (Eaton, 2007).

The emergence of cross-border higher education providers, including branch campuses and online programs open to students in any country, presents new challenges for accreditation. Program accreditors in large fields, like business and engineering, have undertaken global responsibilities. For example, the Association to Advance Collegiate Schools of Business (AACSB) and the Accreditation Board for Engineering and Technology (ABET) are program accreditors that have a global scope and recognize programs in multiple continents. However, both organizations are headquartered in the United States and have a long tradition in this country. These international developments have prompted accreditors to coordinate and share ideas about responding to an increasingly international higher education landscape. These responses include national organizations, such as CHEA in the United States, taking a more proactive role internationally as a result of the many activities that U.S. accreditors undertake around the world. Another response has been the development of the International Network for Quality Assurance Agencies in Higher Education, an international organization that groups many accreditors around the world in order to respond to international challenges and new developments.

U.S. ACCREDITATION AND THE DOMESTIC CRISIS OF CONFIDENCE

Post-secondary accreditation presents a paradox of perception. In the United States, institutional accreditation has faced a public relations crisis for at least the past decade. Criticism against accrediting agencies has ranged from a lack of adequate oversight of online providers, resulting in an accreditation agency losing federal recognition, to claims of discrimination against historically Black colleges and universities or HBCUs (Fain, 2016; Kreighbaum, 2019). Two recent books communicate in their titles and subtitles a sense of urgency: *Accreditation on the Edge* (Phillips and Kinser, 2018) and *How It's Changing, Why It Must* (Gaston, 2013). Popular media and scholarly sources in the United States portray accreditation as a broken system in urgent need of reform. The U.S. Department of Education (2018) has further eroded the credibility of accrediting agencies by stating that "the current focus on minutiae may 'check boxes,' but it does not necessarily demonstrate to the Department that the accreditor is a reliable authority as to the quality of education or training provided by its accredited institutions" (p. 4). Given this state of affairs, how can we explain the fact that these very accreditors constantly receive requests from international HEIs to review their operations, or from governments in other countries to train their newly developed quality assurance agencies? How are we to understand that U.S. accrediting agencies, often criticized at home, receive so many inquiries that they need to state publicly, as the Middle States Commission on Higher Education (2009) and the Western Association of Schools and Colleges (WASC) Senior College and University Commission (2018) have, that they are currently not taking new international applications?

Despite the ongoing scrutiny in the United States, U.S.-based accrediting agencies enjoy a robust and long-standing reputation as the "gold standard" of quality assurance (Jackson et al., 2010, p. 9). A research article explored the discursive web of legitimation that U.S. accreditation agency leaders employed to justify their international activities in the following terms (Blanco Ramírez, 2015b). The study concluded that "the current approach of U.S. agencies has been to continue their regular activities and taken-for-granted perspectives but opening those up to international institutions" (p. 955). Put another way, U.S. accreditors engage internationally as long as they can establish the terms of such engagement and as long as their practices remain unchanged. This logic follows from the assumption that "adapting standards would be equated to lowering standards" (p. 951), and that would be considered a blemish in the credibility of U.S. accreditation agencies.

On the global stage, the challenge for U.S. accreditation agencies is not the need to overcome a negative perception but the need to remain relevant while the spectacle of global rankings (Chang and Osborn, 2005), nearly reaching the level of obsession, captures the attention of prospective students and university administrators alike. In this context, the following has been observed: "The emergence of global university rankings . . . makes evident a new reality in which countries compete against each other in the pursuit of excellence, which is purported to be captured in the metrics of rankings. Rankings are perhaps the most extreme manifestation of excellence as the technology of neoliberal ideology since they reduce everything about a university—staff, students, research—into a single ordinal number" (Saunders and Blanco Ramírez, 2017, p. 402).

Inside the U.S. context, rankings do not and cannot replace accreditation, because accreditation plays an important role for the recognition of degrees and the eligibility of institutions to receive federal funding. However, from a global perspective, the functions of accreditation can include reputation seeking, market segmentation, and student recruitment. It is in this global field that accreditation and rankings compete as indicators of higher education quality. In this context, U.S. accreditation agencies, the accreditors that H. R. Kells (1983) studied for the first time nearly four decades ago, struggle to articulate a coherent strategy for international engagement before the effects of their reputation and relevance abroad wear out completely. In the following sections, I take a critical look at the efforts by U.S. program accreditors to engage globally and the assumptions that U.S. agencies bring into such engagement efforts. As the following section explains, this task can only be completed after acknowledging the role of the United States as the sole empire, or global hegemon, since the disintegration of the Soviet Union (Friedman, 2011) and as the heir of the place once held by the British Empire (Said, 1978). Consequently, postcolonial theory serves as a powerful analytical framework for understanding the privileged role that U.S.-based accreditors play in the global competition for higher education quality.

POSTCOLONIAL THEORY AND INTERNATIONAL HIGHER EDUCATION: A FRAMEWORK

In this section, I review and expand a framework for understanding quality assurance in higher education from a postcolonial standpoint. The first element in this framework involves recognizing that the world is divided into two, unclear and at times overlapping, regions: North and South. The Global South corresponds to formerly or currently colonized peoples and territories. Conversely, the Global North involves European powers that held or hold colonies, and their White-settler heirs such as Australia, Canada, and the United States. Given that the Global North often holds the monopoly over writing history and setting the standards for civilization (Chakrabarty, 2009), I intentionally center the experience of the Global South.

Spivak (1993) offers a clear-eyed perspective on how power and university intersect, from the perspective of the southern/postcolonial/subaltern individual: "the aggregative apparatus of Euro-American university education, where weapons for the play of power/knowledge as *puissance/connaissance* are daily put together, bit by bit, according to a history rather different from our own" (pp. 58–59). The university, Spivak's *teaching machine*, is also a "global sorting machine" (Lee and Cantwell, 2012, p. 47) with mechanisms devised to exclude, separate, and self-legitimize. Rather than asking whether global power continues to shape the contemporary hierarchies of higher education, which I believe has clearly been established, I seek to investigate how these mechanisms operate within a specific set of practices: institutional and programmatic accreditation, a subset of higher education quality assurance.

THE VISUAL DISCOURSE OF INTERNATIONAL ACCREDITATION

In order to understand the processes discussed in the previous section, I use textual and visual critical discourse analysis to study the rationales that U.S. accrediting agencies present in relation to their international activities. Unlike prior studies that focused exclusively on institutional accreditation (Blanco Ramírez, 2015a), also known as regional accreditation, here I seek to analyze program accreditation schemes, as well as the coordinating body that represents many accreditation agencies in the United States. The work of C.J.W. Ng (2014, 2016) on university corporate branding influenced my approach to this project. In particular, I was very taken by the way visual and textual discourse are interwoven in his work. My approach to textual analysis was further influenced by Gavriely-Nuri's (2012) cultural approach to critical discourse analysis. Accordingly, discourse is understood as the retrieval from a database, and discourse analysis involves identifying patterns stored in said cultural database. Visual research methods are complex and rooted in different disciplinary traditions but are increasingly utilized in higher education research (Metcalfe and Blanco, 2019). My visual analysis relied primarily on Metcalfe's (2015) method of visual juxtaposition, given the way such an approach combines visuality as theory and method.

For the present analysis, I focused on two regional agencies that conduct institutional accreditation, two specialized or program accreditation organizations, and the national organization that coordinates and represents most institutional and program accreditation associations. I believe these organizations capture collectively main approaches present among U.S. accreditors. Thus, the study analyzes public documents, reports, and websites from the following organizations: (a) the Commission on Colleges of the Southern Association of Colleges and Schools (SACS-COC), (b) WASC, (c) AACSB, (d) ABET, and (e) CHEA-IQG. These organizations were selected because their official documents include evidence of international engagement beyond North America in recent years.

The present analysis revealed a significant split between the accreditors conducting specialized accreditation, focused on programs, and those engaging with institutional accreditation. Both AACSB and ABET have embraced global engagement as part of their organizational brands through aspirational goals of building "a better world" (ABET) or promoting "global prosperity" (AACSB). In contrast, regional accreditors appeared more subdued, limiting their information to the contact information for "extraterritorial" accredited institutions (SACS-COC), and in one case making clear they are "not entertaining applications from new international institutions" (WASC). Across the documents analyzed, a set of discourses and taken-for-granted ideas about the role of U.S. accreditation in the current global context became clear. The first of these discourses characterizes U.S. accreditation as an "international gold standard of quality in higher education." The second discourse justifies the central role of U.S accreditation in terms of building trust or ensuring confidence. In this section, I present more details about the contrast between program and institutional accreditors and further develop both of the main discourses identified.

Before proceeding with the next section, an important note is warranted. The examples stemming from ABET and AACSB became more salient as the project advanced, and I allowed this imbalance to be reflected when reporting the study's results. Rather than presenting an artificially balanced set of findings, with equal focus on each of the five organizations, the findings reflect a naturally occurring imbalance by which the internationalization discourses of programmatic accreditors are louder and more visible.

U.S. Program Accreditation Embraces a Global Brand

Through the prominent display of world maps on their official websites, both AACSB and ABET embrace a global identity, making their international activities a core component of their organizational culture and casting themselves as global enterprises. AACSB is focused on accrediting business and accounting education and conducts activities in over one hundred countries and territories. ABET is focused on the accreditation of STEM (science, technology, engineering, and mathematics) programs located in thirty-two countries.

AACSB incorporated a global identity into its website's brand identity. The organization's three physical locations reveal a geographic strategy: Tampa, USA, with a focus on the Americas; Rotterdam, Netherlands, with a focus on Europe, the Middle East, and Africa; and Singapore, with a focus on Asia-Pacific. This information exemplifies how AACSB operates as a global enterprise, in sharp contrast with the institutional accreditors, such as SACS or WASC. SACS, which is headquartered in Decatur, Georgia, makes it very clear that this is not only an American organization, but also a southern one.

The websites for ABET and AACSB show striking similarities, and both are also similar to the institutional websites for research-intensive universities in the United States (Cf. Blanco and Metcalfe, 2020). These websites emphasize numbers—for example, 100+ countries and territories for AACSB and 4,005 accredited programs for ABET. Both websites rely on the visual metaphor of the map with slight variations. AACSB differentiates regions by using the organization's branded colors (different shades of green and turquoise). ABET, probably as a nod to the computer science accreditation it provides, turned the map into dots, resembling pixels or bits against a black background, resembling perhaps a computer screen. These visual interpretations of course could be contested; however, they are reinforced over and over through the textual data. In one instance, ABET's global expansion appears to be simply a logical consequence of time: "We began as the educational standard . . . in the United States. . . . Today, after more than 80 years, our standards continue to play this fundamental role and have become the basis of quality for STEM disciplines all over the world." AACSB has embraced internationalization not only as part of its activities but also in its core identity ("a global nonprofit association") and in its vision "to transform business education for global prosperity." A "global mindset" is also presented as one of AACSB's statements of values.

The Market and Consistency as Sources of Legitimacy

The discourses employed to explain the program accreditors' international activities tend to be self-legitimizing: "Our purpose is to assure confidence. . . . Our approach . . . inspires confidence in those who aim to build a better world" (ABET). "Be confident" reads a sign in all uppercase, bolded text. ABET explains that its legitimacy is demonstrated because the accreditation it offers is "sought worldwide." In the AACSB case, accreditation takes on a fetishistic character, in the same sense that Naidoo (2016) uses the term: "By simply integrating the new AACSB Accreditation seal and Business Education Alliance logo into your marketing and communications efforts, you are demonstrating your commitment to improving the quality and value of business education." This example illustrates what Naidoo defines as a fetish: "an irrational belief in magical powers which are invested in an object to protect from harm or to make wishes come true" (p. 1). Moreover, these claims attributed to the display of the AACSB seal only make sense in a neoliberal context, in which the benevolence of the market is taken for granted (Saunders, 2014). Under such circumstances, if a service or product is sought after, especially if it is "sought worldwide" as ABET accreditation is, then that is enough legitimacy, because if a service were not strong or adequate, it would wither away.

A second source of international legitimacy for U.S. accreditors is a sense of consistency. In other words, U.S. accreditors pride themselves in not adapting their processes for international programs or institutions seeking accreditation, because that would water down the process. This has been found in previous research regarding institutional accreditation (Blanco Ramírez, 2015a). WASC states the following: "International institutions must meet the same standards as all other WSCUC members and participate in institutional improvement activities, including educational programming and peer review." The same process seems to be at play among program accreditors: "The ABET accreditation process for programs located outside of the United States (U.S.) *is identical to the accreditation process for programs within the U.S.*" (emphasis in original). This statement captures very clearly that international accreditation relies on geopolitical power. U.S. accreditation is desirable, not because of the standards or the procedures but because it is U.S. based.

Language constitutes an application of this legitimizing consistency. AACSB and ABET require all key documentation to be provided in English, including "faculty handbooks...codes of conduct; student handbooks...syllabi" (AACSB). ABET has a similar policy: "Programs must be able to prepare for and receive a visiting review team conducting activities in English. All visit activities will be conducted in English." Of course, these expectations seem to be straightforward and reasonable. However, this is not the only possible approach. For example, CHEA, the coordinating body for most U.S.-based agencies, provides translations of a core document, the International Quality Principles, in six different languages, including Arabic, Chinese, and Russian. My argument is not that expecting communication is unfair or impractical. This example serves to illustrate that, in light of the strong sense of internationalization presented in the documents discussed, those aspirations and the English-only policies can only be reconciled if the status of English as the sole academic lingua franca is taken for granted. This assumption has been questioned recently (e.g., Björkman, 2013; Jenkins, 2013).

U.S. Standards

The idea that U.S. accreditation constitutes the gold standard of quality assurance in higher education may very well be based on decades of high performance by U.S. HEIs, as Brittingham (2009) argues. Nevertheless, as this chapter's introduction indicates, this high-performance record is not unquestioned. As a result, the directionality of the argument matters. Tempting as it may be, it is not the same to say that the accreditation of U.S. providers enjoys a strong reputation due to the demonstrated effectiveness of its practices and standards as it is to claim that these standards and practices are effective because they are connected to U.S. accreditation. In practice, both American universities and the American accreditation system benefit from the circularity of this argument. U.S. accreditors tend to judge the quality of international institutions on the basis of how similar their practices are to American institutions (Blanco Ramírez, 2015b). This approach places privilege in the Americanness of universities, regardless of the soundness of the practices or their responsiveness to the local context. This reality invites higher education leaders to question assumptions of quality and reimagine quality standards in light of local values and understandings.

As Spivak (1993) forcefully argues: "The old ways, of imperial adjudication and open systemic intervention, cannot sustain unquestioned legitimacy. Neocolonialism is fabricating its allies by proposing a share of the center in a seemingly new way" (p. 63). Applied to higher education, the idea of sharing or diversifying the top spots in rankings and opening up U.S. accreditation to institutions in other countries are reasonable goals. Global circulation is the currency of the new era, and therefore some amount of sharing is necessary. Nevertheless, as long as the norms remain based on U.S. standards and traditions, how diverse can quality in higher education become? The situation revealed in this study suggests that it is unacceptable to continue to uncritically embrace the privileged position of U.S. accreditation as a global norm or gold standard when this status is based, albeit not exclusively, on geopolitical power. For non-U.S.-based practitioners it would simply suffice to read the specialized and popular media dealing with the many challenges that U.S. accreditation faces to emerge with a more realistic perspective.

Embracing Uncertainty

As the examples of ABET presented in this chapter indicate, accreditors encourage confidence, a rare commodity in these times, especially after the stressors that COVID-19 has brought to HEIs around the world. Higher education media report with alarming frequency the closure or loss of accreditation of HEIs, along with mergers and layoffs. This happens in a context where the credibility of many social institutions is being eroded.

At a time when universities face uncertainty, providing a sense of security—like the authoritative tone that U.S. accrediting agencies employ, and that I have analyzed here—is an easy way out to extend our survival. The current lack of confidence presents a serious challenge, but the role of higher education cannot be, and does not have to be, that of an intellectual placebo. After all, universities are among the most resilient social institutions. Just as accreditation standards and practices adapt to respond to new realities, such as the introduction of online delivery and massive open online courses (MOOCs), while retaining a set of values, even if aspirational, the value of higher education may reside precisely in preparing individuals to face an uncertain world, rather than making them believe that change can be avoided.

In the immediate aftermath of COVID-19, accreditors and universities continued their activities, and accreditation review teams conducted virtual site visits and made decisions based on them. Likewise, regional accreditors introduced greater flexibility. It is uncertain how long these practices will remain in place. These examples illustrate that change is possible. As a result, it should not be considered unrealistic to expect substantial change in which the internationalization of accreditation does not mean the wholesale imposition of U.S. academic culture, norms, and expectations.

Future Directions

The international roles that U.S. accreditors have undertaken constitute a mixture of approaches. ABET and AACSB present encouraging examples of how U.S.-based organizations can adopt global identities and make internationalization core to their identities. Nevertheless, U.S. accreditors continue to be caught in the trap, identified in prior research (Blanco Ramírez, 2015a), of assuming that adaptation equals lowering standards. If this assumption is not revisited, global engagement will remain superficial and unable to reap the benefits of true international engagement: the possibility of encountering truly novel ways to solve problems and posing questions not yet presented from our necessarily limited national perspective.

This chapter fundamentally calls to question the role of quality assurance in higher education as one of primarily inspiring confidence. This discourse was so salient in the data that it influenced the overall direction of this study. Is accreditation an alibi to hide the fact that HEIs have concerns about their own survival? As part of this debate, it is worthwhile to return to Naidoo's (2016) rejection of fetishistic approaches to higher education and to make a canonical interpretation of higher education accreditation: "There can be no general theory of cannons. Cannons are the condition of institutions and the effect of institutions. Canons secure institutions as institutions secure canons" (Spivak, 1993, p. 304). Likewise, we can identify a similar co-dependent relationship between accreditation standards and practices (the canon) and higher education (the institution). While the opening up of U.S. accreditors is a reason for hope, given the possibilities of new ideas and practices, just as universities have been present in radically different ways in different cultures, we must also pursue this opening up to the world at more than just at the surface. Depictions of maps on websites can only go so far. Spivak (1993) goes on to trace a parallel between canon and authority; she reminds us that "the world has changed too much" (p. 305), and the least we can do in higher education is to act accordingly.

CONCLUSION

Accreditation plays a crucial role in higher education quality assurance and has a significant impact on reputation building and maintenance within a globally competitive environment. Accreditation, as a practice of higher education quality assurance, serves an important role—especially during uncertain times. While U.S. accreditation has made many significant contributions to set and uphold standards of quality, our scholarly responsibility requires shedding light on those instances where unearned privilege and unequal power relations exist.

The examples presented in this chapter tell a story of geopolitical power at the core of the legitimation processes underpinning U.S. accreditation. The dominant role of U.S. accreditation practices favors American assumptions about higher education and what a university should look and feel like. These assumptions need to be re-evaluated if we are to take seriously higher education's much-touted commitment to diversity and inclusion. Institutional diversity in a global context has intrinsic value. Careful consideration of the strengths of U.S. accreditation would suggest that it is precisely the ability to apply and adapt a set of standards paying attention to the local context and institutional mission that has made accreditation so successful. Therefore, the same adaptability is needed when pursuing an international perspective for higher education accreditation. The discussion presented in this chapter stands as an invitation to imagine new standards and indicators of quality that are more congruent with local and regional values. In a context of rapid change, standards of quality that are contingent on local needs and interests may be better suited than standards that purport to be permanent and rigorous in the traditional sense. As we seek those new standards, we would be well served by acknowledging the rich traditions of universities in the Global South that are too often suppressed when we focus narrowly on traditional metrics of research outputs and student success.

REFERENCES

Barrett, B., Fernandez, F., and Gonzalez, E. M. (2019). Why universities voluntarily pursue US accreditation: The case of Mexico. *Higher Education*. Advance online publication. https://doi.org/10.1007/s10734-019-00427-y

Björkman, B. (2013). *English as an academic lingua franca: An investigation of form and communicative effectiveness.* Boston, MA: Walter de Gruyter.

Blanco Ramírez, G. (2014). Trading quality across borders: Colonial discourse and international quality assurance policies in higher education. *Tertiary Education and Management, 20*(2), 121–134.

———. (2015a). Translating quality in higher education: US approaches to accreditation of institutions from around the world. *Assessment & Evaluation in Higher Education, 40*(7), 943–957.

———. (2015b). US accreditation in Mexico: Quality in higher education as symbol, performance and translation. *Discourse: Studies in the Cultural Politics of Education, 36*(3), 329–342.

Blanco Ramírez, G., and Metcalfe, A. S. (2020). Visualizing quality: University online identities as organizational performativity in higher education. *The Review of Higher Education, 43*(3), 781–809.

Brittingham, B. (2009). Accreditation in the United States: How did we get to where we are? *New Directions for Higher Education* (145), 7–27.

Chakrabarty, D. (2009). *Provincializing Europe: Postcolonial thought and historical difference* (New ed.). Princeton, NJ: Princeton University Press.

Chang, G. C., and Osborn, J. R. (2005). Spectacular colleges and spectacular rankings: The 'US News' rankings of American 'best' colleges. *Journal of Consumer Culture, 5*(3), 338–364.

Council for Higher Education Accreditation. (2019). Databases and directories: Institutions. Retrieved from https://www.chea.org/search-institutions

Council for Higher Education Accreditation International Quality Group. (2019). CIQG membership list. Retrieved from https://www.chea.org/ciqg-membership-list

Eaton, J. S. (2007). An international accreditation space. In J. Tres and B. Sanyal (Eds.), *Higher education in the world 2007: Accreditation for quality assurance; What is at stake?* (pp. 159–165). New York, NY: Palgrave-Macmillan.

———. (2009). Accreditation in the United States. *New Directions for Higher Education, 145,* 79–86.

Fain, P. (2016). Education secretary drop recognition of accreditor. *Inside Higher Ed.* Retrieved from https://www.insidehighered.com/quicktakes/2016/12/13/education-secretary-drops-recognition-accreditor.

Friedman, G. (2011). *The next decade: Where we've been . . . and where we're going.* New York, NY: Anchor.

Gaston, P. L. (2013). *Higher education accreditation: How it's changing, why it must.* Sterling, VA: Stylus.

Gavriely-Nuri, D. (2012). Cultural approach to CDA. *Critical Discourse Studies, 9*(1), 77–85.

Harvey, L., and Newton, J. (2007). Transforming quality evaluation: Moving on. In *Quality assurance in higher education* (pp. 225–245). Dordrecht, Netherlands: Springer.

Jackson, R. S., Davis, J. H., and Jackson, F. R. (2010). Redesigning regional accreditation: The impact on institutional planning. *Planning for Higher Education, 38*(4), 9–19.

Jenkins, J. (2013). *English as a lingua franca in the international university: The politics of academic English language policy.* New York, NY: Routledge.

Kells, H. R. (1983). *The accreditors: A characterization of institutional accrediting boards.* Washington, DC: Council on Postsecondary Accreditation.

Kreighbaum, A. (2019). UNCF president calls for scrutiny of accreditors. *Inside Higher Ed.* Retrieved from https://www.insidehighered.com/quicktakes/2019/03/06/uncf-president-calls-scrutiny-accreditors

Lee, J. J., and Cantwell, B. (2012). The global sorting machine: An examination of neoracism among international students and postdoctoral researchers. In B. Pusser, K. Kempner, S. Marginson, and I. Ordorika (Eds.), *Universities and the public sphere: Knowledge creation and state building in the era of globalization* (pp. 47–63). New York, NY: Taylor and Francis.

Metcalfe, A. S. (2015). Visual juxtaposition as qualitative inquiry in educational research. *International Journal of Qualitative Studies in Education, 28*(2), 151–167.

Metcalfe, A. S., and Blanco, G. L. (2019). Visual research methods for the study of higher education organizations. In M. Paulsen and L. Perna (Eds.), *Higher education: Handbook of theory and research* (Vol. 34, pp. 153–202). Dordrecht, Netherlands: Springer. doi:doi.org/10.1007/978-3-030-03457-3_4

Middle States Commission on Higher Education. (2009). *Becoming accredited: Handbook for applicants & candidates for accreditation*. Philadelphia, PA: Author.

Naidoo, R. (2016). The competition fetish in higher education: Varieties, animators and consequences. *British Journal of Sociology of Education, 37*(1), 1–10. doi:10.1080/01425692.2015.1116209

Ng, C.J.W. (2014). Semioticizing capitalism in corporate brand enactment: The case of Singapore's corporatized universities. *Critical Discourse Studies, 11*, 139–157.

———. (2016). 'Hottest brand, coolest pedagogy': Approaches to corporate branding in Singapore's higher education sector. *Journal of Marketing for Higher Education, 26*(1), 41–63.

O'Reilly, G. (2019). *Aligning geopolitics, humanitarian action and geography in times of conflict*. Cham, Switzerland: Springer.

Patil, A., and Codner, G. (2007). Accreditation of engineering education: Review, observations and proposal for global accreditation. *European Journal of Engineering Education, 32*(6), 639–651.

Phillips, S. D., and Kinser, K. (Eds.). (2018). *Accreditation on the edge: Challenging quality assurance in higher education*. Baltimore, MD: Johns Hopkins University Press.

Prasad, A., Segarra, P., and Villanueva, C. E. (2019). Academic life under institutional pressures for AACSB accreditation: Insights from faculty members in Mexican business schools. *Studies in Higher Education, 44*(9), 1605–1618.

Romero, E. J. (2008). AACSB accreditation: Addressing faculty concerns. *Academy of Management Learning & Education, 7*(2), 245–255.

Said, E. (1978). *Orientalism*. New York, NY: Vintage.

Saunders, D. B. (2014). Exploring a customer orientation: Free-market logic and college students. *The Review of Higher Education, 37*(2), 197–219.

Saunders, D. B., & Blanco Ramírez, G. (2017). Against "Teaching Excellence": Ideology, Commodification, and Enabling the Neoliberalization of Postsecondary Education. *Teaching in Higher Education, 22*(4), 396–407. doi:10.1080/13562517.2017.1301913

Spivak, G. C. (1993). *Outside in the teaching machine*. New York, NY: Routledge.

U.S. Department of Education. (2018). *Rethinking higher education: Accreditation reform*. Retrieved from https://www.insidehighered.com/sites/default/server_files/media/White%20Paper%20on%20Accreditation%20Reform%2012.19.18.pdf

Western Association of Schools and Colleges Accrediting Commission for Senior Colleges and Universities. (2012). *A guide toward WASC accreditation for institutions incorporated and operating primarily outside of the United States*. Alameda, CA: Author.

PART 2 NATIONAL AND GLOBAL RESEARCH

5 ◆ GEOPOLITICAL TENSIONS AND GLOBAL SCIENCE

Understanding U.S.-China Scientific Research Collaboration through Scientific Nationalism and Scientific Globalism

JOHN P. HAUPT AND JENNY J. LEE

To be a major player on the current geopolitical stage, a country must possess a strong knowledge economy. Unlike in past decades, in which reliance on natural resources and unskilled manual labor were leading determinants of economic power (Powell and Snellman, 2004), knowledge production—namely, scientific and technological (S&T) innovation—is a main driver of economic growth. Universities, as well as research institutes and commercial organizations, play a key role in facilitating such growth (McMahon, 2009). Governments, keenly aware of the interrelationship between knowledge production and country advancement, have established policies to develop and enhance domestic S&T capabilities to meet national needs as well as to be competitive in the global economy (Cantwell and Grimm, 2018; Sá and Sabzalieva, 2018).

From a geopolitical perspective, knowledge production not only fuels domestic growth but also allows for comparative advantage over other countries. Domestic development and global competition are not so easily separable. Evidence of such global competition manifested itself during the Cold War as the United States and the Soviet Union competed to advance their domestic S&T capabilities as a means to promote national security, strengthen economic advantage, and spread influence throughout the world (Sá and Sabzalieva, 2018; Wang, 2002). Experts have labeled the rising tensions between the United States and China as a "New Cold War" (Allison, 2018) as the Trump administration positioned China as an adversary and a threat to U.S. prosperity and security as opposed to a strategic partner (Allison, 2018). With this stance, U.S. foreign policy toward China shifted from a positive-sum to a zero-sum strategy, leaving room for only one winner (Lee and Haupt, 2020).

Tensions between the United States and China have escalated into a contentious trade war, which has directly impacted both countries' S&T enterprises (San, 2020). These tensions have also impacted global S&T more broadly as they have threatened to limit global cooperation to halt the spread of COVID-19 (Crowley, Wong, and Jakes, 2020). The United States has accused China of attempting to steal its way to economic dominance at the expense of the United States (Dennis, 2019), a claim that the Chinese have vehemently denied (Reuters, 2018). Similarly, in May 2020, the U.S. Federal Bureau of Investigation (FBI) and the Cybersecurity and Infrastructure Security Agency accused China of trying to steal U.S. intellectual property and public health data on COVID-19 (FBI, 2020). The United States has taken a particularly strong stance against Chinese tech companies, such as Huawei and ZTE, claiming these companies pose security threats to the United States; U.S. agencies have been banned from doing business with them (Sharma, 2019). Furthermore, the United States has tried to limit China's access to the U.S. S&T enterprise by scrutinizing the ties and activities of graduate students and research scientists who participate in federally funded research projects (Trump, 2020; U.S. Senate, 2019). Additionally, President Trump issued a presidential proclamation suspending and limiting F and J visas for Chinese nationals with ties to China's military-civil fusion strategy (Trump, 2020). Actions such as these have been rationalized by the FBI as preventing the Chinese from engaging in espionage and intellectual property theft and maintaining U.S. security and economic prosperity (Dennis, 2019; IP Commission Report, 2017).

What has gone missing in much of the political rhetoric surrounding current U.S. and China tensions is the positive impact that U.S.-China S&T cooperation has for both countries and the world. This cooperation is vital in addressing global problems, such as COVID-19. Although national governments set policies primarily to enhance domestic capabilities and to increase their comparative advantage, many, including the United States, also promote global engagement via science. Governments have long supported their research scientists in partaking in international research collaboration networks, and at the same time, have sought to attract top global research talent to strengthen research capacity and advance their technological capabilities (Rhoads, Baocheng, Chang, Shi, and Wang, 2014). Engagement in international research collaborations provides scientists with access to expertise, resources, and equipment, all of which are necessary for scientists to partake in cutting-edge research (Bozeman and Boardman, 2014). The knowledge created through these global research networks can be utilized to advance the interests of individual countries as well as the interests of the broader global community.

Given the geopolitical tensions between the United States and China surrounding S&T, including the pressing need to find solutions to the COVID-19 crisis during the writing of this book, this chapter investigates the impact that these tensions may have on national and global S&T development. To do so, it analyzes the nature of U.S.-China S&T research collaboration leading up to the U.S. trade war, which began in mid-2018, as well as U.S.-China collaboration patterns on COVID-19 research during the first half of 2020. The chapter focuses on U.S.-China S&T research collaboration because of the countries' positions as top global producers of S&T research. Together, they accounted for approximately 37 percent of published S&T articles in 2018 (National Science Foundation [NSF], 2020). Additionally, they are the world's top research and development (R&D) performers, with the United States' and China's 2017 R&D spending constituting 25 percent and 23 percent, respectively, of global spending (NSF, 2020). Further, the United States and China are also the top international collaborators of scientific research (first and third, respectively), and they collaborate with each other more than with any other countries (NSF, 2020). Therefore, policies meant to limit S&T collaboration between the United States and China may negatively impact the domestic output of both countries as well as the output of the global scientific community.

INTERNATIONAL RESEARCH COLLABORATION IN SCIENCE

Today, most scientific research studies and publications are collaborative (Bozeman and Boardman, 2014). This propensity toward collaboration is not limited to collaboration between scientists located within one country. Across all S&T fields there has been an increase in international scientific research collaboration (NSF, 2020). In the past decade, the percentage of worldwide publications from international collaboration rose from 16.7 percent to 21.7 percent (NSF, 2020).

This rise in international research collaboration is attributable to numerous social, cognitive, economic, and technological factors (Bozeman and Boardman, 2014). Collaboration allows researchers to gain access to expertise, resources, and equipment that they might not otherwise have access to (Bozeman and Boardman, 2014). Pooling expertise, resources, and equipment has become increasingly essential to compete for research funding and engage in cross-disciplinary, applied science (Coccia and Bozeman, 2016; Coccia and Wang, 2016). Additionally, advancements in information and communication technology have allowed for successful collaboration between scientists located throughout the world, making international collaboration more common today than ever before (Bozeman and Boardman, 2014). Further, international research collaborations have shown to result in higher-quality research with a broader scope (Georghiou, 1998). Internationally co-authored publications gain on average more citations than domestic co-publications, resulting in increased prestige and visibility for scientists (Adams, 2013; Chinchilla-Rodrígueza, Vargas-Quesadab, Hassan-Monterob, González-Molinab, and Moya-Anegóna, 2010; Leta and Chaimovich, 2002; Smith, Weinberger, Bruna, and Allesina, 2014). In sum, international research teams yield access to wider specialized skills, knowledge, and technology; a larger international audience; and diverse perspectives, leading to studies that are cited more frequently, increasing the prestige and visibility of scientists involved.

Although international research collaboration has increased globally, the rate of growth in relation to domestic research varies. Adams (2013) found that increases in research publications for U.S. and Western European countries have been attributable to international co-authorships, as domestic output (papers listing only authors from the home country) has stagnated in these countries. In contrast, Adams found that domestic output in emerging economies is expanding. In the case of China, it produced approximately 10,000 domestic outputs in 1991, whereas in 2011 it produced approximately 125,000 domestic outputs, an increase of over 1,000 percent. Although Adams stresses that international collaboration remains key for all countries, including emerging economies, it is evident that high-income economies have become more reliant than emerging economies on international research collaboration to grow their scientific outputs.

Foreign-Born Researchers' Contributions to Domestic Outputs

In addition to the importance of international collaborations to high-income economies' growth in scientific output, these countries have also benefited immensely from the continuous inflow of academic talent from abroad. Pertaining to the United States, this inflow of talent, working in a variety of research positions, has supported growth in scientific output and helped the United States maintain its position as a top global producer of science. The United States has seen a rise in the number of foreign-born faculty holding academic positions, and research has shown that they produce more research than their domestic-born peers (Kim, Wolf-Wendel, and Twombly, 2011; Mamiseishvili and Rosser, 2010). Additionally, the United States has benefited from a large number of international postdocs who are an inexpensive yet productive source of labor, which allows the United States to keep costs down but production up (Cantwell and Lee, 2010; Cantwell and Taylor, 2015). Finally, although there has been a decline in recent years, international students make up a large portion of students enrolled in U.S. S&T graduate programs (NSF, 2018). In 2017, international students constituted 36 percent of all students enrolled in U.S. S&T graduate programs (NSF, 2018). This figure was even higher in computer science, engineering, mathematics, statistics, and economics at 47 percent of all students (NSF, 2018). These graduate students promote growth through their contributions to supervisors' projects (Cantwell, Lee, and Mlambo, 2018; Lee and Rice,

2007) as well as through their own research projects. In sum, the United States' ability to attract international talent has been instrumental for the growth of its scientific output and further highlights the importance of collaboration between foreign nationals for the advancement of scientific knowledge overall.

THE "CHINA THREAT" AND ACADEMIC SCIENCE

The perception that China is a threat to the United States has been perceived for decades owing to China's rapid economic development over the past twenty years. The "China Threat" argues that as China increases its economic and military power, it is likely to pursue interests within its region and globally that are counter to U.S. interests (Roy, 1996, p. 758). Initially, the "China Threat" focused on China's rise in relation to U.S. interests in Asia, as China's rise was seen as conflicting with the U.S. objective to prevent any country from gaining overwhelming power in the region (Bernstein and Munro, 1997). However, the "China Threat" as viewed today has expanded its focus to include U.S. interests around the world owing to China's highly publicized global initiatives and its ever-increasing involvement with countries on all continents. This perceived conflict of interest positions the United States and China as global adversaries, with some arguing that armed conflict between the nations is more likely than not (Allison, 2017).

From the beginning, proponents of the "China Threat" view have suspected China of malicious efforts to acquire U.S. knowledge and technology, which they considered to be a threat to U.S. security (Wang, 2002). The perceived threat applied to not only Chinese nationals in the United States but also Americans of Chinese descent (Wang, 2002). In 1999, the FBI indicted Wen Ho Lee, a Taiwanese-born Chinese American physicist who once worked at Los Alamos National Laboratory, on charges of transmitting technology to Chinese scientists. Lee had failed to notify officials of contacts with Chinese scientists attempting to deceive officials and had failed to properly safeguard classified material. Lee was jailed and kept in solitary confinement for nine months, but ultimately the case against him was dropped because the FBI admitted to making false statements and no substantial evidence was found to prove he engaged in espionage (Wang, 2002). Additionally, during the same year, the U.S. Congress released the Cox Report, which stated, "Threats to national security can come from PRC scientists, students, business people, or bureaucrats, in addition to professional civilian and military intelligence operations" (U.S. House of Representatives [USHR], 1999, p. 2). The report indicated that Chinese nationals attending U.S. universities posed a risk owing to their access to high-performance computers used by national weapons laboratories (USHR, 1999). Moreover, Chinese scholars who remain in the United States could serve as assets to the Chinese government's efforts to collect science and technology information (USHR,

1999). The report stated that to combat Chinese efforts, the United States can allow only U.S. citizens to access data, limit universities' access, and enhance security and security education at universities (USHR, 1999).

Twenty years later, the "China Threat" to the U.S. S&T enterprise has garnered renewed attention because of the U.S. trade war with China. Similar to decades ago, China is viewed as a threat to U.S. security and prosperity through its purported attempts to acquire U.S. knowledge and technology (U.S. Senate, 2019). The United States has argued that China has exploited the United States' openness to advance its own national economic and military interests (U.S. Senate, 2019). It has done this through talent recruitment programs, such as the Thousand Talents Plan, which recruits U.S.-based researchers, scientists, and experts to share knowledge and technology with China in exchange for monetary compensation and other benefits (U.S. Senate 2019). Once again, the United States has identified its universities as targets of Chinese efforts to acquire knowledge and technology and has accused the Chinese of engaging in academic espionage (U.S. Senate, 2019).

Because of these concerns, the FBI and federal granting agencies, such as the National Institutes of Health, have been in contact with universities to warn against and prevent espionage and intellectual property theft by China (Ackerman, 2018). U.S. agencies have accused federal grant recipients with ties to China of failing to report funding from and ties to the Chinese government, removing thousands of electronic files before traveling to China, sharing grant application information with collaborators in China, filing patents based on U.S. government-funded research, stealing proprietary defense information related to U.S. military jets, and agreeing to give Chinese institutions intellectual property rights that overlap with research conducted at U.S. institutions (Brumfiel, 2020; Kaiser and Malakoff, 2018; U.S. Senate, 2019). Numerous scientists have been investigated for violating reporting rules, including at Harvard University (Brumfiel, 2020), Temple University (Brumfiel, 2020), University of Texas MD Anderson Cancer Research Center (Hvistendahl, 2019), Emory University (Malakoff, 2019), and Baylor College of Medicine (Mervis, 2019). Almost all of those reportedly accused of violating reporting rules, whether eventually dismissed from their positions or cleared of charges, have been of Chinese descent.

This intense scrutiny of research ties with China and the accusations against scientists of Chinese decent have led to criticisms that Chinese students and scientists are being exclusively and unfairly treated based on their ethnicity (Hvistendahl, 2019). Several Chinese scientific communities and Chinese American leaders have spoken against the purported racial profiling, which they say is un-American and can have devastating effects not only on individual careers but also on the Chinese American scientific community (Committee of 100, 2019, para. 2; Lu et al., 2019). These are sentiments that were also expressed by the Asian American community in 1999 during the prosecution of Wen Ho Lee

(Wang, 2002). Moreover, university leaders have voiced concerns about the potential impact that an anti-Chinese climate would have on U.S. universities' ability to attract students and researchers of Chinese decent (American Association for the Advancement of Science [AAAS], 2019; Williams, 2019). University leaders have also reaffirmed their commitment to open science and the value of their institutions' international communities while at the same time addressing security concerns raised by the U.S. government. They warn that the United States has much to lose if scientists of Chinese descent avoid studying and working in the United States, because of the significant contributions these scientists have made to the U.S. S&T enterprise (Brumfiel, 2020; Wang, 2002).

SCIENTIFIC NATIONALISM AND SCIENTIFIC GLOBALISM

Science has long been a geopolitical tool utilized by nation-states to promote national interests. In the case of the Cold War, scientific cooperation and technology transfers were utilized by the United States and Soviet Union to spread influence throughout the world (Wang, 2002). The United States and Soviet Union were actively pursuing scientific nationalism, or the state support of science to primarily provide benefits to the nation-state and promote national interests abroad (Cantwell and Grimm, 2018; Nakayama, 2012). According to scientific nationalism, both scientific and technological advancement are seen as necessary for national security, strengthening economic advantage, and signaling national prestige (Sá and Sabzalieva, 2018). Scientific competition is conceptualized within a zero-sum framework for the advancement of certain states and the demise of others (Cantwell and Grimm, 2018; Sá and Sabzalieva, 2018).

The "China Threat" view similarly conceives scientific competition between the United States and China through a zero-sum framework. Some binary rationales are as follows: An increase in China's S&T capabilities is a threat to U.S. security and prosperity (U.S. Senate, 2019). U.S. investments in S&T should primarily benefit the United States and strengthen its military and economic advantage over other countries. The U.S. scientific community must be suspicious of collaborations with Chinese scientists on U.S. federally funded research projects, as they may steal the output of the research and use it to their own advantage. Thus, China is positioned as an adversary rather than an ally, and the gains of one country result in a loss for the other.

Although this zero-sum perspective positions the United States and China as rivals, the reality is that zero-sum perspectives exist alongside positive-sum perspectives (Marginson, 2018) depending on the scenario, interpretation of context, and strategies employed by nation-states (Christensen, 2006). Taking the positive-sum concept further, U.S. and China scientific competition can be alternatively viewed through the lens of scientific globalism. Scientific globalism perceives science as universal, or not being bound by political borders or belonging to certain groups of people. Science is guided by the norms established within the scientific community, and the knowledge derived through scientific inquiry should be available to all (Sá and Sabzalieva, 2018). Within this logic of scientific globalism, international cooperation, and even competition, S&T advancement is beneficial to all nations and supports mutual socioeconomic development (Sá and Sabzalieva, 2018). Therefore, scientific globalism applies a positive-sum perspective to U.S. and China scientific competition in which both parties can benefit without the demise of the other.

Depending on the perspective taken, U.S. scientific research collaboration with China represents an opportunity or a threat. If policymakers espouse scientific nationalism's zero-sum logic, collaboration with China provides the Chinese with an opportunity to gain access to knowledge and technology at the frontiers of science, which they can use to compete against the United States and hurt its global standing. Such a view justifies attempts to limit international research. On the contrary, if policymakers adopt scientific globalism's positive-sum logic, collaboration with China is an opportunity for mutual growth and essential for the development of knowledge and technology that can be utilized in addressing global challenges. These contrary yet coexisting logics can be utilized to understand how policies and programs might promote or inhibit a country's S&T research capabilities and its international partnerships. Regarding the current geopolitical tensions between the United States and China, it is possible to gain insight into how policies or programs meant to limit U.S. research collaboration with China may impact the future of the United States, China, and global S&T production.

U.S.-CHINA RESEARCH COLLABORATION

This chapter elaborates on the results from a portion of our previous study (Lee and Haupt, 2020) that analyzed the patterns and nature of research collaborations between the United States and China from 2014 to 2018, through the frameworks of scientific nationalism and scientific globalism. International research collaboration is arguably especially important during periods of global crisis. Thus, this chapter extends this research by providing a snapshot of U.S.-China collaboration patterns on COVID-19 research specifically. Research collaboration was measured by using Scopus to gather data on co-authored peer-reviewed journal article publications that included at least one scholar affiliated with a U.S. institution (U.S. scholar) and one scholar affiliated with a Chinese institution (China scholar). Co-authorship was selected as a measure of collaboration because it is a commonly accepted scientific indicator for measuring and evaluating research collaboration patterns (Katz and Martin, 1997). Data retrieved on co-publications included the total number of U.S. and China S&T publications from 2014 to 2018 as well as each country's total number of S&T publications on

COVID-19 during the first half of 2020, the total number of S&T publications that included both U.S. and China scholars during both time periods, and the total number of S&T publications that included U.S., China, and third-country scholars during both time periods. In addition to the total number of publications, data also included all collaborating authors' university affiliations, the funding sponsors of each article, and the number of times an article had been cited. Utilizing the data from 2014 to 2018, we measured the growth of co-publications between U.S. and China scholars, the extent to which these co-publications impacted the growth of U.S. and China S&T publications, and the country affiliations of first authors on the top-cited 500 co-publications. With the COVID-19 data, we measured the rate of collaboration between U.S. and China scholars and the country affiliations of first authors on all co-publications.

GROWTH IN U.S.-CHINA RESEARCH COLLABORATION

Similar to global trends identified in past research, the number of co-authored publications including U.S. and China scholars steadily increased from 2014 to 2018, with a 55.7 percent increase in annual publications when comparing 2014 and 2018 co-publications. In total, there were 175,655 U.S.-China co-publications, representing approximately 10 percent of all U.S. and China S&T publications during the time period. The results also indicate that the majority of co-publications that included U.S. and China scholars were bilateral, meaning they included only U.S. and China scholars. Of the total U.S.-China co-authored publications, 75 percent were bilateral collaborations versus only 25 percent for multilateral collaborations including scholars from other countries. However, both forms of co-authorship grew over the five-year time period, with bilateral collaborations in 2018 increasing by 52.5 percent compared with 2014, and multilateral collaborations in 2018 increasing by 65.6 percent compared with 2014.

THE ROLE OF RESEARCH COLLABORATION IN THE GROWTH OF U.S. AND CHINA S&T PUBLICATIONS

Beyond growth in co-publications, the study sought to understand the value that collaboration brings to the two countries by analyzing growth in each country's S&T publications with and without the other country. The data show that both countries positively contributed to each other's growth in publications; however, U.S. growth was dependent on collaborations with China scholars, while China's growth was enhanced by but not dependent on collaborations with U.S. scholars. For the United States, when excluding articles with China scholars, U.S. scholars produced 6,405 fewer articles, or a 2.03 percent decrease, between 2014 and 2018. In contrast, when including articles with China scholars, U.S. scholars produced 8,876 more articles, or a 2.59 percent increase, across the same

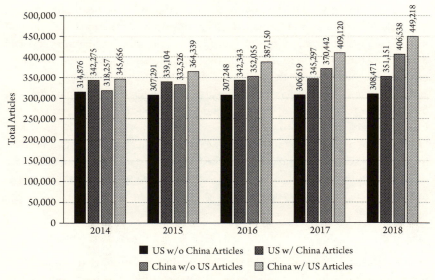

FIGURE 5.1. U.S. and China S&T article publications with and without the other country, 2014–2018.

time span. In other words, U.S. growth was attributable to collaborations with China. On the other hand, China publication data present a different story across the same time period. The number of articles published by China scholars, excluding those with U.S. scholars, increased by 27.74 percent from 2014 to 2018. When including publications with U.S. scholars, China scholars produced 29.96 percent more articles in 2018 than in 2014. Thus, Chinese output grew regardless of whether collaboration occurred with U.S. scholars, and publications with U.S. scholars contributed only slightly to this growth (see figure 5.1).

INTELLECTUAL LEADERSHIP IN U.S.-CHINA RESEARCH COLLABORATION

Proponents of the "China Threat" view argue that China scholars are engaged in espionage and stealing U.S. intellectual property without acknowledging the role that scholars from both countries play in the development of new knowledge and the advancement of science. When analyzing the top 500 cited articles produced from 2014 to 2018 for U.S. and China bilateral collaborations, the findings show that China scholars were first authors on a higher percentage of publications than U.S. or U.S.-China dual affiliated authors. China scholars were first authors on almost half of the publications, or 49 percent, while U.S. and U.S.-China dual affiliated scholars were first authors on roughly a quarter of the publications, 28 percent and 23 percent, respectively. Moreover, when analyzing

Geopolitical Tensions and Global Science

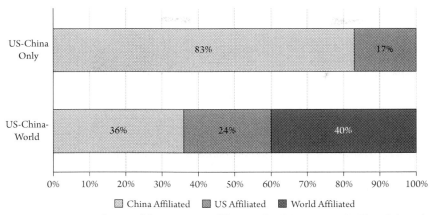

FIGURE 5.2. First authors and their country affiliations for COVID-19 U.S.-China bilateral and multilateral co-publications.

the top 500 cited articles from 2014 to 2018 for U.S. and China multilateral collaborations, U.S. and China scholars were first authors on approximately the same percentage of publications, 35 percent and 32 percent, respectively. Scholars from other countries were first authors on 22 percent of publications, and U.S.-China dual affiliated scholars were first authors on 11 percent of publications. These findings demonstrate that while collaborating with U.S. scholars, China scholars are playing leading roles in the production of high-impact research (Larivière et al., 2016).

U.S.-China Collaboration during the COVID-19 Global Pandemic

As of the end of June 2020, a total of 9,366 S&T articles had been published on COVID-19. Of these articles, China scholars and U.S. scholars authored approximately the same number of articles, 2,078 (22.3%) and 2,004 (21.4%), respectively. Scholars affiliated with both countries collaborated on 227 articles, or 10.9 percent of China's COVID-19 publications and 11.3 percent of the United States' COVID-19 publications. This is a slight increase compared with collaboration patterns from 2014 to 2018. Of the 227 co-publications, 136 (59.9%) were bilateral collaborations, which is 15 percent lower than the 2014–2018 pattern. Thus, U.S. and China scholars are engaged in more multilateral collaborations on COVID-19 than they were leading up to the trade war. Moreover, regarding first-authorship patterns, 83 percent of bilateral U.S.-China co-publications were first-authored by a China scholar (see figure 5.2), whereas for multilateral co-publications, China scholars first-authored 36.2 percent and U.S. scholars first-authored 24.2 percent. Unlike the 2014–2018 collaboration patterns, there is a noticeably higher proportion of both bilateral and multilateral COVID-19 co-publications that were first-authored by China scholars.

DISCUSSION

This study utilized the patterns and nature of co-publications between U.S. and China scholars leading up to the current trade war and on COVID-19 research to understand how policies and programs designed to limit collaboration between U.S. and China scholars might impact each country's scientific outputs as well as global science more broadly. Framed in reference to scientific nationalism and scientific globalism, the results of the study show the United States and global science have much to gain if the former chooses to promote open science and not limit collaboration with China. In fact, the publication data leading up to the trade war indicate that if the United States is to solely adopt a nationalistic, zero-sum perspective on research with China and tries to limit collaboration, it risks negatively impacting its rate of growth in future S&T output. Comparing the number of U.S. annual publications in 2014 with that in 2018, excluding co-publications with China scholars, resulted in a slight decline, whereas including co-publications with China scholars resulted in a slight increase. Moreover, limiting collaboration would also likely negatively impact the advancement of global science as both U.S.-China bilateral collaborations and multilateral collaborations steadily increased, producing more scientific output in 2018 than in 2014. This same negative impact would also likely be felt on global science surrounding COVID-19 since U.S. and China COVID-19 co-publications include a higher proportion of third-country scholars than collaborations from 2014 to 2018 did. Thus, viewing collaboration with China through scientific globalism's positive-sum perspective instead of scientific nationalism's zero-sum perspective is likely to result in opportunities for growth in future U.S. S&T output and further advances in global scientific knowledge.

Similarly, the findings from the analysis of first authorship patterns show that U.S. S&T output benefits from the knowledge and skills that China scholars bring to the collaborations. On publications from 2014 to 2018, for U.S.-China bilateral collaborations, China scholars were lead authors on half of the publications, and for multilateral collaborations, they were lead authors on nearly one-third of them. Regarding COVID-19 research, China scholars' leading roles grew substantially on bilateral collaborations but only slightly on multilateral collaborations. These results demonstrate that China scholars have played and continue to play important roles in the creation of new scientific knowledge (Larivie et al., 2016), including in times of global crisis. Further, these results run counter to the "China Threat" rhetoric that often characterizes China scholars as engaging in collaboration with U.S. scholars to gain access to and steal scientific knowledge and technology. From a scientific globalism perspective, collaborations with China scholars provide U.S. scholars with access to knowledge, skills, and labor that they might not otherwise have access to. This is true for both bilateral and multilateral collaborations; however, with multilateral collaborations, U.S. scholars may lose access to the knowledge and skills provided by both China and third-country scholars. Thus, espousing a scientific nationalism perspective and limiting research collaboration with China could result in U.S. scholars' reduced access to specialized knowledge and skills that may be necessary to engage in groundbreaking, cutting-edge research to advance the United States' S&T capabilities as well as solve pressing global problems, such as COVID-19.

Future U.S. efforts to collaborate with China are especially imperative as China is considering reducing its "excessive reliance" on the Science Citation Index (SCI) (Sharma, 2020, para. 1). In the spirit of scientific nationalism, President Xi Jinping indicated that China should have its own academic standards, rather than follow the standards dictated by the West. Less reliance on SCI publications would mean fundamentally new requirements in "awarding doctoral degrees, hiring new researchers, promoting young researchers to a higher rank or determining academics' bonuses, research funding or their application for academic prizes or rewards" (Huang, 2020). With less governmental pressure to publish in international journals, international collaboration will inevitably drop, not only for China (Huang, 2020) but, as our research has demonstrated, for the United States as well. Thus, scientific nationalism can affect the extent of scientific collaboration, as in the cases of the United States and China.

Despite the potential benefits of scientific globalism, we are not suggesting that the United States, or any country for that matter, completely abandon concerns related to national security and intellectual property. It is imperative for the advancement of national science systems and global science that scientists adhere to scientific norms for the recognition of scholarly contributions to one's respective field as well as to globally agreed-upon standards for intellectual property rights. Doing so helps ensure that national governments will continue funding scientists to engage in cutting-edge research and that scientists will possess the trust necessary for collaboration to occur.

In conclusion, our research shows that the extent to which U.S. agencies and organizations promote scientific nationalism, scientific globalism, or some combination of both will likely have ramifications on the future of U.S., China, and global S&T production. If the United States continues to view China primarily as a threat and develops policies to limit engagement with China, it may undermine the security, growth, and prosperity it is hoping to achieve. It is clear that U.S. scholars benefit from access to the skills and knowledge of China scholars and that collaborations with China scholars contribute to U.S. S&T growth. The United States also must consider the impact of a hostile climate against ethnic Chinese scientists on the U.S. S&T enterprise. A hostile climate is likely to make it harder for the United States to attract and retain top global talent (Lee, 2019), and if history repeats itself, to attract U.S.-born ethnic Chinese to work in S&T positions that receive federal funding (Wang, 2002). Owing to the possible negative long-term impact on its S&T enterprise, the United States must determine how to best facilitate and leverage research collaborations with China to advance its own S&T capabilities, as China has been doing for so long (Marginson, 2018). The United States would yield greater benefits from engaging in scientific globalism and remaining open to collaboration with China. Maintaining and increasing collaboration with China has the potential to provide greater benefits to the United States while also advancing global science, which is necessary to help solve present and future global challenges.

REFERENCES

Ackerman, T. (2018, August 8). MD Anderson ousts 3 scientists over concerns about Chinese conflicts of interest. *Houston Chronicle*. Retrieved from https://www.houstonchronicle.com/news/houston-texas/houston/article/MD-Anderson-fires-3-scientists-over-concerns-13780570.php.

Adams, J. (2013). The fourth age of research. *Nature*, 497, 557–560.

Allison, G. (2017). *Destined for war: Can America and China escape Thucydides' trap?* Boston, MA: Houghton Mifflin Harcourt.

———. (2018, October 12). The U.S. is hunkering down for a new cold war with China. Retrieved from https://www.belfercenter.org/publication/us-hunkering-down-new-cold-war-china

American Association for the Advancement of Science. (2019, September 4). Multicity letter on foreign influence [PDF file]. Retrieved from https://www.aaas.org/sites/default/files/2019-09/Multisociety%20Letter%20on%20Foreign%20Influence_9-4-2019.pdf

Bernstein, R., and Munro, R. (1997). The coming conflict with America. *Foreign Affairs*, 76(2), 18–32. doi:10.2307/20047934

Bozeman, B., and Boardman, C. (2014). *Research collaboration and team science: A state-of-the-art review and agenda*. New York, NY: Springer.

Brumfiel, G. (2020, February 19). Harvard professor's arrest raises questions about scientific openness. *National Public Radio*. Retrieved from https://www.npr.org/2020/02/14/806128410/harvard-professors-arrest-raises-questions-about-scientific-openness

Cantwell, B., and Grimm, A. (2018). The geopolitics of academic science. In B. Cantwell, H. Coates, and R. King (Eds.). *Handbook on the politics of higher education* (pp. 130–148). Cheltenham, UK: Edward Elgar Publishing.

Cantwell, B., and Lee, J. J. (2010). Unseen workers in the academic factory: Perceptions of neo-racism among international postdocs in the US and UK. *Harvard Education Review*, 80(4), 490–517.

Cantwell, B., Lee, J. J., and Mlambo, Y. (2018). International graduate student labor as mergers and acquisitions. *International Student Journal*, 8(4), 1483–1498.

Cantwell, B., and Taylor, B. J. (2015). Rise of the science and engineering post doctorate and the restructuring of academic research. *The Journal of Higher Education*, 86, 667–696.

Chinchilla-Rodríguez, Z., Vargas-Quesadab, B., Hassan-Monterob, Y., González-Molinab, A., and Moya-Anegóna, F. (2010). New approach to the visualization of international scientific collaboration. *Information Visualization*, 9, 277–287.

Christensen, T. J. (2006). Fostering stability or creating a monster? The rise of China and U.S. policy toward East Asia. *International Security*, 31, 81–126.

Coccia, M., and Bozeman, B. (2016). Allometric models to measure and analyze the evolution of international research collaboration. *Scientometrics*, 108, 1065–1084.

Coccia, M., and Wang, L. (2016). Evolution and convergence of the patterns of international scientific collaboration. *Proceedings of the National Academy of Sciences USA*, 113, 2057–2061.

Committee of 100. (2019, April 7). Committee of 100 condemns Chinese American racial profiling [Press release]. Retrieved from https://www.committee100.org/press_release/committee-of-100-condemns-chinese-american-racial-profiling-2/

Crowley, M., Wong, E., and Jakes, L. (2020, March 22). Coronavirus drives the U.S. and China deeper into global power struggle. *The New York Times*. Retrieved from https://www.nytimes.com/2020/03/22/us/politics/coronavirus-us-china.html

Dennis, S. T. (2019, July 24). FBI chief says China is trying to 'steal their way' to economic dominance. *Time*. Retrieved from https://time.com/5633390/fbi-christopher-wray-china-counterintelligence/

Federal Bureau of Investigation. (2020, May 13). People's Republic of China (PRC) targeting of COVID-19 research organizations. Retrieved from https://www.fbi.gov/news/pressrel/press-releases/peoples-republic-of-china-prc-targeting-of-covid-19-research-organizations

Georghiou, L. (1998). Global cooperation in research. *Research Policy*, 27(6), 611–626.

Huang, F. (2020, February 26). China is choosing its own path on academic evaluation. *University World News*. Retrieved from https://www.universityworldnews.com/post.php?story=20200226122508451

Hvistendahl, M. (2019, April 19). Exclusive: Major U.S. cancer center ousts 'Asian' researchers after NIH flags their foreign ties. *Science*. Retrieved from https://www.sciencemag.org/news/2019/04/exclusive-major-us-cancer-center-ousts-asian-researchers-after-nih-flags-their-foreign

IP Commission Report. (2017, February 27). *The theft of American intellectual property: Reassessments of the challenge and United States policy*. Retrieved from http://ipcommission.org/report/IP_Commission_Report_Update_2017.pdf

Kaiser, J., and Malakoff, D. (2018, August 27). NIH investigating whether U.S. scientists are sharing ideas with foreign governments. *Science*. Retrieved from https://www.sciencemag.org/news/2018/08/nih-investigating-whether-us-scientists-are-sharing-ideas-foreign-governments.

Katz, J. S., and Martin, B. R. (1997). What is research collaboration? *Research Policy*, 26(1), 1–18.

Kim, D., Wolf-Wendel, L., and Twombly, S. (2011). International faculty: Experiences of academic life and productivity in U.S. universities. *The Journal of Higher Education*, 82, 720–747.

Larivière, V., Desrochers, N., Macaluso, B., Mongeon, P., Paul-Hus, A., and Sugimoto, C. (2016). Contributorship and division of labor in knowledge production. *Social Studies of Science*, 46(3), 417–435.

Lee, J. J. (2019). Beyond Trumpism: The underlying U.S. political climate for international students and scholars. Trends and Insights, A Special Edition by the 2018–19 NAFSA Senior Scholars. Retrieved from http://www.nafsa.org/Professional_Resources/Research_and_Trends/Internationalization_in_a_Time_of_Global_Disruption/.

Lee, J. J., and Haupt, J. P. (2020). Winners and losers in US-China scientific research collaborations. *Higher Education*, 80, 57–74.

Lee, J. J., and Rice, C. (2007). Welcome to America? International student perceptions of discrimination. *Higher Education*, 53(3), 381–409.

Leta, J., and Chaimovich, H. (2002). Recognition and international collaboration: The Brazilian case. *Scientometrics*, 53, 325–335.

Lu, S., Han, Z., Hung, M., Xu, J., Xu, Y., Zheng, P., ... Zheng, H. (2019). Racial profiling harms science [Letter]. *Science*, 363(6433), 1290–1292.

Malakoff, D. (2019, May 23). Emory ousts two Chinese American researchers after investigation into foreign ties. *Science.* Retrieved from https://www.sciencemag.org/news/2019/05/emory-ousts-two-chinese-american-researchers-after-investigation-foreign-ties

Mamiseishvili, K., and Rosser, V. (2010). International and citizen faculty in the United States: An examination of their productivity at research universities. *Research in Higher Education, 51*(1), 88–107.

Marginson, S. (2018). National/global synergy in the development of higher education and science in China since 1978. *Frontiers of Education in China, 13,* 486–512.

McMahon, W. (2009). *Higher learning, greater good: The private and social benefits of higher education.* Baltimore, MD: Johns Hopkins University Press.

Mervis, J. (2019, April 26). U.S. universities reassess collaborations with foreign scientists in wake of NIH letters. *Science.* Retrieved from https://www.sciencemag.org/news/2019/04/us-universities-reassess-collaborations-foreign-scientists-wake-nih-letters

Nakayama, S. (2012). Techno-nationalism versus techno-globalism. *East Asian Science, Technology and Society, 6*(1), 9–15.

National Science Foundation. (2018). Science and engineering indicators 2018. Retrieved from https://nsf.gov/statistics/2018/nsb20181/report/sections/higher-education-in-science-and-engineering/graduate-education-enrollment-and-degrees-in-the-united-states

———. (2020). Science and engineering indicators. Retrieved from https://ncses.nsf.gov/pubs/nsb20203

Powell, W. W., & Snellman, K. (2004). The knowledge economy. *Annual Review of Sociology., 30,* 199–220.

Reuters. (2018, December 20). China denies 'slanderous' economic espionage charges from US, allies. Retrieved from https://www.cnbc.com/2018/12/21/china-denies-economic-espionage-charges-from-us-allies.html

Rhoads, R., Baocheng, J., Chang, Y., Shi, X., and Wang, X. (2014). *China's Rising Research Universities: A New Era of Global Ambition.* Baltimore, MD: Johns Hopkins University Press.

Roy, D. (1996). The "China Threat" issue: Major arguments. *Asian Survey, 36,* 758–771.

Sá, C., and Sabzalieva, E. (2018). Scientific nationalism in a globalizing world. In B. Cantwell, H. Coates, and R. King (Eds.), *Handbook on the politics of higher education* (pp. 130–148). Cheltenham, UK: Edward Elgar Publishing.

San, W. (2020, January 13). A delicate truce in the U.S.-Chinese trade war: What both sides must do to forge a better peace. *Foreign Affairs.* Retrieved from https://www.foreignaffairs.com/articles/united-states/2020-01-13/delicate-truce-us-chinese-trade-war

Sharma,Y. (2019, February 11). Top US research universities freeze ties with Huawei. *University World News.* Retrieved from https://www.universityworldnews.com/post.php?story=20190211124159161

———. (2020, February 25). China shifts from reliance on international publications. *University World News.* Retrieved from https://www.universityworldnews.com/post.php?story=20200225181649179

Smith, M. J., Weinberger, C., Bruna, E. M., and Allesina, S. (2014). The scientific impact of nations: Journal placement and citation performance. *PLoS One, 9*(10), 1–6.

Trump, D. J. (2020, May 29). Proclamation on the suspension of entry as nonimmigrants of certain students and researchers from the People's Republic of China. Retrieved from https://www.whitehouse.gov/presidential-actions/proclamation-suspension-entry-nonimmigrants-certain-students-researchers-peoples-republic-china/

U.S. House of Representatives. (1999). US national security and military/commercial concerns with the People's Republic of China. Retrieved from https://www.govinfo.gov/content/pkg/GPO-CRPT-105hrpt851/pdf/GPO-CRPT-105hrpt851.pdf

U.S. Senate. (2019, November 18). Threats to the U.S. research enterprise: China's talent recruitment plans. Retrieved from https://www.hsgac.senate.gov/imo/media/doc/2019-11-18%20PSI%20Staff%20Report%20-%20China's%20Talent%20Recruitment%20Plans.pdf

Wang, Z. (2002). Chinese American scientists and U.S.-China scientific relations: From Richard Nixon to Wen Ho Lee. In P. Koehn and X. Yin (Eds.), *The expanding roles of Chinese Americans in U.S.-China relations: Transnational networks and trans-Pacific interactions* (pp. 207–234). Armonk, NY: M.E. Sharp.

Williams, R. (2019, March 21). Chinese-American scientist societies fear racial profiling. *The Scientist*. Retrieved from https://www.the-scientist.com/news-opinion/chinese-american-scientist-societies-fear-racial-profiling-65627

6 • CONCEPTS FOR UNDERSTANDING THE GEOPOLITICS OF GRADUATE STUDENT AND POSTDOC MOBILITY

BRENDAN CANTWELL

Research universities in the United States have long been at the center of the academic science enterprise globally. International students and researchers make extraordinary contributions to U.S. academic science (Stephan, 2012), are sought after by universities wishing to improve their research performance, and enhance the global competitiveness of U.S. higher education (Cantwell and Lee, 2010; Cantwell, Lee, and Mlambo, 2018; Taylor and Cantwell, 2015). Each year, U.S. universities attract tens of thousands of graduate students and early-career researchers from abroad. In 2017 over 230,000 international graduate students enrolled in science, engineering, and health-related (S&E) fields, totaling approximately 35 percent of S&E graduate students. That same year, U.S. universities employed nearly 35,000 international postdocs, accounting for approximately 55 percent of all S&E postdoctoral researchers (National Science Foundation [NSF], 2019). By their numbers and talents, internationally mobile researchers propel research. These same researchers also establish links between academic systems, support the global development of higher education, and are actors in internationalization. As Jenny Lee argues in the introduction to this book, internationalization processes are directed by social and political power.

This chapter considers how the inflow of international graduate students contributes to the global dominance of the United States in academic science and considers implications for the near future. The inflow of graduate students and postdocs to the United States during the end of the twentieth and the start of the twenty-first century strengthened the U.S. academic research system and contributed to American scientific and academic dominance. Growing isolation in U.S. higher education, driven by a nationalist policy environment and rhetoric, is associated with declining demand of U.S. higher education among students from abroad (Redden, 2019), and the rate of growth among inbound postdocs appears to be stalled. Overall, international graduate students and postdoctoral researcher numbers have been substantively flat since 2010. This chapter was composed and revised during 2019 and 2020, during the time that U.S. immigration policy was tumultuous with drastic changes proposed and some implemented. At times, higher education has been at the center of nationalist immigration policies, including a temporary suspension of the H-1B skilled visa program. Mounting confusion, complexity, and above all nationalist hostility underwrite current immigration policy. What these policies mean for higher education in the longer term is, of course, not certain. What is clear is that growth in the aggregate number of international researchers migrating to the United States has slowed in the second decade of the twenty-first century relative to the previous few decades. Nationalist exclusion through xenophobic immigration policy targets and harms current and perspective educational migrants. Flat growth may also reflect the relative weakening of U.S. academic science globally.

International mobility, including large inflows of early-career academics, has strengthened higher education and provided opportunities for individual mobile researchers. Drawing on recent scholarship about power relations in global higher education, I explore the complicated and sometimes contradictory implications of international graduate education and postdoctoral training in a shifting and increasingly nationalist political environment. Relevant concepts include neo-nationalism (Lee, 2017; Lee, Jon, and Byun, 2017), which considers how ethnonational identities shape the way individuals are included and excluded in higher education systems, techno-nationalism, and scientific nationalism (Cantwell and Grimm, 2018), which addresses the way states use academic science to capture advantage, and the geopolitics of higher education (Hazelkorn, 2016).

In this chapter, I synthesize secondary news reports, primary source documents, and empirical literature in arguing that the internationalization of graduate education and scientific training is an example of the way American institutions have exploited globalization processes to leverage individual, institutional, and national advantages from the labor and expertise of internationally mobile graduate students and postdocs. My goal is to develop arguments supported by evidence rather than to uncover new empirical findings. I argue that traditional center-periphery models for explaining international processes in higher education are insufficient to explain the geopolitics of international postdocs and graduate students in the United States. To understand the role of international postdocs and graduate students in the United States, I consider inbound mobility through various concepts of nationalism—including techno-nationalism and neo-racism. The chapter concludes by considering what this topic suggests about the place of U.S. academic science and engineering in the world.

INTERNATIONAL PHD STUDENTS AND POSTDOCS: A DATA PROFILE

The U.S. NSF (2019) collects information through the annual Survey of Graduate Students and Postdoctorates in Science and Engineering. The survey has near-census coverage of U.S. colleges and universities that engage in graduate education and research. Numbers for graduate students are likely to be highly precise. Counting postdocs is more complicated because the definition of postdoc appointments is not always consistent (Einaudi, Heuer, and Green, 2013). Also, the NSF survey covers only science and engineering fields for the postdoc counts, including the social sciences and medical-related fields but excluding the arts and humanities. Despite these limitations, NSF data are a high-quality and reliable source for understanding the inflow of graduate students and postdocs to the United States. To supplement NSF data, I draw from other sources such as the data from the Council of Graduate Schools.

International Doctoral Education

Nearly one in three earned doctoral degrees in the United States are awarded to temporary visa holders, the category of people generally referred to as "international." In 2017, over 16,300 international students earned a doctoral degree from a U.S. university. Growth in the number and share of all doctoral degrees awarded to temporary visa holders was spectacular during what might be called the global era in higher education, the period of time between the end of the Cold War and the first fifteen years of the twenty-first century. In 1987, a few years before the fall of the Soviet Union and subsequent acceleration of globalization processes, some 5,600 doctoral degrees—17 percent of the total—were awarded to international students. Between 1987 and 2017 the number of awards to international students nearly tripled, and the share among all doctoral awards nearly doubled.

Fields that awarded an above average share of all doctoral degrees to international students include engineering (52% in 2017), mathematics and computer science (50%), and physical and earth sciences (35%). Heavily internationalized fields are typically quantitative and, at least in the cases of engineering and computer science, are tightly linked with labor markets. The least internationalized

TABLE 6.1   Postdocs employed at U.S. universities, 2011–2016

	2011	2012	2013	2014	2015	2016
All surveyed fields	62,639	62,851	61,942	63,593	63,861	64,712
U.S. citizens and permanent residents	29,712	29,864	29,546	30,095	28,726	29,810
Temporary visa holders	32,927	32,987	32,396	33,498	35,135	34,902
Share international	53%	52%	52%	53%	55%	54%
Science and engineering	44,121	43,841	43,395	44,623	45,295	45,737
U.S. citizens and permanent residents	20,340	20,214	20,257	20,453	19,593	20,205
Temporary visa holders	23,781	23,627	23,138	24,170	25,702	25,532
Share international	54%	54%	53%	54%	57%	56%

fields are education (11% in 2017), the arts and humanities (13%), and psychology and the social sciences (19%). These lesser internationalized fields are often described as "soft," a term that is misleading about content and rigor but nonetheless demonstrates perceptions (misplaced as they may be) of rigor and importance. Independent of assessments about which fields are most valuable, these data and secondary research show (a) international students constitute a large share of all doctoral awards, (b) international doctoral students are heavily concentrated in science and engineering fields, and (c) the country, universities, and individual faculty members benefit from the contributions made by international doctoral students (Stephan, 2012).

Despite the continued high proportion of doctoral degrees awarded to international students, recent enrollments have dipped. Data collected by the Council of Graduate Schools show that first time international graduate school enrollments declined by 3.7 percent from the fall of 2016 to 2017. Total international applications and the proportion of all graduate students who were international also declined (Council of Graduate Schools, 2018). The dip in graduate enrollments has been greeted by the press as evidence of a so-called Trump effect, or a chill in the international appeal of the United States resulting from xenophobic politics. It is likely that nationalist politics are at least partially driving away international graduate students. NSF data, however, show that international doctoral degree awards peaked around the time of the Great Recession. In other words, gradual de-internationalization of U.S. doctoral education may be occurring naturally based on economic terms and shifting political power but is likely accelerated by, and the political implications amplified by, the current hostile environment (see Table 6.1).

INTERNATIONAL POSTDOCS

Postdocs are central to the U.S. academic research enterprise. As highly skilled researchers who are generally not well paid and employed on short-term contracts, postdocs make cost-effective contributions to academic science. Over the past several decades, the number of postdocs employed at U.S. universities has swelled. Growth was driven by increases in federal funding for research and intensified competition for research dollars (Cantwell and Taylor, 2013). Universities, and the individual investigators therein, hired postdocs to perform research funded by grants and then relied on the contributions of postdocs to secure further funding. Postdocs became central to U.S. research performance, and by the early 1990s, the majority of postdocs came from abroad. In other words, this highly internationalized group of scientific workers has become central to the U.S. science and engineering enterprise and to the country's standing in global science.

Table 6.2 and Figure 6.1 show postdoctoral employment figures. In 2016 there were 64,712 postdocs employed at U.S. colleges and universities, as reported by the NSF survey of Graduate Students and Postdoctorates in Science and Engineering. Of those, 34,902, or 54 percent, were temporary visa holders. Among the "Science and Engineering" category, which includes the social sciences but excludes health fields, international postdocs accounted for 56 percent of the total. Between 2011 and 2016 the total number of postdocs and the share who are international have fluctuated a bit from year to year but over the period have generally held steady. Over a longer period, the number of postdocs employed and the share who are international have grown tremendously. In 1980 there were fewer than 19,000 science and engineering postdocs in the United States, of which 35 percent were international. While both PhD students and postdocs are internationalized, postdoc ranks have long been more internationalized. In fact, it is likely that postdocs are the most international group in U.S. higher education (Cantwell and Lee, 2010).

As with PhD students, internationalization among postdocs may have peaked. In 2003, 58 percent of all science and engineering postdocs were international. In 2009, the share of postdocs who were international dipped below 54 percent for the first time since the late 1990s. Again, we do not have certain causal explanations for why this happened. Financial strain placed on higher education after the Great Recession may be one factor, as may the fact that China and other countries have expanded their research operations and, in doing so, have created attractive opportunities outside the United States. Nor do we know that the de-internationalization trend is permanent. It is possible that the long-term average for postdocs could settle in at around 55 percent, which would indicate continued strong international pull to the United States among early-career researchers.

TABLE 6.2 Doctoral degrees awarded at U.S. universities by citizenship status and field of study in selected years: 1987–2017

Field of study and citizenship status	1987	1992	1997	2002	2007	2012	2017
All fields	32,365	38,886	42,539	40,031	48,132	50,944	54,664
U.S. citizen or permanent resident	24,585	28,005	31,097	27,737	29,501	32,981	35,791
Temporary visa holder	5,660	9,980	9,194	9,747	15,123	14,784	16,323
Unknown	2,120	901	2,248	2,547	3,508	3,179	2,550
Share international	17%	26%	22%	24%	31%	29%	30%
Life sciences	5,783	7,172	8,421	8,478	10,702	11,964	12,592
U.S. citizen or permanent resident	4,529	5,106	5,987	5,850	7,009	8,184	8,857
Temporary visa holder	939	1,956	2,058	2,121	3,039	3,197	3,329
Unknown	315	110	376	507	654	583	406
Share international	16%	27%	24%	25%	28%	27%	26%
Physical sciences and earth sciences	3,811	4,517	4,550	3,875	4,956	5,419	6,081
U.S. citizen or permanent resident	2,657	2,857	3,034	2,358	2,567	3,148	3,717
Temporary visa holder	929	1,572	1,297	1,330	2,059	1,959	2,156
Unknown	225	88	219	187	330	312	208
Share international	24%	35%	29%	34%	42%	36%	35%
Mathematics and computer sciences	1,189	1,927	2,032	1,729	3,042	3,496	3,843
U.S. citizen or permanent resident	673	997	1,150	868	1,241	1,627	1,746
Temporary visa holder	445	876	771	789	1,591	1,617	1,931
Unknown	71	54	111	72	210	252	166
Share international	37%	45%	38%	46%	52%	46%	50%
Psychology and social sciences	6,063	6,562	7,369	6,925	7,309	8,498	9,079
U.S. citizen or permanent resident	4,846	5,189	5,796	5,363	5,272	6,319	6,874
Temporary visa holder	726	1,158	1,080	1,110	1,482	1,601	1,680
Unknown	491	215	493	452	555	578	525
Share international	12%	18%	15%	16%	20%	19%	19%

(continued)

TABLE 6.2   (continued)

Field of study and citizenship status	1987	1992	1997	2002	2007	2012	2017
Engineering	3,712	5,438	6,114	5,081	7,749	8,469	9,843
U.S. citizen or permanent resident	1,915	2,521	3,333	2,169	2,546	3,579	4,339
Temporary visa holder	1,539	2,749	2,555	2,650	4,591	4,355	5,070
Unknown	258	168	226	262	612	535	434
Share international	41%	51%	42%	52%	59%	51%	52%
Education	6,453	6,677	6,577	6,508	6,448	4,803	4,823
U.S. citizen or permanent resident	5,665	6,018	5,748	5,417	5,358	4,040	4,047
Temporary visa holder	430	559	411	479	601	460	536
Unknown	358	100	418	612	489	303	240
Share international	7%	8%	6%	7%	9%	10%	11%
Humanities and arts	3,478	4,387	5,285	5,297	5,085	5,561	5,290
U.S. citizen or permanent resident	2,929	3,745	4,452	4,320	3,894	4,434	4,290
Temporary visa holder	282	542	561	705	797	761	693
Unknown	267	100	272	272	394	366	307
Share international	8%	12%	11%	13%	16%	14%	13%
Other	1,876	2,206	2,191	2,138	2,841	2,734	3,113
U.S. citizen or permanent resident	1,371	1,572	1,597	1,392	1,614	1,650	1,921
Temporary visa holder	370	568	461	563	963	834	928
Unknown	135	66	133	183	264	250	264
Share international	20%	26%	21%	26%	34%	31%	30%

MOBILE RESEARCHERS AND THE GEOPOLITICS OF HIGHER EDUCATION

To what extent does the inflow of international graduate students and postdoctoral researchers support the geopolitical position of the United States? It is challenging to know exactly how much geopolitical power to attribute to higher education (Cantwell, 2016). Higher education can contribute indirectly to clear sources of state power including economic and military dominance, but it is awfully difficult to claim that higher education, let alone the inflow of postdocs and graduate students, causes advantage in those domains. Academic research

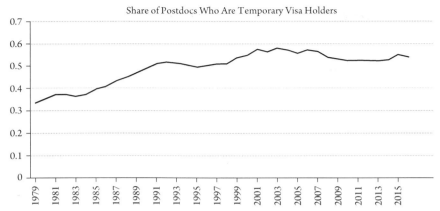

FIGURE 6.1. Share of postdocs who are temporary visa holders.

can support the military and a national security, and the U.S. Department of Defense was budgeted to spend a massive sum of $95 billion on research and development in fiscal year 2019, but only about $927 million was specifically budgeted for university-based activities (Association of American Universities [AAU], 2019). Military capabilities can be developed without a globally engaged academic research system. North Korea, for example, was able to develop nuclear weapons without an internationally recognized university system and while attracting few, if any, postdocs or graduate students from abroad.

Human capital development and knowledge creation are now seen as more important than raw materials for economic production (World Bank, 2002), and economists are able to demonstrate high individual and social returns from higher education (McMahon, 2009). Commercial and national security interests are intertwined, and sometimes touch higher education—for example, the Chinese technology firm Huawei, which has contracts with several research universities and has been accused by the U.S. government of being a security threat because of the alleged potential that the company could spy on consumers for the Chinese government (Sharma, 2019).

International graduate students and postdoctoral researchers add to the country's stock of intellectual capability and scientific knowledge. Specific political and industrial disputes—such as the tension between the United States and China—are remote from the exchange of students and scholars, but internationalization is not insulated from political succession. The U.S. government is now scrutinizing every aspect of U.S.-China academic exchange. Exchange and collaboration are often represented by American officials as foreign individuals and governments taking advantage of U.S. intellectual property and knowledge. Recent research by Lee and Haupt (2020), however, demonstrates that U.S. academic science has benefited tremendously from collaboration with China. It is difficult to measure the direct contribution of international graduate students and postdoc researchers, but it is evident that the United States benefits from the inflow of talent.

Holding the position of an attractive place for advanced study and research contributes to American prestige and influence in the world. In other words, the United States likely benefits from attracting international graduate students and postdocs. By standing as the premier location to study, the United States can set standards for global higher education because other countries emulate the American model (Lo, 2011). Hosting large numbers of international postdocs and graduate students, then, is likely a source of soft power for the country, as well as a difficult-to-measure but likely real material advantage. As with the material advantage enjoyed by attracting human capital, soft power and academic prestige cannot be precisely measured, but generally support the idea that hosting international graduate students and postdocs advances U.S. interests in the world.

Center-Periphery Models Are Not Enough

Center-periphery models have for decades been a mainstay for explaining the dynamics of higher education globally (Altbach, 1981). Center-periphery models assume a global center is responsible for global value-added production and quality control, upon which the global periphery is dependent. In operation, it assumes that North America, and to a lesser extent Western Europe, Australasia, and Japan, serves as the global center of higher education upon which other systems rely. To a large extent, the center-periphery models accurately, if only partially, describe global dynamics. International students and postdocs in the United States come from all over the world, but populous middle- and lower-income countries such as China and India supply a majority of the inbound students and researchers. By contrast, few Americans study or work in these countries. Asymmetric exchange is a hallmark of center-periphery models.

Center-periphery models may not fully explain the geopolitics of international student and postdoc flows. Dependency theory is the progenitor of the center-periphery model for understanding global higher education. Dependency theory is an economic model from the mid-twentieth century that was developed to explain persistent inequality among countries and underdevelopment in what was then called the Third World. Dependency theory holds that raw materials are extracted in the periphery by unskilled labor and exported to the core, where skilled labor and technology transform materials into value-added finished goods (Smith, 1979). Countries in the periphery relied on core countries for foreign exchange ("hard currency" such as U.S. dollars or British pounds) and, because countries in the periphery have underdeveloped economic capacity, were also dependent on core countries for imported goods. Periphery countries are locked in a pattern of dependence because they rely on the core for both money and the goods perchance with cash. As manufacturing has moved to lower-income countries, the dependency model has been modified to reflect that research and development and intellectual property are retained in the core while assembly takes place in the periphery. The well-known phrase found on the back of Apple products—"Designed in California, assembled in China"—is emblematic.

Does the internationalization of doctoral education and postdoctoral employment at U.S. universities reflect a dependency relationship as one may deduce using the center-periphery model? Perhaps. Reliance on the United States for knowledge-intensive activities like scientific training certainly fits the dependency pattern. To follow the analogy crudely, skilled individuals—researchers who leave their home countries to study and work in the United States—are the raw materials transformed into finished products (fully developed scientists). Countries in the periphery are unable to produce their own high-end scientists and instead have to use foreign exchange to import scientific production. My own collaborative research with Jenny Lee bares some of the hallmarks of dependency thinking when analyzing the use of international postdocs (e.g., Cantwell and Lee, 2010; Cantwell, Lee, and Mlambo, 2018).

The limits of a dependency is that it (a) does not fully account for the extent to which the periphery contributes to production and (b) underestimates agency in the periphery. The United States is an attractive place to learn and work (Janger, Campbell, and Strauss, 2019), but U.S. universities also seek international students and researchers to increase their own status and contribute to productivity (Taylor and Cantwell, 2015). Internationalization is a two-way street that requires both supply and demand. Researchers have to want to come to the United States, and U.S. universities and faculty have to want to host students and scholars from abroad. Although outflows of students and researchers have contributed to brain drain, internationally mobile scholars who return home, move to a third country, or participate in transnational academic networks have contributed to global academic development and have not benefited the United States exclusively.

Import substitution industrialization is a common response to dependency (Bruton,1998). The idea is that countries in the periphery put up high import taxes on manufactured goods and support the domestic industry to develop national productive capacity. International higher education is quite the opposite of the import substitution strategy. Numerous countries, including in Asia and Europe, have encouraged academic mobility through specific policies and by nurturing a culture that values international engagement precisely to develop a domestic higher education system. And, at least in some cases, it seems to have worked. It is hard to imagine the contemporary power of Chinese academic research absent decades of global engagement led by Chinese students and researchers who studied and worked abroad. To be direct, there is little evidence that strategic protectionism works in higher education. Global engagement in higher education is rife with the dynamics of power, and the benefits for engagement may be accrued asymmetrically, but backing out of cross-border exchange is unlikely to net a better result.

NATIONALISMS AND HIGHER EDUCATION

If center-periphery models are insufficient for understanding the geopolitical implications of international graduate education and postdoctoral employment, then which models are appropriate? Rather than advance a metaphor-as-model that seeks to explain the entire global system, I propose the use of multiple concepts—each of which touches on different concepts of geopolitical power—to explain the geopolitics of international graduate education and postdoctoral employment. I consider technological nationalism (Cantwell and Grimm, 2018) as a possible explanation for both sending countries and the United States. I also explore the use of neo-nationalism (Lee and Rice, 2007) to explain the usage and treatment of international PhD students and postdocs in the United States.

Technological Nationalism

Technological nationalism is a state-centric concept that partially confronts neoliberal accounts of globalization and academic science (Ostry and Nelson, 1995). The basic idea is that nation-states support, and seek to control, science and technology, not spur innovation for the economic and social benefits themselves but for the state to harness the power of science for national advantage (Cantwell and Grimm, 2018). It assumes that states want to steer and harness science in order to become relatively more powerful than rival nations. Technological nationalism, or techno-nationalism, is a political philosophy that assumes "the state of affairs in which technology is promoted by a nation state and for the sake of national interest" (Nakayama, 2012, p. 11). The purpose of science, research, and technology development is to advance state power.

Using the concept of techno-nationalism, a plausible analysis is that sending countries encourage—and in many cases directly support—PhD students and postdocs migrating to the United States for advanced training as a means of technology transfer. Rather than focusing on the human capital lost, as with brain drain concepts, a technology transfer view sees the social networks established by mobility as conduits for knowledge and know-how to flow back to the sending country. This approach is quite similar, for example, to China's well-known practice of using direct foreign investment as a way to acquire technology developed abroad (Mowery and Oxley, 1995). A techno-nationalist model also applies to higher education (Liu and Jiang, 2001). Unlike using strategic protectionism through import substitution industrialization to develop domestic capacity, by sending nationals abroad, techno-national approaches to internationalization seek to capture the benefits of open-global engagement for relative national advantage. Taking into consideration the vast flows of Chinese PhD students and postdocs to the United States over the past several decades, along with the meteoric development of the Chinese academic research enterprise, the claim that China has benefited from internationalization of U.S. universities as much as the United States has is entirely plausible.

Adopting a techno-nationalism frame gives focus to the ways that nation-states use global science and technology to secure geopolitical advantage. From this perspective, higher education internationalization is not only about global connections and openness but also about establishing conduits to transfer technology and knowledge between countries. It is related to the center-periphery model in that it highlights transfer from the United States to other parts of the world but does not assume a development trap through dependence.

NEO-NATIONALISM

Jenny Lee (2016, 2017) founded the study of neo-nationalism in higher education internationalization. Lee finds that international students are understood by host countries based not exclusively on individual attributes but on perceptions of national identity within the global system. "Simply put, neo-nationalism is defined as discrimination based on national identity. With increasing internationalization, national identity is being reintroduced and reconceptualized as forms of global competition" (Lee, 2016, p. 23). International students and scholars are incorporated into the U.S. higher education system at least partly within the parameters of neo-national ideology.

The concept of neo-nationalism helps clarify the treatment of international PhD students and postdocs, who simultaneously are recruited by, and face discrimination within, U.S. universities. By recruiting international students and postdocs, but keeping them in positions of subordination, either by treating them as hired hands or via outright discrimination, higher education adopts a nationalist stance toward internationalization. Of course, it is true that postdocs and graduate students, national and international alike, can experience bad treatment and uncertain prospects. But research by Jenny Lee and me (Cantwell and Lee, 2010; Cantwell, Lee, and Mlambo, 2018; Lee 2017) shows direct expressions of neo-nationalism. One such example is the proclaimed preferences by a professor for Chinese postdocs because they "work their socks off" (Cantwell and Lee, 2012). That and other examples show the imposition of perceptions about various countries on individuals.

Unlike dependency theory and center-periphery models, which give little attention to culture and national identity, neo-nationalism shows how claims to cultural supremacy attached to the structure of the global economy shape higher education internationalization. Neo-nationalism has allowed universities in the United States, for example, to extract value from the talent and skills of PhD students and postdocs. Neo-nationalism maps onto de-colonial and human capital / knowledge economy approaches to the geopolitics of higher education.

CONSIDERING AGENCY

A common feature of geopolitical theories is that they tend to obscure individuals and limit the potential for human agency as explanatory factors. Even the traditional "push-pull" models of academic mobility tend to render the internationally mobile as passive bodies swept by political and economic tides. Push-pull models imply a strong structure and limited agency among the internationally mobile. Understanding internationalization of doctoral education and postdoc work through a human agency framework foregrounds individuals as sovereign. In outlining a concept of inferential mobility as "self-formation," Marginson (2014) explains, "The student is understood as typically a strong agent piloting the course of her/his life" (p. 12). In making decisions about what to do and how, individual internationally mobile students and researchers shape the networks and pathways that link academic systems, thereby contributing to the structure of global higher education as well as the geopolitics of the sector.

In a study of international postdocs in the United States and the United Kingdom, I found that early-career researchers made employment decisions based on self-defined parameters about the best professional and scientific opportunities as well as the best available opportunities for living and establishing a personal/family life (Cantwell, 2011). This does not mean that mobility and opportunity are fully open or that anyone can do whatever they want. What it does suggest is that "mobility is shaped as much by the individuals, institutions, and states that seek academic migrants in a global higher education market and competition arena as by the individuals who physically move. The situated negotiation of actors within this arena highlights that the transnationally mobile are not entirely autonomous but nor are they [un]able to exercise agency" (Cantwell, 2011, p. 443). Individual actors are self-regulating and subject to state authority, but are able to exercise agency, negotiate structure, and in doing so, shape, in a small way, the geopolitics of higher education.

Agency-based approaches foreground the importance of individuals in the geopolitics of internationalization. Agency self-formation concepts understand the geopolitics of higher education not as totalizing structures that impose deterministically on individuals but rather as apparatuses that enable and constrain individual actions and life courses. Agency-based approaches map onto soft and disciplinary concepts of geopolitical power.

CONCLUSION

The United States has long been a major destination for internationally mobile graduate students and postdocs. Data from the NSF and other sources show that graduate education and the research enterprise, especially in science and engineering disciplines, are substantially internationalized. The flow of scientific talent has geopolitical implications. Traditional center-periphery models of higher education suggest that the presence of large numbers of international students and scholars in the United States indicates dependency patterns, wherein the rest of the world is dependent on the United States for scientific training. Dependency accounts do not accord with prevailing developments. The flow of international graduate students and postdocs to the United States has slowed in recent years, and the power of the U.S. academic research enterprise seems to be in decline, at least in relative terms. What is more, U.S. politics now seem to shirk international leadership and engagement in favor of a more inward-looking nationalism.

At the same time, countries in the periphery, most notably China, are on the rise and no longer seem dependent on the United States. This dynamic of the United States becoming increasingly, if only partially, isolated in academic and scientific matters as does the growing positions of China and other countries. A recent report published by the National Science Board explicitly acknowledge the decline of U.S. dominance. The introduction states: "Growth of S&T [science and technology] capabilities in other nations has outpaced that of the United States along several dimensions, enabling some countries to converge with, or even to be poised to overtake, the United States in developing specific areas of S&E expertise. This has resulted in a regional shift in S&T performance and capabilities from the United States, Western Europe, and Japan to other parts of the world, notably to China and other Southeast Asian economies" (Khan, Robbins, and Okrent, 2020, p. 3). A decline in the U.S. position of dominance in global academic science was probably inevitable. To the extent that the leading position has been supported and extended by the inflow of graduate students and postdocs, ebbing of inward mobility may accelerate decline.

In this chapter I argue that we need new concepts to understand the geopolitics of international graduate education and the research enterprise. Of note, I suggest neo-nationalism, techno-nationalism, and agency-based models can lead to a more nuanced and complete understanding of the state of affairs. Models that assume static relations, or zero-sum outcomes, fail to explain the complexity of an emerging multipolar higher education environment.

REFERENCES

Altbach, P. G. (1981). The university as center and periphery. *Teachers College Record, 82*(4), 601–621.
Association of American Universities. (2019). AAU summary of the president's FY2020 budget. Retrieved from https://www.aau.edu/key-issues/aau-summary-presidents-fy20-proposed-budget
Bruton, H. J. (1998). A reconsideration of import substitution. *Journal of Economic Literature, 36*(2), 903–936.
Cantwell, B. (2011). Transnational mobility and international academic employment: Gatekeeping in an academic competition arena. *Minerva, 49*(4), 425–445.

———. (2016). The geopolitics of the education market. In E. Hazelkorn (Ed.), *Global rankings and the geopolitics of higher education* (pp. 309–323). Abingdon, United Kingdom: Routledge.

Cantwell, B., & Grimm, A. (2018). The geopolitics of academic science. In B. Cantwell, H. Coates, & R. King (Eds.), *Handbook on the politics of higher education* (pp. 130–148). Cheltenham, United Kingdom: Edward Elgar Publishing.

Cantwell, B., and Lee, J. (2010). Unseen workers in the academic factory: Perceptions of neoracism among international postdocs in the United States and the United Kingdom. *Harvard Educational Review, 80*(4), 490–517.

Cantwell, B., Lee, J. J., and Mlambo, Y. A. (2018). International graduate student labor as mergers and acquisitions. *Journal of International Students, 8*(4), 1483–1498.

Cantwell, B., Marginson, S., and Smolentseva, A. (Eds.). (2018). *High participation systems of higher education*. Oxford, UK: Oxford University Press.

Cantwell, B., & Taylor, B. J. (2015). Rise of the science and engineering postdoctorate and the restructuring of academic research. *The Journal of Higher Education, 86*(5), 667–696.

Council of Graduate Schools. (2018). Trends in first-time international graduate enrollment. Retrieved from https://cgsnet.org/trends-international-first-time-graduate-enrollment

Einaudi, P., Heuer, R., and Green, P. (2013). *Counts of postdoctoral appointees in science, engineering, and health rise with reporting improvements*. Arlington, VA: National Science Foundation.

Hazelkorn, E. (Ed.). (2016). *Global rankings and the geopolitics of higher education: Understanding the influence and impact of rankings on higher education, policy and society*. Milton Park, United Kingdom: Taylor & Francis.

Janger, J., Campbell, D. F., and Strauss, A. (2019). Attractiveness of jobs in academia: A cross-country perspective. *Higher Education, 78*(6), 991–1010.

Khan, B., Robbins, C., & Okrent, A. (2020). *The State of US Science and Engineering*. Washington, D.C.: National Science Board.

Lee, J. J. (2016). Neo-nationalism: Challenges for international students. *International Higher Education* (84), 23–24.

———. (2017). Neo-nationalism in higher education: Case of South Africa. *Studies in Higher Education, 42*(5), 869–886.

Lee, J. J., and Haupt, J. P. (2020). Winners and losers in US-China scientific research collaborations. *Higher Education, 80*(1), 57–74.

Lee, J., Jon, J. E., and Byun, K. (2017). Neo-racism and neo-nationalism within East Asia: The experiences of international students in South Korea. *Journal of Studies in International Education, 21*(2), 136–155.

Lee, J. J., and Rice, C. (2007). Welcome to America? International student perceptions of discrimination. *Higher Education, 53*(3), 381–409.

Liu, H., and Jiang, Y. (2001). Technology transfer from higher education institutions to industry in China: Nature and implications. *Technovation, 21*(3), 175–188.

Lo, W. Y. W. (2011). Soft power, university rankings and knowledge production: Distinctions between hegemony and self-determination in higher education. *Comparative Education, 47*(2), 209–222.

Marginson, S. (2014). Student self-formation in international education. *Journal of Studies in International Education, 18*(1), 6–22.

McMahon, W. W. (2009). *Higher learning, greater good: The private and social benefits of higher education*. Baltimore, MD: Johns Hopkins University Press.

Mowery, D. C., and Oxley, J. E. (1995). Inward technology transfer and competitiveness: The role of national innovation systems. *Cambridge Journal of Economics, 19*(1), 67–93.

Nakayama, S. (2012). Techno-nationalism versus techno-globalism. *East Asian Science, Technology, and Society, 6*(1), 9–15.

National Science Foundation. (2019). Survey of graduate students and postdoctorates in science and engineering. Retrieved from https://www.nsf.gov/statistics/srvygradpostdoc/

Ostry, S., and Nelson, R. R. (1995). *Techno-nationalism and techno-globalism: Conflict and cooperation.* Washington, DC: Brookings Institution.

Redden, E. (2019, November 18). Number of new international students drops. *Inside Higher Education.* Retrieved from https://www.insidehighered.com/admissions/article/2019/11/18/international-enrollments-declined-undergraduate-graduate-and

Sharma, Y. (2019, February 11). Top US research universities freeze ties with Huawei. *University World News.* Retrieved from https://www.universityworldnews.com/post.php?story=20190211124159161

Smith, T. (1979). The underdevelopment of development literature: The case of dependency theory. *World Politics, 31*(2), 247–288.

Stephan, P. E. (2012). *How economics shapes science.* Cambridge, MA: Harvard University Press.

Taylor, B. J., and Cantwell, B. (2015). Global competition, US research universities, and international doctoral education: Growth and consolidation of an organizational field. *Research in Higher Education, 56*(5), 411–441.

World Bank. (2002). *Constructing knowledge societies: New challenges for tertiary education.* Washington, DC: Author.

PART 3 UNIVERSITY INTERNATIONALIZATION STRATEGIES

7 • EXPLORING GEOPOLITICS IN U.S. CAMPUS INTERNATIONALIZATION PLANS

CHRYSTAL A. GEORGE MWANGI, SEAN JUNG-HAU CHEN, AND PEMPHO CHINKONDENJI

The increasing commitment to internationalization through mission statements, strategic plans, and special task forces is well documented among U.S. higher education institutions (HEIs) (Childress, 2009; Helms, Brajkovic, and Struthers, 2017), with the pursuit of internationalization becoming more of an expectation rather than a choice (Brandenburg and de Wit, 2011). With the increasing amount of time and resources HEIs are expending to pursue internationalization, it has become critically important to understand the motivations, perceived benefits, and actual impact of those pursuits. While scholars describe campus internationalization as a tool to engage in practices ranging from diplomacy (Peterson, 2014) to hegemony (Kim, 2011), less is empirically understood about how the language U.S. HEIs use to define their internationalization efforts connects to these broader geopolitical concepts. Therefore, there is a lack of understanding about how universities are connecting internationalization to their global influence, relations, and power. This is dangerous, given that higher education (HE) internationalization not only is an insular campus effort but is outwardly connected to global economic, cultural, social, and political forces (Lee, Vance, Stensaker, and Ghosh, 2020) that can lead to unequal power dynamics and hegemonic outcomes within other parts of the world (George Mwangi, 2017). For example, the COVID-19 pandemic demonstrated the globally interconnected nature of public health that subsequently reduced student/academic mobility and study abroad around the world given increased travel restrictions, more stringent visa policies, and negative economic impact (Toner, 2020). Yet, the pandemic's impact reified and amplified existing power structures, making responsive measures and overall consequences of COVID-19 unequal across individuals, communities, HEIs, and nations (Bassett and Arnhold, 2020; Marinoni and de Wit, 2020).

In this chapter, we center on the internationalization outcomes of global power and dominance by demonstrating how U.S. HEI internationalization strategies are framed as a geopolitical tool. Using extant literature and findings from our empirical study of U.S. HEI internationalization strategies, we argue that these strategies are often geopolitically centered on financial gain and reputational influence for institutions and their local communities, over the pursuit of national or institutional diplomacy and allyship. We conclude with recommendations for campus leaders and scholars engaged in research and practice related to internationalization strategies for U.S. HEIs.

INTERNATIONALIZATION APPROACHES AND IMPLEMENTATION

HEIs engage in internationalization for various reasons and motivations. Knight and de Wit (1997) outlined four main rationales that drive internationalization: academic, social/cultural, political, and economic. De Wit (1999) later pointed out that the rationales for internationalization over the past century have shifted from an emphasis on academic and social/cultural rationales to an emphasis on political and economic rationales. In particular, the rise of the United States as a world power has driven American universities to take on internationalization in order to maintain global influence. Additionally, from an economic perspective, internationalization not only brings in a global workforce and international research and development dollars but also increases the revenue for institutions owing to the growing commodification of HE (de Wit, 1999).

Given the wide range of rationales for internationalization, much scholarship has attempted to investigate the approaches to campus internationalization and provided models for its planning and implementation. For instance, Childress (2009) interviewed dozens of HEIs and identified three general types of internationalization plans: institutional strategic plans (ISPs), distinct documents (DDs), and unit plans (UPs). The findings indicated that factors influencing HEIs' choices of ISP, DD, or UP include the size of the institution, their phases in the internationalization cycle, goals and purposes of internationalization, and campus stakeholders' buy-in (Childress, 2009). In addition, among the types of internationalization plans, the ISP was found to be the most common (Childress, 2009). This is consistent with Bartell's (2003) study, which proposed a top-down approach to the internationalization process, emphasizing the roles of campus leadership and university-wide strategic plans. Bartell argued that institutions that are responsive to external change are more likely to bring about a successful internationalization process than internally oriented institutions. In other words, institutions that rely mostly on internal maintenance and fail to respond to external environmental change tend to take on truncated and tokenizing international processes, and thus fail to bring about successful internationalization.

Recognizing that internationalization is a constantly changing process, Zhou (2016) took a dynamic systems approach to examine the process and argued that successful internationalization must happen at five levels: global, national, institutional, program, and personal. In addition, each level should consist of its own purposes, programs, outcomes, approaches, and projects (Zhou, 2016). The American Council on Education (ACE) also contributes to the literature with its proposed model for the implementation of comprehensive internationalization, which emphasizes the interconnectedness of six pillars: (1) articulated institutional commitment; (2) administrative leadership, structure, and staffing; (3) curriculum, co-curriculum, and learning outcomes; (4) faculty policies and practices; (5) student mobility; and (6) collaborations and partnerships (Helms, Brajkovic, and Struthers, 2017). Among the six pillars, student mobility has recently become a central focus of many HEIs' internationalization efforts, as ACE's 2016 Mapping Survey findings suggest that education abroad and international student recruitment are the top two priority activities in which HEIs most frequently engage (Helms et al., 2017). Although approaches to internationalization processes vary, university leadership and faculty buy-in/engagement are identified as among the most important drivers for successful internationalization (Bartell, 2003; Childress, 2009; Hudzik, 2011). Other conducive forces for successful internationalization include written commitment and clear goals and purposes (Childress, 2009; Hudzik, 2011).

CRITIQUE OF U.S. HEI INTERNATIONALIZATION

In today's globalized world, internationalization continues to be a central part of institutional and national programming, policies, and strategies. Despite that it seems to be a "high-profile" and important part of policy, it is a concept that is ambiguous, is misunderstood, and serves as a "catchall phrase...losing its meaning and direction" (Knight, 2011, p. 14). Brandenburg and de Wit (2011) also posit that internationalization has not only deteriorated and lost its form and substance but also "become a synonym of 'doing good'" (p. 16). HEIs from across the globe are constantly under pressure to have internationalized curriculums, activities, and campuses.

Green and Schoenberg (2006) state that this pressure has led to the mushrooming of internationalization strategies and activities to the point that almost all U.S. HEIs pursued internationalization. These forms of internationalization range from informal activities among various institutions to extensive curriculum changes and student exchanges (Vavrus and Pekol, 2015). However, research shows that behind the intensification of internationalization, there are implicit assumptions (Knight, 2011), economic and social imperatives (Vavrus and Pekol, 2015), and a lack of scrutinization of the underpinnings of internationalization programs and ideologies (Stier, 2004).

Knight (2011) discussed and exposed five myths or implicit assumptions that are embodied in HEIs' internationalization processes: foreign students as internationalization agents, international reputation as proxy for quality, international institutional agreements, international accreditation, and global branding. Unfortunately, the picture that is painted is different from the reality on the ground. Although it is not the case in all universities, foreign students struggle socially and academically, especially when facing racial tensions and resistance from domestic students. Knight (2011) states that the recruitment of foreign students, although done with good intentions, is a mask for improving rankings and generating revenue for HEIs. Concurringly, Brandenburg and de Wit (2011) state that in the past two decades, internationalization in HE has experienced a massive change in its activities, from its basic exchange of students to "the big business of recruitment" (p. 15).

According to Vavrus and Pekol (2015), the present intensity on internationalization among HEIs overlaps with neoliberal policies contributing to the decrease in funding for universities across the globe. With the fight for private funds and need for revenue, institutions shifted their focuses to implement strategies and activities that could lead to the "importing of full-paying students" (p. 6). Conversely, institutions in the Global South did not have access to similar financial resources, nor were they labeled with the global reputations of Global North HEIs. Many Global South HEIs continue to depend on international aid, regional partnerships, and partnerships with Global North HEIs.

Drawing from decolonial scholarship, Stein, Andreotti, Bruce, and Suša (2016) posit that there is a need to examine the practice and nature of HE internationalization. The authors explain that most HEIs operate through a global dominant imagery from which issues of racial hierarchies and economic inequalities in the field are harbored. It is critical for scholars and practitioners to conduct research that critically addresses the challenges and inequalities related to HE internationalization processes.

U.S. HEI INTERNATIONALIZATION STRATEGIES: A CRITICAL DISCOURSE ANALYSIS

A recent study that we conducted on how U.S. campuses frame their internationalization strategies provides additional evidence to demonstrate the contemporary ways in which U.S. HEIs engage in geopolitics. Our team analyzed the internationalization strategies of seventy-eight Association of International Education Administrators member institutions using critical discourse analysis. These strategies were collected before the COVID-19 pandemic. We start with a discussion of the patterns and themes that emerged in how the internationalization strategies defined the purpose of internationalization, followed by the ways in which these documents presented how internationalization would be (or is being) implemented at HEIs. We end with how the documents describe the desired impact of their internationalization strategies.

Purpose of Internationalization

There were two dominant discourses regarding how institutions framed the purpose of pursuing internationalization. The first was to use their capital and resources in service to a global society (i.e., altruism discourse), and the second was to reap benefits and increase standing (i.e., prestige discourse). The University of Illinois Chicago presents an example of the altruism discourse: "UIC will serve the citizens of Chicago and the world by being an international leader in research, scholarship, and innovation, and by creating a globally connected campus community which supports faculty, staff and students as they address the challenges and opportunities of the 21st century." However, it is important to note that the only institutions that emphasized a solely altruistic orientation throughout the purpose of their internationalization strategies were liberal arts and/or Jesuit institutions. For example, the University of St. Thomas's document states, "The University of St. Thomas will actively promote global engagement in teaching, learning, research and service in an ethical and socially responsible manner," and Xavier University of Louisiana articulates "Xavier's mission is to promote a more just and humane society and to prepare students for leadership and service in a global society. . . . Adoption of the Internationalization Strategic Plan: 2013–2018 . . . will move Xavier closer toward meeting its mission." These institutions specifically described internationalization as a civic or social responsibility integrated into their university mission. All other documents described either a solely prestige discourse or both an altruism and prestige discourse, with a predominant focus on internationalization serving to benefit the university.

When institutions described their strategic purpose of pursuing internationalization as a benefit to the university (prestige discourse), this included language focused on competition and reputation. For example, expressing a commitment to internationalization will make universities an "investment of choice" to global stakeholders; prepare their students for an "increasingly globalized, connected, and competitive workforce"; and make them a "premier destination" for international scholars/students. Each of these statements illustrates the goal of status attainment and reputation building as major drivers of internationalization strategies. This is reflected in the University of Evansville's statement that internationalization will serve "to expand and enrich the University's international programs and engagement to achieve national prominence." Interestingly, the University of Evansville and a number of other universities described a desire to use internationalization to increase their rankings and prestige within the U.S. context rather than a global context, which may reflect how U.S. standards are at the forefront of ways to become more global or "world-class" universities (see chapter 4 by Blanco).

In tandem with reputation building, the purpose of internationalization was discussed as a revenue driver. This fiscal rationale for internationalization reflected developing a strategy that could produce additional financial resources for the institutions, as described by the University of Illinois Urbana-Champaign: "The global impact and 'brand' of universities are increasingly important to the financial sustainability of higher education institutions such as Illinois as noted by Moody's Investor's Services in its 2018 outlook for the higher education sector."

Overall, the strategic purpose of internationalization for the majority of institutions was expressed through competing discourses: (1) internationalization as both a social responsibility and service (altruism discourse) and (2) internationalization as a means of status and resources (prestige discourse). The altruism discourse engages a tone assuming that U.S. universities have the solution to the world's challenges, particularly in areas of the world deemed less privileged, and that internationalization will give these universities the platform to provide solutions. Whereas the prestige discourse focuses on enhancing the standing and rankings of universities, which serves to increase their power and positionality among HEIs globally. Yet, both discourses emerge as geopolitical tools that position the United States as a power player and other regions as vulnerable.

When countries outside the United States were discussed, discourses regarding internationalization's purpose were framed primarily in three ways: (1) homogenously or not at all, (2) as strategic priority areas, or (3) as partners and collaborators. Most documents that we analyzed did not discuss any specific countries in describing the purpose of their internationalization strategies. Alternatively, institutions discussed vaguely that they would pursue global engagement broadly to achieve their goals. For example, the University of Colorado, Colorado Springs discussed that its work with (unnamed) other countries would "support education abroad opportunities in order to build cultural understanding and to develop the global competencies of the UCCS community." The University of Iowa did not name any specific countries that it would engage with in its document either, but discussed engagement with "developing countries" broadly as "encouraging economic development initiatives in developing countries and in countries with strong UI and Iowa ties." Although internationalization requires working across borders with other areas around the world, the documents we reviewed often did not discuss with specificity any regions or countries.

When documents did include specific countries or regions, they were discussed as strategic priority areas similar to the University of Nebraska's statement on the purpose of its internationalization strategy in part as "leveraging partnerships and relationships in priority nations" and to "strategically choose country and/or institution-specific collaboration." Likewise, Virginia Commonwealth University's document stated it will "increase resources to support the study of foreign languages, world regions, and international affairs, particularly for those languages and regions tied to VCU's international partnerships and considered of growing global strategic interest." The University of North Carolina named two specific regions, Asia and Africa, owing to Asia's strengthening position as a powerful world region and the potential the university sees in Africa's future: "Because Asia holds greater potential benefits and challenges for the United States than any other part of the globe, Carolina graduates—regardless of their chosen career path—must understand the relevance of Asia to be competitive in a rapidly changing world. New emerging trends in Africa are of increasing global importance, and echo the early rise of Asia as a global economic factor. Unlike our delayed response to Asia, UNC must commit early to understanding how these changes will ultimately determine Africa's future place in the world." Alternatively, some institutional documents used a partnership or collaborative approach to discuss engagement with other countries through internationalization. The University of Denver explained an interest in "creating deep institutional partnerships with a number of universities across the globe, involving faculty, students and administrators on exchanges, short visits and research collaboration." The University of Hawaii had historical and cultural connections to regions it named in pursuing internationalization: "The University's campuses, schools, and departments have thriving partnerships with sister institutions throughout the Asia-Pacific region and beyond. Especially important are our longstanding ties with Japan, Korea and China." Yet, even the development of partnerships could be framed as other countries/regions being used to facilitate the needs of the U.S. university, as demonstrated by the University of Texas at Dallas's statement that "global support services will include programs for international students and faculty, as well as partnerships with universities, organizations and alumni abroad to attract the best talent to UT Dallas."

Implementation of Internationalization

Based on the analysis of the institutional strategic plans for internationalization, two major themes emerged from these data that focused specifically on implementation, which include traditional forms of implementation (long-standing best practices in internationalization as defined by international education associations such as study abroad and international student recruitment) and formulaic forms of implementation (the specific steps and strategies to pursue internationalization goals). The findings also indicate that through the traditional and formulaic approaches to implementation, most institutions either centralized or decentralized the implementation process at the U.S. universities. Furthermore, the data show that the various forms of implementation were mostly inward facing rather than outward facing. This means that most of the programs and activities implemented were designed to primarily benefit domestic students rather than international students and scholars and foreign universities.

Traditional forms of implementation. The traditional forms of implementation include the long-established activities and projects that HEIs incorporate at their campuses to enhance student exchange and to internationalize the curricular and campus operations. Some of the traditional forms of implementation outlined in the strategic plans include the recruitment of international students, study abroad programs, English language/foreign language programs, faculty mobility, integration of international content within the curriculum, and partnerships with foreign universities.

To achieve the internationalization of the curriculum, some institutions created certificate programs in global or international studies so that their students could have the option of specializing their education. For instance, some of the proposed activities at Xavier University of Louisiana include "creating an inventory of courses with significant global content, establishing a Global Certificate Program, expanding education abroad opportunities, effective utilization of partners abroad, and encouragement of international student research." Some of the other institutions that aimed to introduce certificate programs to strengthen their internationalization strategies include Baylor University (certificate program in global engagement), Cornell University (global studies major and an international scholarship certificate), and Hillsborough Community College (global studies certificate). Similarly, the Ohio State University's strategy was to ensure that "international aspects are integrated into all majors for all students."

In addition to internationalizing the curriculum, the recruitment of foreign students and the mobility of domestic students and faculty were major activities identified among the traditional forms of implementation. In elaborating their recruitment of international students, some institutions were very particular about the nature of international students they were interested in recruiting. For instance, universities often emphasized a focus on recruiting and enrolling "high achieving" and "highly qualified" international students.

Many of the documents also focused on establishing partnerships with foreign universities and implementing English/foreign language programs. Through its collaborations with foreign universities, the College of Coastal Georgia helps the domestic students at the campus find internships and opportunities to teach English abroad. Similarly, Emporia State University implemented the Intensive English Program (IEP), which provides English instruction to nonnative speakers and prospective foreign students to prepare them for studies in the United States. As its mission, the IEP "prepares students in the English language for academic purposes. In addition to language skills, students become familiarized with academic teaching styles, teaching methods and classroom expectations common to most U.S. university environments."

Formulaic forms of implementation. Formulaic forms of implementation emerged from the documents as the second major theme of the internationalization plans, in which institutions developed distinct procedures and approaches ("formulas") to guide the implementation of internationalization at their campuses, and which differed from solely naming the activities and practices (traditional forms). The Virginia Commonwealth University (VCU) presents an example of formulaic implementation: "The Provost's Global Advisory Network, as the continuation and institutionalization of the Task Force for Comprehensive Internationalization, plays a vital role in the future progress of internationalization at VCU. With the support of the Executive Director of GEO, it will be the Global Advisory Network's responsibility to prepare an implementation plan, including resource needs and timeline, as well as regularly monitor and gauge progress toward goal achievement in each of these areas." For institutions like VCU, the creation of task forces was a specialized effort that allowed an appointed group of faculty, staff, and sometimes students to make recommendations on how their campus would develop better programs and initiatives toward internationalization. Hofstra University's Internationalization Taskforce, together with other subcommittees, consulted with different stakeholders on campus to create recommendations that promote the institution's global engagement. The team used surveys to collect data from faculty, staff, and administrators, which were later adapted into a student survey. The task force and other subcommittees worked together to review the results of the survey and the various offices/documents on campus to make recommendations for internationalization. As part of this process, Hofstra University's task force sought to redefine the university's mission, goals, and vision for internationalization because these did not previously put forth a clear picture of the institution's "international identity."

Furthermore, other institutions, such as the University of Illinois Urbana-Champaign and the University of Illinois Chicago, also centralized their internationalization efforts to minimize duplication, have clear methods to measure success, and eliminate bureaucratic and campus obstacles. Contrastingly, the University of Denver's approach was to decentralize its implementation by having each academic unit actualize the internationalization plan. On the other hand, Indiana University's strategic plan "acknowledges the organizational complexities arising from the varying mix of centralized and decentralized control over international activities. For each university-wide goal, the *Plan* sets forth action items for the Office of the Vice President for International Affairs

(OVPIA), other centralized administrative units, and objectives and recommendations for academic units." Despite the fact that most institutions were explicit about who would implement the internationalization strategies, and how they would do so, some institutional strategic plans were vague and unclear on how the goal of internationalization was to be achieved. For example, the University of Texas at Dallas was not clear on who would do the implementing, but it did discuss three kinds of goals/initiatives the institution would focus on: global education, global conversations, and global support services. Similarly, the University of South Florida did not state who will implement its plans, but the institution set a budget and assessment procedures that would support the internationalization strategies.

Impact of Internationalization

Three main discourses regarding the impact of the pursuit of internationalization emerged from this study. The first one centered on how the pursuit of internationalization would benefit the U.S. campus community—namely, the university itself, as well as its students, faculty, and staff. The second discourse addressed the benefits the pursuit of internationalization would bring to the local region and state where the institution was located. The third discourse was in regard to how the internationalization efforts pursued by HEIs in the United States would improve conditions and challenges faced by regions and countries outside the United States.

Impact on university. The internationalization plans emphasized that internationalization would impact university stakeholders and the U.S. university as a whole in positive ways. For example, internationalization was viewed as status-building to the institution's global reputation and standing, as described by the University of Georgia: "Collaborations with universities and institutions with a global reach also advance the university's reputation at home and abroad which in turn attracts even stronger students, scholars, and faculty to the campus." Many other institutions echoed this status-building impact of internationalization. In particular, Kansas State University envisioned that its internationalization efforts would enhance its place in major world university ranking systems, as it described one of its long-term goals to "position in world university rankings commensurate with our benchmark institutions."

Besides an improved reputation and elevated rankings, most internationalization plans in this study also depicted the students, faculty, and staff as stakeholders who would gain the most from internationalization. More specifically, the impact of internationalization was frequently described as preparing students, faculty, and staff to become "global citizens" equipped with the intercultural and global competencies necessary in an increasingly globalized (and competitive) world/job market. For instance, the University of Iowa stated that internationalization would provide its students with opportunities that would help them "develop cross-cultural competences" and "learn to function successfully and with ease in global environments." However, most plans, when discussing the positive impact on students, focused on the benefits for domestic students. International students, on the other hand, were often mentioned as a catalyst for the institutions.

A similar "beneficial" rhetoric can also be found in describing the multitude of international research and funding opportunities that internationalization could potentially expose faculty to. For instance, a priority in the University of Georgia's internationalization plan was "to promote international research and teaching opportunities for UGA faculty." Internationalization was described as not only impacting faculty professional development (e.g., improving their inter- and cross-cultural competences, increasing research opportunities) but also influencing how faculty would be evaluated. More specifically, many internationalization plans indicated a goal to incorporate faculty members' performance regarding international collaborations into their evaluation process. For example, Ramapo College of New Jersey, in its internationalization plan, stated one of its targets was to "revise promotion & tenure guidelines to include recognition of a faculty member's engagement with comprehensive internationalization of Ramapo College." The Ohio State University echoed this practice in its plan by suggesting that international engagement should be included in tenure and promotion decisions as an incentive, because, otherwise, "faculty are likely to discount the importance of international engagement."

Impact on local community. Many of the documents, particularly those from public/land-grant institutions, portrayed internationalization as impacting institutions' state or local area. The University of California, Riverside, for example, states that, through internationalization, it will "advance our land-grant mission by assisting the City of Riverside and the state of California in their strategic international economic partnerships." Similarly, the University of Georgia states that "as a land grant flagship university, UGA has a responsibility to internationalize for our community and state" and that one of its goals is "to support the advancement of the community and state through internationalization."

As institutions discuss the purpose of internationalization as serving the local communities immediately beyond their campus walls, they suggest that their internationalization strategies are about developing or reinforcing the engagement and relations of their towns, states, and regions with other countries around the world. Universities explained that their internationalization efforts would impact their communities in the local region or state in beneficial ways, such as increasing international collaborative opportunities for local organizations and connecting local communities to the world. For example, Rutgers University, in its internationalization plan, made "catalyzing New Jersey's cultural, economic, and social vitality through international engagement, bringing the innovative ingenuity of Rutgers and New Jersey to bear on issues that transcend national borders" a central intended outcome. Similarly, the University of North Carolina added to this conversation, proposing that "UNC's success will benefit North Carolina by expanding global connections, increasing opportunities for international collaboration and innovation."

Impact on international community. The third discourse stressed U.S. HEIs' roles in impacting the world. In particular, the pursuit of internationalization by U.S. HEIs was intended to also contribute to the solutions of many global problems. For example, the University of Illinois Urbana-Champaign stated that "a globalization strategy will also create conditions for innovative and culturally appropriate research that enhances understanding and solutions to global issues confronting the world's populations." The global issues mentioned in these plans often suggested problems faced by "developing countries" or the "Global South." For instance, Georgia Institute of Technology indicated that it was "regularly asked to assist developing countries in the building of their national 'science and technology literacy' ecosystems." In a more specific example, the internationalization plan of State University of New York at Buffalo introduced a Zimbabwean student at UB, who was the first person to earn a doctoral degree in pharmacy in Zimbabwe. The document stated, "As his nation's first clinical pharmacist, he is using lessons learned at UB to improve treatment of his countrymen infected with HIV/AIDS, about 18 percent of the adult population."

It is not surprising that almost all of the documents adopt a positive and beneficial rhetoric about internationalization. However, it is unknown and unacknowledged in these plans whether the pursuit of internationalization could bring negative impacts. For example, while most plans in this study stated that the pursuit of internationalization would connect their local regions and states to the world, what this connection might entail was not fully discussed. Furthermore, these beneficial outcomes and impacts mostly align with the U.S. universities' interests. Although some plans mentioned their aims to establish "mutually beneficial" partnerships, these partnerships were only possible on the condition that they aligned with the U.S. institutions' interests. For instance, the University of Nebraska stated: "Build on existing agreements and create new strategic partnerships in order to develop mutually beneficial education, research, and other forms of collaboration with institutions, governments and businesses outside the U.S. on key areas of importance to the state of Nebraska and the university." In addressing the impacts of international efforts on the international community, a dominant discourse depicted the U.S. HEIs as the benevolent with advanced knowledge and technology. The impact of internationalization was depicted as helping solve challenges faced by the world, while regions and countries outside the United States were viewed as in need of help from the United States. Overall, the ideas of benefits and U.S. dominance and superiority permeated how the impacts of internationalization were constructed in the documents.

DISCUSSION

In our study, a number of discourses emerged as geopolitical tools in which internationalization strategies mostly reflected one-sided benefits in favor of U.S. universities and their states/regions, with limited mention of possible benefits for their international partners. In this sense, other regions and countries around the world were described as factors that could support these benefits, rather than through a lens of mutual benefit and reciprocity. Other scholars have confirmed the unequal power dynamics present within internationalization practices (e.g., George Mwangi, 2017; Stein et al., 2016; Vavrus and Pekol, 2015), but our findings demonstrate that this practice is not unintentional. Internationalization strategies act as guiding documents for U.S. institutions' global engagement, and the fact that some language used in these documents is embedded with hegemonic discourse is troubling. While we understand that the purpose of the documents is to center on the U.S. institutions and present a rationale for internationalization, these strategies are also action oriented and meant to be implemented, which means they have implications for the ways these U.S. institutions conduct work abroad, as well as for the people and places they work with (Bartell, 2003; Childress, 2009). Because of this global interaction, internationalization strategies cannot be understood in a vacuum apart from those around the world that are on the receiving end of these strategies.

There are a number of factors that should be unpacked in how we understand U.S. HEI internationalization strategies given the context of geopolitics. One is how these documents engage the concept of competition. Themes within the internationalization strategies were clearly grounded in competition for dominance and positioning, better rankings and reputation, and the demonstration of quality education. Yet, the strategies were often defined as competition with other U.S. universities (e.g., a focus on national rankings). Given this, other HEIs around the world, but particularly in the Global South, appeared to be positioned as cogs in U.S. HE's drive for a competitive edge via internationalization. Similarly, rather than seeing other nations as equals in a competitive market, the colonialist perspective views "the other" through a lens of exploitation (Said, 1979). The impact on specific countries or HEIs abroad was treated as an afterthought or not discussed at all. Further, while the internationalization strategies discussed U.S. universities' global engagement as having a positive impact on the world, these assertions were broad and vague. Extant scholarship demonstrates that indicators of "quality" in HE, such as rankings and accreditation standards, are heavily influenced by the Global North, and many institutions around the world are seeking accreditation by U.S. agencies (Blanco Ramirez, 2014, 2015). While this can inequitably stratify Global South HE systems, our findings also demonstrate how further stratification can happen given the internationalization discourse by U.S. HEIs using their engagement with Global South countries/HE systems to gain greater standing.

A second theme that underpins our analysis is how U.S. HE internationalization engages politics. Locally, most public and land-grant HEIs were using their internationalization strategies as a means of affirming a commitment to their city, state, or region. In these instances, campus internationalization was described as being in service to the interests of local constituencies. States continue to divest in U.S. HE, and internationalization is one way that universities create alternative revenue streams (Altbach and Knight, 2007; George Mwangi, 2013). However, demonstrating the utility of internationalization to local areas can also be used to strengthen political ties with local policymakers who make decisions about funding streams that will impact not only a university's internationalization efforts but also the overall university budget. Furthermore, convincing local companies and philanthropists that internationalization is an asset to the city, state, and/or region can be used to develop alliances with key stakeholders who can invest resources into the institutions.

Our findings also demonstrate that U.S. colleges and universities are attempting to navigate and negotiate politics on a global scale. Internationalization strategies discussed universities' ability to educate international students and build collaborations with HEIs abroad. This can be interpreted as a political move given that internationalization strategies have been used historically to socialize students and scholars from abroad into Western thought and promote allyship with the United States (de Wit, 1999). For example, the Fulbright-Hays Act of 1961, which drives educational and cultural exchange between the United States and other nations, was created to "promote international cooperation for educational and cultural advancement, and thus to assist in the development of friendly, sympathetic, and peaceful relations between the United States and the other countries of the world" (McAllister-Grande, 2008, p. 22). Interestingly, though, the internationalization documents did not typically frame internationalization as a benefit to the United States' national priorities in any specific ways. This lack of a focus on national priorities may be due to national- and state-level plans for educational internationalization within the United States being new or nonexistent and "given that most efforts at the federal, state, and institutional level have been piecemeal, usually without the interest or support of powerful lawmakers and, perhaps most importantly, a presidential administration or a farsighted governor" (Douglass and Edelstein, 2009, p. 20). Instead, the impact of internationalization within the reviewed documents remained at the institutional, city, state, and regional levels, with global relationships and partners described as being able to improve the universities' local areas rather than the nation.

Finally, our findings elucidate how international relations can be understood through the internationalization strategy documents. The strategies were drafted with language that assumes international students will want to come to their universities and that other countries will welcome U.S. faculty and research collaborations. This hubris by U.S. institutions is further reinforced by the documents demonstrating that the greatest benefits of internationalization are to U.S. institutions and their local communities. Rarely were the local contexts of particular countries abroad discussed, although they will inevitably be impacted by U.S. HE's internationalization efforts.

When particular countries or regions of the world were discussed in the internationalization documents, they were located in the Global South and within target areas that the universities believed were becoming influential. Patel (2017) provides an interpretation: "Internationalization is marketed as a revenue generating machine that has become a hegemonic force, overwhelming developing communities on the promise of a quality education designed in the West, leading to quality of life in their local contexts" (p. 67). Working together, the reputation, resources, and messaging around internationalization from U.S. HE reflect a persuasive approach to asserting influence within other countries, and yet does not provide clear benefits to other countries within internationalization strategies.

The need for internationalization was discussed in the strategic documents as an imperative to improve the world's environmental, educational, and economic problems and as a means of developing graduates who will positively transform the world. There was no tone of restraint in describing the impact of global engagement, but instead a focus on HE internationalization as "doing good" for itself and the rest of the world (Brandenburg and de Wit, 2011, p. 16). This lack of caution in internationalization is further reinforced in many of the institutional implementation strategies, which emphasize "comprehensive internationalization" that infuses one's internationalization strategy into all facets of the college or university along with necessary resources, leadership, and support (Helms et al., 2017). In this way, internationalization becomes embedded within university values and practices as a guiding paradigm without questioning its potential shortcomings. However, the pre-COVID-19 pursuit of comprehensive internationalization ground to a halt as the pandemic forced U.S. HEIs to closely examine the possibilities for global engagement when human mobility becomes severely reduced (Toner, 2020). Although our analysis was conducted before the pandemic, we view the post-COVID-19 context as an opportunity for HEIs to revisit their internationalization strategies and consider new possibilities.

For example, our analysis revealed that nearly all of the internationalization plans examined in this study placed a great emphasis on "inward" benefits—meaning these plans generally focused on the benefits to the U.S. HEIs. We suggest that future administrators and policymakers consider developing internationalization plans in a language that is more multilaterally inclusive and beneficial. As suggested in previous sections, internationalization plans are meant to be action oriented, serving as guidelines for the actual implementation. Thus, incorporating multilaterally inclusive and beneficial language into the purposes, implementation, and potential impacts of internationalization plans would be the first step to building mutually beneficial and sustainable collaborations. One way to engage this practice would be by U.S. HEIs collaborating with partner countries/HEIs in developing their internationalization strategies moving forward. Given the reduced budgets and other fiscal challenges resulting from the COVID-19 pandemic, strategic planning for a streamlined version of internationalization may become necessary at many HEIs. Yet, by homing in on establishing fewer, but stronger and more engaged, partnerships with global stakeholders that have a role in their strategic planning process, U.S. HEIs may be more inclined to acknowledge and work to mitigate power differentials and pursue mutual outcomes.

Our study also pointed out that internationalization is never merely "the process of integrating an international, intercultural, or global dimension into the purpose, functions or delivery of postsecondary education" (Knight, 2003, p. 2). Instead, power dynamics and global in/equalities permeate U.S. HEIs' pursuit of internationalization. Therefore, we suggest that U.S. institutions demonstrate awareness of these dynamics and inequalities when developing broader policies and practices related to internationalization—for example, by reflecting on what it means and what impacts it may have on the state, in the internationalization plans, and in its strategic location/regions with which the institution wishes to build partnerships and recruit international students. This reflexive engagement will assist U.S. HEIs in moving away from a description of internationalization as only a positive effort, and instead take a more holistic perspective when framing internationalization strategies in order to pursue feasible and socially responsible goals.

Although our findings provide a rich description, it is limited to the discourse(s) created within the U.S. context alone. Further research is needed to look at the effects of internationalization of HE in other countries, particularly within the Global South. There was a lack of detailed attention to Global South countries and HE systems in the documents we reviewed for this study. Understanding how Global South nations frame their own HE internationalization strategies would be useful in understanding their geopolitical positioning and how forces of globalization are shaping their international engagement. Future research could also explore a methodology that compares the internationalization strategies of two different countries to examine the purpose, implementation, and impact of those strategies.

Furthermore, our study investigated internationalization strategies, but not how these documents were actualized or the outcomes of their implementation. Future research should focus on conducting an in-depth inquiry that identifies a select number of HEIs to analyze and explores the process of actualizing their internationalization plans. Scholars could investigate the traditional or formulaic forms of implementation separately to fully understand and capture what these processes of internationalization entail. Researchers could also capture qualitative experiences and observations with faculty, students, and staff at the universities to better understand the influence and impact of internationalization.

REFERENCES

Altbach, P. G., and Knight, J. (2007). The internationalization of higher education: Motivations and realities. *Journal of Studies in International Education*, 11(3/4), 290–305.

Bartell, M. (2003). Internationalization of universities: A university culture-based framework. *Higher Education*, 45(1), 43–70.

Bassett, R. M., and Arnhold, N. (2020, April 30). COVID-19's immense impact on equity in tertiary education. *Education for Global Development: World Bank Blogs*. Retrieved from https://blogs.worldbank.org/education/covid-19s-immense-impact-equity-tertiary-education

Blanco Ramirez, G. (2014). Trading quality across borders: Colonial discourse and international quality assurance policies in higher education. *Tertiary Education and Management*, 2, 121–134.

———. (2015). International accreditation as global position taking: An empirical exploration of U.S. accreditation in Mexico. *Higher Education*, 69(3), 361–374.

Brandenburg, U., and de Wit, H. (2011). The end of internationalization. *International Higher Education*, 62, 15–17.

Childress, L. K. (2009). Internationalization plans for higher education institutions. *Journal of Studies in International Education*, 13(3), 289–309.

de Wit, H. (1999). Changing rationales for the internationalisation of higher education. *International Higher Education*, 15, 1–2.

Douglass, J. A., and Edelstein, R. (2009). *The global competition for talent: The rapidly changing market for international students and the need for a strategic approach in the U.S.* (Center for Studies in Higher Education, Research & Occasional Paper Series). Retrieved from http://cshe.berkeley.edu/publications/docs/ROPS.JD.RE.GlobalTalent.9.25.09.pdf

George Mwangi, C. A. (2013). The impact of state financial support on the internationalization of public higher education: A panel data analysis. *Higher Education in Review*, 10, 61–77.

———. (2017). Partner positioning: Examining international higher education partnerships through a mutuality lens. *Review of Higher Education*, 41(1), 33–60.

Green, M. F., and Shoenberg, R. (2006). *Where faculty live: Internationalizing the disciplines*. Washington, DC: American Council on Education.

Helms, R. M., Brajkovic, L., and Struthers, B. (2017). *Mapping internationalization on U.S. campuses: 2017 edition*. Washington, DC: American Council on Education.

Hudzik, J. (2011). *Comprehensive internationalization*. Washington, DC: NAFSA, Association of International Educators.

Kim, J. (2011). The birth of academic subalterns: How do foreign students embody the global hegemony of American universities. *Journal of Studies in International Education*, 16(5), 455–476.

Knight, J. (2003). Updating the definition of internationalization. *International Higher Education*, 33, 2–3.

———. (2011). Five myths about internationalization. *International Higher Education*, 62, 14–15.

Knight, J., and de Wit, H. (Eds.). (1997). *Internationalisation of higher education in Asia Pacific countries*. Amsterdam, Netherlands: European Association for International Education.

Lee, J. J., Vance, H., Stensaker, B., and Ghosh, S. (2020). Global rankings at a local cost? The strategic pursuit of status and third mission. *Comparative Education*. doi: 10.1080/03050068.2020.1741195

Marinoni, G., and de Wit, H. (2020, June 8). A severe risk of growing inequality between universities. *University World News*. Retrieved from https://www.universityworldnews.com/post.php?story=2020060815405140

McAllister-Grande, B. (2008). *The historical roots of internationalization*. Retrieved from http://www.nafsa.org/_/File/_/ac08sessions/GS089.pdf

Patel, F. (2017). Deconstructing internationalization: Advocating glocalization in international higher education. *Journal of International and Global Studies*, 8(2), 64–82.

Peterson, P. M. (2014). Diplomacy and education: A changing global landscape. *International Higher Education*, 75, 2–3.

Said, E. W. (1979). *Orientalism*. New York, NY: Vintage Books.

Stein, S., Andreotti, V., Bruce, J., and Suša, R. (2016). Towards different conversations about the internationalization of higher education. *Comparative and International Education / Éducation Comparée et Internationale*, 45(1), 1–18.

Stier, J. (2004) Taking a critical stance toward internationalization ideologies in higher education: Idealism, instrumentalism and educationalism. *Globalisation, Societies and Education*, 2(1), 1–28.

Toner, M. (2020, April 1). Internationalization, interrupted. *International Educator*. https://www.nafsa.org/ie-magazine/2020/4/1/internationalization-interrupted.

Vavrus, F., and Pekol, A. (2015). Critical internationalization: Moving from theory to practice. *Forum for International Research in Education*, 2(2), 5–21.

Zhou, J. (2016). A dynamic systems approach to internationalization of higher education. *Journal of International Education and Leadership*, 6(1), 1–14.

8 • THE LIFE CYCLE OF TRANSNATIONAL PARTNERSHIPS IN HIGHER EDUCATION

DALE LAFLEUR

As U.S. institutions of higher education seek to internationalize their campuses, the use of entrepreneurial behavior has become standard practice. The most common entrepreneurial initiatives include targeted international student recruitment, the merger of curriculum and modes of teaching with other institutions abroad, the development of international alumni networks, and the pursuit of transnational partnerships (Deschamps and Lee, 2014). The motivations are often driven by increasing international student recruitment targets and the desire to expand existing transnational partnerships in order to fulfill goals stated in institutional-level strategic plans (LaFleur, 2018). Developing transnational partnerships between institutions of higher education has become a more prominent internationalization strategy used in the past few decades. The inherent nature of transnational partnerships allows the parties involved to gain access to new resources, pursue collaborative research, and share students. Considering the impact of the recent COVID-19 pandemic on higher education globally, institutions are being driven to innovate, explore new terms of engagement, and reimagine the higher education paradigm. With careful consideration and recognition of respective geopolitical contexts and motivations, transnational partnerships can be successful for and beneficial to all stakeholders and provide outlets for new opportunities. Without checks and balances of motivations, ethics, values, and assessment of desired outcomes, however, transnational partnerships can run the risk of becoming lopsided, with benefits largely going to one partner to the detriment of the other.

The root causes of this entrepreneurial behavior stem from economic instability for institutions of higher education. When considered through a critical lens, several potentially unfavorable circumstances are revealed. First, U.S. public institutions of higher education have become reliant on the tuition revenue generated by international students, especially from key countries such as China and India (Cantwell, 2015; Choudaha and Chang, 2012; Gai, Xu, and Pelton, 2016; Ozturgut, 2013). If current downward international student enrollment trends in the United States continue and student mobility flows shift to other countries as a result of COVID-19, these institutions will be placed in a precarious financial position. Second, entrepreneurial behavior is weakened by the inconsistent approach to program assessment that could be used to inform practices and improve student experiences and program outcomes (LaFleur, 2018). The lack of focus on assessment by U.S. institutions of higher education is an indicator that the underlying motivations relate more to short-term economic benefits than to the long-term sustainability of the programs, student experiences and outcomes, or growth of transnational partnerships.

TRANSNATIONAL PARTNERSHIPS

Transnational partnerships enhance the ability of individual institutions to share resources and expertise in order to pursue new opportunities globally. By definition, partnerships are "cooperative agreements between a higher education institution and another distinct organization to coordinate activities, share resources, or divide responsibilities related to a specific project or goal" (Kinser and Green 2009, p. 4). When partnerships involve institutions in different countries, they become transnational. Proponents of transnational partnerships in higher education highlight that they provide opportunities for scholars and students to exchange ideas and information in order to advance teaching, learning, and research to address today's global challenges. The sudden adoption of teaching online during the COVID-19 pandemic has positioned institutions to be able to pursue more virtual collaboration than had been pursued previously. However, critics contend that there are other factors at play that influence the behaviors of institutions as well as of scholars and students themselves. Survival of institutions, academic programs, and a focus on local community engagement has put a strain on some international partnership activities (International Association of Universities, 2020).

The desire to solidify and improve an institution's global status is a common motivation for institutions of higher education that influences their approach to transnational partnerships. For example, one study found that transnational partnerships with U.S. institutions are often pursued by international institutions in Latin America seeking to enhance their prestige and increase their global rankings (Arroyo Perez, 2017). In exchange, the U.S. institutions are rewarded with access to new student markets, which bring economic benefits (Arroyo Perez, 2017). Another study noted the strategic approach to partnership development by Chinese institutions seeking to improve their prestige through transnational partnerships (Montgomery, 2016). In this study, elite institutions of higher education in China systematically sought partnerships with high-ranking institutions in the United Kingdom and globally to increase their own prestige (Montgomery, 2016). The elite institutions in China were primarily located in the urbanized and wealthy regions of the country, thus exacerbating the rural versus urban divide and the unequal distribution of access to higher education and elite institutions across the country (Montgomery, 2016).

The existence of asymmetrical power dynamics or the "donor-recipient" paradigm is another challenge supported by research on north-south development projects that involve transnational higher education partnerships (Koehn, 2012; Koehn and Obamba, 2014; Samoff and Carrol, 2004). These partnerships may involve governmental organizations, nongovernmental organizations, higher education institutions, and others. George Mwangi (2017) conducted a study on international higher education partnership dynamics and engagement supported by the Higher Education for Development (HED) program. The HED program supported 400 partnerships in the United States and majority world nations to address global development challenges (George Mwangi, 2017). The study focused on partnerships across Eastern Europe, sub-Saharan Africa, Southeast Asia, South Asia, the Middle East, and Mexico, with a majority involving U.S. public institutions. Results indicated that a perception of what each partner contributes to the project early on led to ongoing unequal power dynamics. At the outset, the majority world partner was often identified as providing research skills and expertise, while the local partner provided knowledge of the local context and access to potential key stakeholders (George Mwangi, 2017). The local partner's knowledge of context and expertise were critical to implementing a program that would match local needs and developmental goals, but they oftentimes were underutilized during partnership development and the goal-setting phase, leading to unrealistic or inadequate project goals and outcomes (George Mwangi, 2017). For some, partnership dynamics evolved over time and became more equitable, but the dominant partner seemed to sustain that role for the duration of most partnerships. Partnerships that demonstrated more equity in project dynamics often had pre-existing relationships with both partners equally involved in the development, implementation, and assessment of the project (George Mwangi, 2017).

Similarly, studies of multistakeholder transnational partnerships, or transnational partnerships that involve different types of organizations coming together to address the United Nations Sustainable Development Goals, found that most multistakeholder transnational partnerships had imbalanced representation and were led by institutions in the north with a lack of representation from the south, and tended to replicate the geographical imbalances that exist in the political arena (Bäckstrand, 2006; Schäferhoff, Campe, and Kaan, 2009). To date, most of the partnerships have failed to deliver on the intended goals, and lack the organizational capacity, resources, and transparency to achieve their objectives (Bäckstrand, 2006; Pattberg and Widerberg, 2016). These circumstances can be attributed to several factors such as the sustainable development program itself having conflicting agendas and norms, diffuse goals, and unclear reporting guidelines. Combined with imbalanced representation in the partnerships, lack of governance and self-regulation processes, and unclear monitoring and reporting mechanisms, the partnerships did not foster intergovernmental relations or inclusiveness, or participation of the marginalized actors in global governance (Pattberg and Widerberg, 2016).

In the corporate world, a study on transnational partnerships between firms in emerging versus developed markets determined that the types of resources each group will pursue vary based on their market context (Hitt, Dacin, Levitas, Arregle, and Borza, 2000). Developed markets in the study included Canada, France, and the United States, and emerging markets included Mexico, Poland, and Romania. Results indicated that firms in developed markets seek transnational partnerships to grow resource endowments and organization learning in order to be competitive in particular markets, while firms in emerging markets seek transnational partnerships for financial capital, technical capabilities, managerial capabilities, and other intangible assets such as firm reputation (Hitt et al., 2000). The different motivations reflect the context in which the firms are embedded and therefore often mirror the existing imbalances between the countries involved in the transnational partnerships.

Though at first glance the pursuit of transnational partnerships in higher education seems like a win-win response to the influences of globalization on higher education, these studies demonstrate that most transnational partnerships are embedded in imbalanced power dynamics, and many are destined to bring about only short-term or lopsided benefits. This chapter highlights the tension between the traditional educational mission of public institutions of higher education and the influences of the external neoliberal environment in which the institutions are situated. This perfect storm is forcing institutions of higher education to balance the traditional mission of public institutions of higher education and the underlying motivations behind the entrepreneurial behavior exhibited through many transnational partnerships. This chapter will explore this complex dynamic while drawing on research outlining the influences of neoliberalism on internationalization strategies being adopted by U.S. higher education institutions.

INTERNATIONAL JOINT/DUAL DEGREE PROGRAMS

One of the leading transnational partnership program models of increasing interest to U.S. institutions of higher education is international joint/dual degree programs (Bhandari and Blumenthal, 2011; Knight and Lee, 2012; Lane and Kinser, 2014). According to the American Council on Education (2014), an international joint degree is "a degree program that is designed and delivered by two or more partner institutions in different countries issuing a single qualification endorsed by each institution," whereas an international dual degree (sometimes referred to as a double degree) is "a degree program that is designed and delivered by two or more partner institutions in different countries where a student receives a qualification from each of the partner institutions." Research has shown that the primary motivations behind the pursuit of international joint/dual degree programs by public institutions of higher education in the United States are recruiting international students, extending an existing transnational partnership, and pursuing objectives in an institutional strategic plan (LaFleur, 2018).

On its surface, international joint/dual degree programs are an expected result of the neoliberal environment influencing higher education institutions in the United States and globally. U.S. institutions have looked abroad to recruit talented international students for decades with the ideals of soft power diplomacy and connections to the future leadership of other countries since the post–World War II era. Faculty have also been partnering with colleagues at institutions abroad through collaborative research, co-supervising graduate students, and providing international graduate students with assistantships that offer many benefits, including a salary, health insurance, and tuition scholarships, in exchange for teaching or research duties. The sentiment that has been introduced in more recent literature is that the values-based proposition of transnational partnerships appears to be secondary to the economics-based proposition, whereby the partner institution that is more advantaged recoups a larger share of the benefits (Arroyo Perez, 2017; Bäckstrand, 2006; George Mwangi, 2017; Hitt et al., 2000; Koehn, 2012; Koehn and Obamba, 2014; Montgomery, 2016; Pattberg and Widerberg, 2016; Samoff and Carrol, 2004; Schäferhoff et al., 2009). These benefits can be financial or positional, but the consequence is that they are not mutual and can be exploitative. There are means by which international joint/dual degree programs, for example, can be balanced and mutually beneficial. It requires intentional design, management, and assessment of programs, as well as alignment with the university culture at both institutions and the geopolitical context in which they are situated. The coordination of these elements is not easy, but when achieved, it can result in positive outcomes for all stakeholders involved.

In the development of sustainable international joint/dual degree programs in the United States, there has been a lack of attention to the assessment of the programs and the student experiences (LaFleur, 2018). This missing piece suggests that once the key motivator, increased recruitment targets, is achieved, the U.S. partner perceives it has met its goal and any additional investment of resources on assessment is not warranted. It brings to light a significant weakness in the adoption of this entrepreneurial behavior toward internationalization being implemented at U.S. public institutions of higher education (LaFleur, 2018). The managerial professionals that are leading many of these efforts at higher education institutions in the United States, though specialists in their fields, are not necessarily skilled entrepreneurs, nor are they provided any training on this new approach (LaFleur, 2018). They are, however, held accountable for achieving results and have introduced seven key strategies to help them achieve their internationalization goals.

KEY STRATEGIES AT U.S. PUBLIC INSTITUTIONS

The evolution of transnational partnerships has prompted the introduction of key strategies at U.S. public institutions of higher education. These strategies include the introduction of new behaviors, organizational adaptations, and the use of conceptual frameworks and paradigms. New behaviors draw on the need to solicit champions at various levels across the institution and to incorporate high-level support through strategic plans and centralized processes at the institutional level. Organizational adaptations stem from the need to establish a centralized administrative infrastructure and appropriate human resources to support the growth of transnational partnerships and balance the underlying tension between education logics and market logics driving these programs. Finally, the use of conceptual frameworks and paradigms aids in the broader understanding of the life cycle of transnational partnership development and how it is influenced by university culture and context in order to achieve overall goals and objectives. Together, these strategies are used to implement internationalization plans at U.S. public institutions of higher education.

Roughly two-thirds of participants at U.S. public institutions of higher education that joined a study on transnational partnerships and international joint/dual degree programs indicated they use key strategies to develop and implement the international joint/dual degree program model as part of their campus internationalization strategy (LaFleur, 2018). The most common strategies used by participants include (1) emphasizing the role of transnational partnership development in institutional strategic plans; (2) meeting with key administrative leadership on campus; (3) having faculty champions—those who have demonstrated success in implementing existing international joint/dual degree programs—share their success stories; (4) providing materials and/or work-

Life Cycle of Transnational Partnerships

University Culture Typology	Faculty Champions	Materials/ Workshops	Key Leadership	On-site Liaisons	College Liaisons	Strategic Plans	Comprehensive Infrastructure
Strong/Internal							
Weak/Internal	✓	✓					
Weak/External	✓	✓	✓	✓	✓		
Strong/External	✓	✓	✓	✓	✓	✓	✓

Institutional Strategies for Implementing
International Joint/Dual Degree Programs

FIGURE 8.1. Institutional strategies by university culture typology.

shops focused on the development of international joint/dual degree programs; (5) utilizing college liaisons; (6) utilizing on-site liaisons; and (7) creating a comprehensive centralized administrative infrastructure that includes approved practices, proposal forms, agreement templates, review committees, and assessment protocols. The introduction of these seven strategies highlights the perceived dependence of U.S. institutions in this study on alternative resources provided by international joint/dual degree programs as a strategic form of international student recruitment, and the organizational adaptations needed to implement the programs successfully.

The university culture typology developed by Sporn (1996) provides a key lens with which to evaluate the potential success of these partnership strategies in different institutional contexts. The primary variables in the typology are the strength and orientation of the university culture. Strength refers to the congruence between the values and goals of the members, hierarchical integration, and the institutional strategies. Institutions of higher education will be either weak or strong. Orientation refers to the values, attitudes, beliefs, and patterns of behavior of the members of the institution of higher education. Orientation will be either external or internal (Sporn, 1996). Participants reported varying levels of success with these strategies based on the university culture that existed on their respective campuses. This is outlined in figure 8.1.

The most common strategies were to utilize faculty champions, marketing materials, and workshops to help promote the program model to other administrators and faculty on campus. Peer-to-peer conversations between faculty and administrators were found to be the most effective way to enlist new support for pursuing transnational partnerships and international joint/dual degree programs. In this way, additional support for the program model is garnered across campus and new opportunities are identified. The next common strategy was to solidify support from key leadership that would be involved in decision-making about the ability to develop and launch international joint/dual degree programs. The people in this category ranged from senior leadership to middle management depending on the institutional organization structure, but all were in a decision-making role when it came to the development of international joint/dual degree programs. Next, the hiring of on-site liaisons, who are housed on the campus of the international partner institutions, and college liaisons, who are housed in the academic colleges on campus, were common strategies that had gained support from the campus community and key leadership. By having professional staff immersed either at the partner institution or in the academic colleges at the U.S. institution who are dedicated to making these programs a success, the administrative unit overseeing international activities is building human networks that will help sustain the programs over time. It was also expressed that this network serves as a mechanism to identify and triage potential conflicts more quickly. Institutions that were identified as externally oriented, regardless of whether they had a weak or strong university culture toward the international joint/dual degree programs, used more of these strategies to varying levels of success. However, institutions with a strong and externally oriented university culture implemented additional strategies. These were the inclusion of international joint/dual degree programs in the institutional strategic plan, and the development of a comprehensive infrastructure to support the implementation of the programs through centralized units staffed by managerial professionals with specialized skills in international education. Most often, these are administrative units that must sustain themselves through a combination of state funds and fee-based revenues. The behaviors of the managerial professionals within these centralized interstitial units, therefore, are often driven by a combination of market logics and educational logics. The tension between these two logics can be challenging to balance when the university culture toward internationalization is weak and does not support internationalization efforts. A strong university culture that is externally oriented and supports internationalization efforts is better positioned to accommodate both logics as they are internalized by the members of the university community, resulting in a higher level of success using the seven strategies. By utilizing the university culture typology, a broader understanding of the likelihood for success and long-term sustainability during times of crisis of the different strategies at institutions can be revealed.

ORGANIZATIONAL ADAPTATIONS

The merger of market- and education-driven logics facing higher education institutions in the United States has introduced organizational adaptations such as the introduction of managerial professionals and centralized interstitial units responsible for internationalization efforts (Gumport and Sporn, 1999; Rhoades and Sporn, 2002). Though the market-driven logic often directs institutional-level decisions, there is also a personal desire on behalf of managerial professionals in these interstitial units to support education logics through international engagement to enhance longer-term benefits of cross-cultural understanding, public diplomacy, and the exchange of knowledge (LaFleur, 2018). For many managerial professionals working in interstitial units supporting internationalization efforts, balancing these differing logics is an inherent challenge of their positions. This is compounded by the fact that many interstitial units are funded primarily through student fees, making them susceptible to cuts when student flows shift. This tension is apparent when considering the perspectives of the managerial professionals based at the home campus versus the on-site liaisons abroad.

One study conducted by Healey (2018) compared the perspectives of senior-level managerial professionals located at home institutions in the United Kingdom with those of managerial professionals located at the partner institutions abroad in Southeast Asia, the Middle East, and China. The study found that home-based senior-level managers considered the offshore transnational partnership programs to be risky and not scalable or sustainable, and perceived that the home institution lacked the institutional capacity to manage quality assurance in the program activity (Healey, 2018). They also relayed that costs had been underestimated, resulting in only modest revenue streams, which led to resistance from university stakeholders and the perception of mission drift (Healey, 2018). The market-based logics compelled the home-based senior-level managers to have an aversion toward offshore programs with international partners. The same study found that in-country senior-level managers differed in age than the home-based senior level managers, often lacked sufficient training, and had little previous experience in management at the home institution before being based abroad. They often had a dysfunctional relationship with colleagues at the home university owing to the perceived lack of empathy toward the context abroad. Colleagues at home lacked the understanding that home-based policies and protocols would not necessarily work at the host institution. The in-country managers also found host country governments to be overly controlling, had a complicated relationship with the partner institution abroad, and had difficulties managing locally based staff and students (Healey, 2018). These findings indicate that the home-based senior-level managers were more negative about developing offshore programs abroad in general owing to market logics, and the in-country senior-level managers were more frustrated and in conflict with those at the home campus rather than having a shared opposition to the transnational partnership overall (Healey, 2018). Being immersed in the geographic location abroad appeared to have created an allegiance more in alignment with the partner institution and local community owing to the managers' bonding with their local peers. This could be attributed to their prioritizing of education logics and the building of relationships with the host community over bottom-line market logics.

Incorporating a formal market analysis protocol, conducted in collaboration with the partner institution abroad, into the program development process and understanding the partner universities' cultures toward transnational partnership ventures will help to balance the varying logics at play in transnational partnership development. In the context of COVID-19 as well as a post-pandemic era, this step cannot be overlooked. An essential element of these efforts is understanding the various stakeholders involved in transnational partnerships and creating a value-add for each one in the development process so that the results yield more than what either partner operating independently could accomplish (Brinkerhoff, 2002). Typical stakeholders include higher education institutions, governments, industry partners, students, and parents (Bolton and Nie, 2010; LaFleur and Regulska, 2018). Within higher education institutions, various stakeholders are involved with the development of transnational partnership programs, including senior leadership, administrators overseeing compliance, academics and research scholars, and advancement professionals (LaFleur and Regulska, 2018). Aligning stakeholder needs and values with the broader internationalization goals and strategies is critical to the overall success of the transnational partnership programs. By clearly articulating and analyzing desired program goals that align with stakeholder needs and values, and housing decision-making authority with a functional governing committee composed of various stakeholders, institutions create a system of checks and balances and are better positioned to make informed decisions about which partnerships to pursue and why. In this way, internationalization efforts can be reframed to respond to competing internal logics and provide opportunities to reimagine higher education not only for international students and faculty who are engaged internationally, but also for domestic students and other stakeholders. In turn, a successful transnational partnership is one that develops its own partnership identity, forming a basis for legitimacy and value for the stakeholders involved (Brinkerhoff, 2002).

Knight (2015, 2018) provides a different perspective for international education professionals to consider that shifts the focus away from power dynamics and competing logics introduced in the academic capitalist framework of the knowledge economy, and focuses more on mutual benefits and gains that can be achieved through knowledge diplomacy. She defines the concept of knowledge diplomacy as "the role that international higher education, research and innovation can play in the strengthening of relations between and among countries" (2018). Ryan (1998) utilized the term "knowledge diplomacy" to discuss intellectual property and trade cooperation as a progression beyond industrial diplomacy and to better support emerging global markets. In his book, he acknowledges the gap in global economies and geopolitical contexts and discusses how various trade laws have attempted to address these barriers to promote the free flow of information. He argues that managing multinational enterprises requires a high level of knowledge of cultural differences economically, politically, and socially. To create the free flow of information that is globally desired by multinational enterprises, governments around the world must utilize knowledge diplomacy (Ryan, 1998). In this chapter, the term "knowledge diplomacy" references Knight's use of the term as a means by which institutions of higher education around the world are seeking talent for collaborating and creating in order to tackle today's grand challenges and respond to future global crises.

TRANSNATIONAL PARTNERSHIP LIFE CYCLE

To develop transnational partnerships that draw on the spirit of entrepreneurialism yet allow the institutions to remain focused on mutual gains, productive student experiences, positive program outcomes, university cultures, and longer-term sustainability, I introduce a framework for transnational partnership development: the transnational partnership life cycle (see figure 8.2).

The transnational partnership life cycle emphasizes the cyclical and entrepreneurial nature of transnational partnerships and the importance of focusing on three distinct phases. Phase 1, development, focuses on partnership identification and conceptualizing and designing opportunities. Phase 2, operational, focuses on negotiating the terms of engagement and implementing the initiatives being pursued. Phase 3, assessment, allows for a review of data and program activity and informs both the development and operational phases of the life cycle. Each of these phases is discussed in more detail with the development of a new international joint/dual degree program in mind.

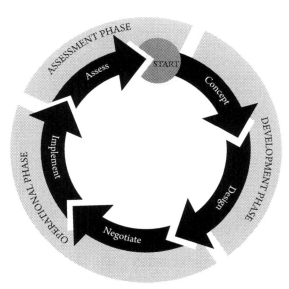

FIGURE 8.2. Transnational partnership life cycle.

Phase 1: Development

In the development phase, it is important that each partner involved communicate clear goals, strategies, any resources available, and the rationale behind the desired outcomes. A certain level of trust and transparency is important during this phase in order to understand the key objectives of the initiative and to determine whether the initiative and the partners are a good match. A market analysis is completed to determine both the feasibility of the initiative and the level of interest of students in the potential programs being designed. It is also critical to understand the university culture and context of each institution, including the roles of the internal and external stakeholders involved in the initiative. Key higher education stakeholders in this phase include the faculty, relevant academic leadership such as department heads and deans, central international office leadership and administrative professionals, and compliance-related administration such as legal counsel, risk management, immigration, accreditation, and technology. These stakeholders will help determine the viability of the proposed project based on respective university policies, protocols, and institutional strategies. Key external stakeholders may include the government, nongovernmental organizations, industry, students, and their parents. The development phase can take time, but it is worthwhile to be as comprehensive as possible at this juncture before moving forward. Doing so can help mitigate potential challenges or misunderstandings in the operational phase. At the end of the development phase a decision is made to either move forward or abandon the project.

Phase 2: Operational

During the operational phase, the partner institutions, and any other relevant stakeholders, will review and negotiate the terms of engagement and outline protocols for implementing and assessing the program. Items may include signing an international memorandum of agreement and completing a business plan. The elements of the business plan may include course articulation charts, timelines for marketing and recruitment, setting target enrollment goals, development of outreach materials, training faculty and staff, and setting up the infrastructure of the program for students to pursue. This is closely followed by the implementation of the business plan and mobility of faculty and students as needed. The operational phase can be chaotic and may require projects to stop and start over. The role of the key stakeholders in this phase includes the review and vetting of any documents created and verification that the documents meet university policies, protocols, and institutional or other relevant requirements before they are signed. Additional stakeholders include review committees, either internal or external, and the signatories for any agreements pursued. Once approved, other stakeholders such as staff that oversee marketing, recruitment, enrollment, and assessment also become involved. Critical elements include strong and clear communication, the ability to be flexible, trust and transparency, and the mitigation of risks.

Phase 3: Assessment

Assessment is a critical element of the overall success of transnational partnership initiatives. Assessment measures outcomes against the desired goals and allows for benchmarking and the early identification of any problems so that adjustments can be made. Assessment of the mechanics of the program itself, the faculty experience, and the student experience, on a regular basis during the program and upon completion of the program, allows for longitudinal data gathering and supports the long-term sustainability of the program. It also provides empirical data to provide to all constituents involved in the transnational partnership as well as any internal and external stakeholders. The role of the key stakeholders in this phase is to determine whether the program objectives are being met and to learn more about the experiences of the people involved in the program. New opportunities and stakeholders may be identified through assessment. If the assessment phase is overlooked, or the data collected are ignored, the long-term success of the initiative and the transnational partnership may be at risk.

If applied comprehensively, the three phases of the transnational partnership life cycle acknowledge the entrepreneurial behavior of higher education institutions and introduce checks and balances to recognize the importance of each university's role in the partnership as well as the respective university cultures, key stakeholders, and geopolitical contexts involved. It requires a sharing of clearly articulated goals and desired outcomes at the outset of the initiative by all parties involved, the transparent negotiation of the terms of engagement, jointly planning the launch of the program, and a shared assessment of the outcomes after the program is up and running. It compels a certain level of trust, ethics, and authenticity between the institutional partners and the inclusion of an exit strategy. At its core, it offers a sustainable approach for developing symmetrical transnational partnerships.

The transnational partnership life cycle, paired with an emphasis on understanding the university culture typology and the knowledge diplomacy paradigm, allows a fresh look at the role of transnational partnerships and an opportunity to redefine their purpose in international higher education. Infusing these lenses into the three phases of the transnational partnership life cycle acknowledges the existing power dynamics and inequities that exist globally and places the development of transnational partnerships in a mutualistic framework. Understanding university culture and the impact of challenges such as COVID-19 will allow for a better institutional understanding of which initiatives and strategies will be supported. Knowledge diplomacy acknowledges the interdependence of the global world and the role international higher education collaboration plays in solving global issues that will not be solved by any one institution or country alone. In turn, transnational partnerships between institutions of higher education rely on collaboration as a key element of success. Though not all transnational partnerships have been designed with mutual benefits in mind, international higher education institutions can adjust their approaches, their goals, and the partnerships they pursue to better align with their university cultures, institutional goals, stakeholder needs and values, and the global context. In fact, it is vital that they do so for the longer-term sustainability of the programs developed and the partnerships themselves, and in the broader scheme, the deconstruction of the knowledge divide that has too often been the result of lopsided transnational partnerships.

CONCLUSION

Recent trends leading up to and including the COVID-19 pandemic indicate that it has become more common for U.S. institutions of higher education to incorporate entrepreneurial internationalization strategies into institutional strategic plans. These trends are prompted by deeper systemic challenges facing institutions of higher education, such as the lack of funding from state and federal resources as well as exposure to the external neoliberal environment that promotes market-like behavior. One common internationalization goal included in institutional strategic plans in the United States is to increase the number of international students on campus, who pay higher tuition fees and bring more revenue to the U.S. institution. The reality of living in a post-COVID-19 environment with the shifting student mobility flows has increased competition globally. To meet this goal, U.S. institutions are now looking to transnational partnerships to extend their reach into new student markets abroad through online or offshore programs. International joint/dual degree programs established through transnational partnerships have the potential to provide access to U.S. degrees to international students at a lower overall price point, but they often fall short because of uneven benefits to the institutional partners involved and false assumptions about programs that will add value to international students and their local communities.

Ultimately, it is the responsibility of the partner institutions and key stakeholders involved in transnational partnerships to conduct a market analysis that considers university culture, local, regional, and global contexts, and partner goals, stakeholder interests, and desired outcomes in the early stages of developing the transnational partnership. Reimagining higher education in a post-COVID-19 world provides an opportunity for transnational partnerships to play a significant role moving forward. The transnational partnership life cycle provides a framework for ensuring that partnership development is carried out in three distinct phases: the development phase, the operational phase, and the assessment phase. It also recognizes the entrepreneurial behavior exhibited by institutions of higher education, the cyclical nature of transnational partnerships, and the various stakeholders involved. Combined with the paradigm of knowledge diplomacy, the transnational partnership life cycle framework can set a new course for transnational partnership development that neutralizes power dynamics and establishes terms of engagement for mutual benefits and longer-term program sustainability.

Of course, the success of any framework is largely dependent on the stakeholders that set goals, influence decisions, and otherwise control the transnational partnership development process. The human element cannot be ignored and will largely determine how any framework or paradigm is adopted. The ethical debate about when and why to pursue transnational partnerships will be unique to each institution, and even to individuals, and it is up to the stakeholders involved on both sides to do their due diligence when vetting a possible new venture and making the decision to move forward. There is potential for institutions of higher education around the world to reconcile their core mission of providing education as a public good with the entrepreneurial behaviors introduced by the free-market economy and reimagining the future of higher education in a new paradigm. It is time to shift gears and focus on an ethical, values-based approach to entrepreneurial behavior that provides more than economic benefits.

REFERENCES

American Council on Education. (2014). *Mapping international joint and dual degrees: U.S. program profiles and perspectives*. Retrieved from http://www.acenet.edu/news-room/Documents/Mapping-International-Joint-and-Dual-Degrees.pdf

Arroyo Perez, A. (2017). *Money for prestige: A geopolitical transaction*. (Publication No. 10743686; Doctoral dissertation, University of Arizona). ProQuest Dissertations and Theses Global.

Bäckstrand, K. (2006). Multi-stakeholder partnerships for sustainable development: Rethinking legitimacy, accountability and effectiveness. *European Environment*, 16(5), 290–306.

Bhandari, R., and Blumenthal, P. (2011). *International students and global mobility in higher education: National trends and new directions*. New York, NY: Palgrave Macmillan.

Bolton, D., and Nie, R. (2010). Creating value in transnational higher education: The role of stakeholder management. *Academy of Management Learning & Education*, 9(4), 701–714.

Brinkerhoff, J. M. (2002). Assessing and improving partnership relationships and outcomes: A proposed framework. *Evaluation and Program Planning*, 25(3), 215–231.

Cantwell, B. (2015). Are international students cash cows? Examining the relationship between new international undergraduate enrollments and institutional revenue at public colleges and universities in the US. *Journal of International Students*, 5(4), 512–525.

Choudaha, R., and Chang, L. (2012). Trends in international student mobility. *World Education News & Reviews*, 25(2), 1–5.

Deschamps, E., and Lee, J. J. (2014). Internationalization as mergers and acquisitions: Senior international officers' entrepreneurial strategies and activities in public universities. *Journal of Studies in International Education*, 19(2), 122–139. doi:1028315314538284.

Gai, L., Xu, C., and Pelton, L. E. (2016). A netnographic analysis of prospective international students' decision-making process: Implications for institutional branding of American universities in the emerging markets. *Journal of Marketing for Higher Education, 26*(2), 181–198. doi:10.1080/08841241.2016.1245233

George Mwangi, C. A. (2017). Partner positioning: Examining international higher education partnerships through a mutuality lens. *The Review of Higher Education, 41*(1), 33–60.

Gumport, P. J., and Sporn, B. (1999). Institutional adaptation: Demands for management reform and university administration. In *Higher education: Handbook of theory and research* (pp. 103–145): Springer, Dordrecht. doi: https://doi.org/10.1007/978-94-011-3955-7_3

Healey, N. M. (2018). The challenges of managing transnational education partnerships: The views of "home-based" managers vs "in-country" managers. *International Journal of Educational Management, 32*(2), 241–256. doi:10.1108/IJEM-04-2017-0085

Hitt, M. A., Dacin, M. T., Levitas, E., Arregle, J.-L., and Borza, A. (2000). Partner selection in emerging and developed market contexts: Resource-based and organizational learning perspectives. *Academy of Management Journal, 43*(3), 449–467.

International Association of Universities. (2020). *Impact of COVID-19 on higher education around the World.* Retrieved from https://iau-aiu.net/IAU-releases-Global-Survey-Report-on-Impact-of-Covid-19-in-Higher-Education

Kinser, K., and Green, M. F. (2009). *The power of partnerships: A transatlantic dialogue.* European University Association, Association of Universities and Colleges of Canada, and American Council on Education. Washington, DC.

Knight, J. (2015). Moving from soft power to knowledge diplomacy. *International Higher Education* (80), 8–9.

———. (2018, February 16). Knowledge diplomacy or knowledge divide? *University World News.* Retrieved from https://www.universityworldnews.com/post.php?story=20180214084632675

Knight, J., and Lee, J. (2012). International joint, double, and consecutive degree programs. In D. K. Deardorff, H. de Wit, and J. D. Heyl (Eds.), *The SAGE handbook of international higher education* (pp. 343–357). Thousand Oaks, CA: Sage Publications, Inc.

Koehn, P. H. (2012). Turbulence and bifurcation in North–South higher-education partnerships for research and sustainable development. *Public Organization Review, 12*(4), 331–355.

Koehn, P. H., and Obamba, M. O. (2014). Asymmetry and symmetry in transnational higher-education partnerships. In *The Transnationally Partnered University* (pp. 71–82). Palgrave Macmillan, New York.

LaFleur, D. (2018). *Transnational partnerships and dual degrees: Entrepreneurial strategies for internationalization.* (Publication No. 10743054; Doctoral dissertation, University of Arizona). ProQuest Dissertations and Theses Global.

LaFleur, D., and Regulska, J. (2018). *A hub and spokes—configuring campus stakeholders for partnership success.* Retrieved from American Council on Education website: https://www.acenet.edu/news-room/Documents/IIA-Intl-Partnerships-Part-3.pdf

Lane, J. E., and Kinser, K. (2014). International joint and double-degree programs. In *Global Opportunities and Challenges for Higher Education Leaders* (pp. 59–62). SensePublishers, Rotterdam.

Montgomery, C. (2016). Transnational partnerships in higher education in China: The diversity and complexity of elite strategic alliances. *London Review of Education, 14*(1), 70–85.

Ozturgut, O. (2013). Best practices in recruiting and retaining international students in the US. *Current Issues in Education, 16*(2), 1–22.

Pattberg, P., and Widerberg, O. (2016). Transnational multistakeholder partnerships for sustainable development: Conditions for success. *Ambio*, 45(1), 42–51.

Rhoades, G., and Sporn, B. (2002). New models of management and shifting modes and costs of production: Europe and the United States. *Tertiary Education & Management*, 8(1), 3–28.

Ryan, M. P. (1998). *Knowledge diplomacy: Global competition and the politics of intellectual property*. Washington, DC: Brookings Institution Press.

Samoff, J., and Carrol, B. (2004). The promise of partnership and continuities of dependence: External support to higher education in Africa. *African Studies Review*, 47(1), 67.

Schäferhoff, M., Campe, S., and Kaan, C. (2009). Transnational public-private partnerships in international relations: Making sense of concepts, research frameworks, and results. *International Studies Review*, 11(3), 451–474.

Sporn, B. (1996). Managing university culture: An analysis of the relationship between institutional culture and management approaches. *Higher Education*, 32(1), 41–61.

PART 4 STUDENTS AND INTERNATIONAL LEARNING

9 • GLOBAL POSITIONAL COMPETITION AND INTEREST CONVERGENCE

Student Mobility as a Commodity for U.S. Academic Imperialism

CHRISTINA W. YAO

Student mobility has emerged as a major economic and political force across the globe. As stated by Altbach (2016), "Not since the medieval period has such a large proportion of the world's students been studying outside their home countries" (p. 90). The Organisation for Economic Co-operation and Development (OECD, 2020a) reported that in 2018, 5.6 million students were engaged in some form of international higher education, which doubled the numbers of mobile students in 2005.

With increasing numbers of students crossing borders for higher education degree programs and study abroad, students began to resemble commodities that are traded between nation-states. The benefits associated with treating students as goods to be imported and exported expressly contribute to the overall global power that sustains a nation-state's positioning as a world leader in education, economics, and politics. As a result, incoming international students serve as imports that contribute to a country's global status as the top destination for students. At the same time, domestic students are sent as exports to absorb an "international consciousness" (Altbach, 2016, p. 125) that will prepare them for future employment in the home country's workforce. Also, higher education institutions and study abroad service providers are increasingly recognizing the material benefits of study abroad, potentially leading to the commercialization of cross-border programs for financial gain (Lewin, 2009). As a result, the commodification of students and their mobility contributes to the overall pursuit of academic imperialism through economic gain, institutional visibility, and international prestige.

Although the quest for global academic imperialism is seldom explicitly stated, the United States stands to gain extensively through the movement of students, both as an import and as an export. Thus, it is essential to question and problematize how students and their mobility choices are perceived and represented as commodities in U.S. international education circles. For example, how often do international education organizations lead with the economic benefits of international students in the United States when making the argument for increased support for this population? Or how do academic leaders push study abroad for U.S. students as a way to meet lofty goals of increasing intercultural competency or enhancing foreign language development, primarily through short-term study tours?

In this chapter, I critique current discourse that commodifies students as imports and exports, all of which contributes to the United States' overall global academic imperialism. I argue that academic imperialism is enacted by and for the United States as an attempt to maintain a global positional competition through interest convergence of viewing students as imports and exports within the higher education market. The interaction between the "macro" forces of global competition and the "micro" processes within higher education such as teaching and learning (Naidoo and Jamieson, 2005) and student exchange must be examined in order to understand the commodification of the modern university. In order to analyze the interaction, public documents, briefs, and current research are used to map the current discourse related to student mobility as a commodity. Although this chapter is not a traditional empirical study, policy briefs from the IIE (2018, 2020a, 2020b), NAFSA (2018a, 2018b), and OECD (2020a, 2020b) are reviewed because of their reputations as primary associations and sources for international education research and advocacy. In addition, current literature, public interviews and statements, and recent news articles are used to inform the analysis. Topics such as international student recruitment, the proliferation of short-term study abroad, and overall student mobility to and from the United States are problematized using a lens that includes positional competition, academic dependency, and interest convergence. I also provide some future directions for practice and policy, with an emphasis on considerations in light of the COVID-19 crisis. At the time of writing this chapter, higher education is in the midst of the COVID-19 pandemic, and higher education institutions around the world are trying to determine how to move forward in current and post-COVID-19 times.

CURRENT LANDSCAPE OF STUDENT MOBILITY IN THE UNITED STATES

Knight (2012) succinctly stated that "there is no question that internationalization, and particularly international student mobility, has transformed the higher education landscape in the last decade" (p. 20). Unprecedented numbers of students are choosing to study outside their home countries, whether for short-term, semester-long, or yearlong study abroad programs or for academic degree granting programs. Thus, student mobility, both inbound and outbound, has received significant attention in recent years. In this section, I offer a brief overview of student mobility to and from the United States to establish some context for the rest of the chapter. For clarification, I operationalize "student mobility" as an umbrella term to include both domestic students currently enrolled at U.S. institutions who participate in study abroad programs and international students who are attending U.S. institutions for degree attainment.

Inbound Student Mobility: International Students in the United States

Enrollment of international students consistently experienced an upward trajectory in the past fifty years, with the United States as the top destination for international students. Yet a downward slope of new international student enrollment was apparent in the 2016–2017 academic year when the numbers dropped 3 percent from the previous year (IIE, 2017). In the 2017–2018 academic year, the United States reached a new high of 1,094,792 total international students enrolled in U.S. higher education (IIE, 2018); however, despite the seemingly large numbers of students, the actual percentage of new international student enrollment dropped 6.6 percent from the previous year. In addition, the Council of Graduate Schools reported that international graduate student enrollments have declined in the past two years (Okahana and Zhou, 2019). Most recently, the number of new student enrollments dropped for the fourth year in a row, currently down 0.6 percent from the previous year (IIE, 2020b). In the 2019–2020 academic year, the United States experienced a 1.8% decline in international student enrollment, which is likely affected by the COVID-19 pandemic.

The first signal of the declining numbers came when IIE released its 2017 *Open Doors* report on November 13, 2017. Multiple media outlets including the *Chronicle of Higher Education* (Fischer, 2017) and *Inside Higher Ed* (Redden, 2017) immediately highlighted the decline in the United States' attraction as a host country for international students. In addition, several higher education institutions demonstrated concern over the potential loss of international students and revenue because of the financial contributions from international student enrollment. The financial resources were significant, according to NAFSA (2018a), which reported that international students contributed $39 billion and helped support over 455,000 jobs in the United States during the 2017–2018 academic year.

In more recent news, several higher education institutions and professional associations are concerned with the current presidential administration's restrictive immigration agenda. Immediately following President Donald J. Trump's executive order in early 2017, "Protecting the Nation from Foreign Terrorist Entry into the United States," colloquially known as the Travel Ban, several associations joined forces to respond with their concerns on how the Travel Ban could affect international student and scholar recruitment (see American Council on Education, Association of American Universities, Association of Public and Land-grant Universities, and the Council on Governmental Relations, 2018). Other statements followed, including a brief of amicus curiae that was submitted in response to the 2018 Supreme Court Case *Trump v. Hawaii* by thirty-three higher education associations against the Travel Ban (see Brief for American Council on Education et al., 2018). NAFSA (2019b) recently released a policy brief titled "Losing Talent: An Economic and Foreign Policy Risk America *Can't Ignore*," which urged policymakers in Congress to support international students and scholars because of the benefits to the United States. Overall, higher education institutions and associations are continually monitoring the trends of student mobility and, more importantly, of how the United States fares as a top host destination for international students and scholars, which is continually shifting owing to current geopolitics.

Outbound Student Mobility: Study Abroad of U.S. Students

According to IIE (2020a), the number of U.S. students studying abroad grew 1.6 percent in the 2018–2019 academic year over the previous year, which includes short-term, mid-length, and long-term study abroad programs. One in ten undergraduate students chooses to study outside the United States during his or her academic studies, and indicators suggest that institutions will continue to emphasize undergraduate study abroad programs. Although U.S. students studying abroad in 2019/2020 were affected by the arrival of the COVID-19 pandemic, IIE (2020b) reported a 1.6% increase of students abroad in 2018/2019, with all indications for strong interest and program growth in study abroad despite the pandemic. Overall, all participation numbers follow an upward trajectory of study abroad participants over the past twenty-five years (IIE, 2020b).

The time spent abroad varies for students, with the majority choosing to participate in short-term programs that last eight weeks or less or take place during the summer months. In 2018–2019, 64.9 percent of study abroad students chose short-term programs (IIE, 2020a), as compared with mid-length programs (one semester, or one or two quarters) at 33.9 percent and long-term programs (academic or calendar year) at 2.2 percent (IIE, 2020a). Short-term programs allow students the opportunity to efficiently engage in international experiences, are gaining in popularity because of the shorter time commitment and potentially lower cost. Europe continues to be the top destination for U.S. students, hosting 51.3 percent of the study abroad population, followed by Latin America and the Caribbean hosting 8.4 percent of U.S. students abroad (IIE, 2020a). In sum, the majority of U.S. students studying abroad tend to choose short-term programs in Europe, another westernized continent that is considered to be part of the Global North.

The purpose of studying abroad includes lofty goals for intercultural learning, international engagement, and global learning for students, especially within the contexts of short-term study. Higher education institutions are focused on "preparing U.S. students to secure jobs after graduation in order to advance their careers, as well as preparing them to thrive in the multicultural global marketplace" (IIE, 2017), and often use study abroad as a way to develop these skills in college students. In addition, governmental policy has taken a role in encouraging more U.S. students to study abroad. For example, former president Barack Obama created the 100,000 Strong Initiative in 2009 as a way to increase the number and diversity of U.S. students who study in China (U.S.-China Strong, 2019). Yet the primary students choosing to study abroad tend to identify as white, constituting 68.7 percent of the total study abroad numbers in 2018–2019 (IIE, 2020a). However, although the total number of racial and/or ethnic minoritized students going abroad has increased over time, the individual racial group representations in 2018–2019 (i.e., Hispanic or Latino(a) [10.9%], Asian or Pacific Islander [8.9%], Black or African American [6.4%], Multiracial [4.7%], and American Indian or Alaska Native [0.4%]) are extremely low when the percentages are disaggregated (IIE, 2020a). Thus, although the overall numbers of students studying abroad are increasing, the questions of overall equity and representation in study abroad are important to consider as U.S. higher education institutions and policy organizations continue to stress the importance of cross-border education.

CONCEPTUAL FRAMEWORK: ACADEMIC IMPERIALISM

Before engaging in the analytical component of student mobility, the concept of *academic imperialism* must be clarified and elaborated. The term "imperialism" conjures the historical image of a dictator or extensive military forces in a physically dominant position over a conquered nation. Yet a contemporary understanding of imperialism must be more broadly understood, especially within today's global dynamics. Simply stated, imperialism is "the subjugation of one people by another for the advantage of the dominant one" (S. H. Alatas, 2000, p. 23) and can be seen in multiple contexts including political, economic, sociocultural, and ideological (Said, 1993). These imperial and colonial actions are evident in both explicit and covert ways in contemporary educational practice, especially in light of higher education as the new imperialism (Naidoo, 2011).

In higher education, the notion of academic imperialism tends to be applied to the privileging and dominance of knowledge, especially in flows of research, ideas, and resources in higher education. Academic imperialism stems from S. H. Alatas's (2000) definition of intellectual imperialism as the "domination of one people by another in their world of thinking" (p. 24). I ascribe to S. F. Alatas's (2003) claim that academic imperialism is closely related to political and economic imperialism. Academic and economic imperialism in higher education are often fanned by the pressures of globalization and internationalization, mostly because higher education as a whole is "a relational environment" (Marginson, 2008, p. 303) that spans the global, national, and local (Marginson, 2008; Marginson and Rhoades 2002; Välimaa, 2004). Within the relational environment in global higher education, the power structures are unevenly oppressive as a result of imperialism that is rooted in uneven relationships and exchanges between what are considered First World and Third World societies (Rhee and Sagaria, 2004).

Academic imperialism includes economic and capitalistic components, especially when placing it within the global educational stage. Globalization of higher education is described as "the economic, political, and societal forces pushing 21st century higher education toward greater international involvement" (Altbach and Knight, 2007, p. 290). As a result, globalization serves as an external force that pushes nation-states to enact imperialistic academic practices under the guise of internationalization. Although the terms "globalization" and "imperialism" may be used interchangeably by other scholars, I view the terms differently, although I do ascribe to Rhee and Sagaria's (2004) overall claim that "imperialism and globalization are premised on both consensual and coercive interaction" (p. 81). In this case, the United States enacts academic imperialism as a result of the pressures of globalization, which maintains a global dominance over the commodification of students as imports and exports within the higher education market.

CURRENT DISCOURSE ON STUDENT MOBILITY FOR ACADEMIC IMPERIALISM: POSITIONAL COMPETITION, INTEREST CONVERGENCE, AND ACADEMIC DEPENDENCY

How do U.S. higher education institutions enact academic imperialism in regard to student mobility to and from the United States? I argue that the U.S. higher education enterprise uses both inbound and outbound mobility as tools that contribute to positional competition, academic dependency, and interest convergence, all of which contribute to academic imperialism. In the following sections, I provide a brief overview of each of the tools and then delve deeper into an analysis of how current discourse from literature, professional associations, and policy organizations contributes to enacting imperialistic practices through student mobility to and from the United States.

Positional Competition
Positional competition (Hirsch, 1977) is defined by "how one stands relative to others within an implicit or explicit hierarchy" (Brown, 2000, p. 633). Rooted within labor and economic sociology, positional competition is clarified by Brown (2000), who defined positional conflict theory as "an understanding of how individuals and social groups mobilise their cultural, economic, political or

social assets in positional power struggles" (p. 638), in which the social elite maintains the advantage. Simply stated, positional competition is the idea of power struggles between groups to outperform or outdo others in order to gain advantage and stay ahead, particularly within times of scarce resources. Positional competition brings in the pressures of globalization and the global knowledge economy (Brown, 2000; Brown, Lauder, and Ashton, 2008; Kim, 2016), which emphasizes the "positional conflict between as well as within societies" (Brown, 2000, p. 639). Because of the pressures of globalization, nation-states, such as the United States, are continually imposing both implicit and explicit actions to maintain global positional competition within "new dynamics between openness and closure" (Kim, 2016, p. 32).

Brown (2000) highlighted three areas that define inclusion and exclusion within positional competition in global markets: membership, meritocratic, and market. *Membership* is based on attributes such as gender, race, class, and national origin, within which an individual is defined in relation to others. The emphasis on the individual is highlighted in *meritocratic* rules, in which individual achievement comes from personal aptitude and effort. Within a meritocracy, structural and systematic forces of inequality within organizations—or in this particular case, in nation-states—are discounted in favor of individuals' personal determination to succeed. And finally, market rules deviate from membership and meritocratic as the emphasis shifts from group and individual attributes. Rather, within *markets*, nation-states "intervene to ensure that the impediments to market competition based on the principles of supply and demand are removed" (Brown, 2000, p. 640). That is, the market rules shift toward an economic impetus for action in order to establish and maintain high positional competition.

When applying the rules of positional competition to international student mobility, the United States maintains a high global status through both implicit and explicit actions to exert its dominance. For example, much of the discourse on declining numbers of international students in the United States comes from a *market* perspective in which the competition for international students as commodities comes to the forefront. Statements from higher education entities indicate the marketization of U.S. higher education in reference to attracting international students and scholars. For example, NAFSA (2018b) believes that the United States is "in a competition for global talent with other countries" and that U.S. higher education institutions must be concerned because "many other countries are proactively introducing national policies and marketing strategies in order to attract these talented individuals." As a result, the United States' "fifth-largest services export is at risk" owing to fewer international students who "create jobs, drive research, enrich our classrooms, strengthen national security, and become America's greatest foreign policy assets" (NAFSA, 2019b, pp. 2, 1).

The United States has always been able to attract global talent over the years, and to a certain extent has benefited from talent from the rest of the world

(Marginson, 2008); however, with the continually changing immigration and visa policies in the United States, its appeal as a host country has waned. The loss of international students and scholars may shift the positional power that the United States has held for many years because internationally mobile students is "a way to tap into a global pool of talent, compensate for weaker capacity at lower education levels, support the development of innovation and production systems and, in many countries, to mitigate the impact of an ageing population on future skills supply" (OECD, 2020a, p. 227). As a result, the fears of U.S. higher education losing its global power position has caused concern for numerous higher education institutions and associations, such as NAFSA (2018a, 2018b, 2019b), American Council on Education, Association of American Universities, Association of Public and Land-grant Universities, and the Council on Governmental Relations (2018).

In regard to U.S. students studying abroad, representation of *membership rules* is apparent in the quest to maintain a high global position. Membership to the United States automatically gives sojourners an advantage when studying in countries outside the United States. For example, in a study on U.S. doctoral students' reflections on conducting international research, Yao and Vital (2018) found that many participants highlighted the power and privilege they brought to their international fieldwork as a result of their U.S.-based academic training, their citizenship, and their use of English as their operating language. U.S. students benefit from membership that gives them "freedom to go anywhere and intervene in other national sites" (Marginson, 2008, p. 308) as a result of the nation's global status.

In addition, the dominance of the United States is reified in how the host countries are chosen and represented by study abroad sojourners. Scholars have critiqued how study abroad sites serve as vacation spots and "island programs," where students tend to socialize only with other study abroad travelers (Lewin, 2009) and gain artificial experiences (Ramírez, 2013). Most alarming is the concern that students, especially those who go to developing countries, end up participating in "a colonialist project of visiting the 'natives,' a kind of poverty tourism that reinforces stereotypes of themselves and others" (Lewin, 2009, p. xv). Students may take pictures of locals as "cultural Others" to demonstrate the exoticism of their travel (Kortegast and Kupo, 2017), reconfirming the student's membership to the dominant U.S. culture when compared with perceived outsiders. Thus, the use of othering in study abroad serves as a hegemonic tool to preserve the U.S.'s global position by maintaining a cultural hierarchy. As stated by Marginson (2008), the hegemony of the United States is "enabled by and expressed in American global geo-strategic mobility" that allows for the "freedom to go anywhere . . . while maintaining territorial control of the homeland" (p. 308). Thus, the global positional competition is maintained by the United States, continuing to push toward increased academic imperialism.

Academic Dependency

Another tool for academic imperialism that is connected to positional competition is the subtle yet explicit imposition of academic dependency on the United States. Academic dependency, like many theories mentioned in this chapter, is rooted in the foundations of economic dependency and capitalism (S. F. Alatas, 2003; Altbach, 1977). Academic dependency is exhibited through the dependence of people from the Global South on those of the Global North, or Western nations such as the United States and the United Kingdom (UK), seeking goods and services related to education. The power differentiation in dependency is connected to the effects of colonialism, which created "an educational dependence on Western intellectual models in the Third World" (Altbach, 1977, p. 188). As a result, the dependency establishes the Western intellectual models as the center, or dominant, force with the dependent nation-states as peripheral members that rely on the center for goods.

Altbach (1977) warned higher education stakeholders of the dangers of academic dependency over forty years ago when he wrote of how education, dependency, and neocolonialism intersected to create a "servitude of the mind" (p. 204) that leads to increasing inequality and chasms between and among nation-states within the global education arena. Yet the United States continued to establish itself as a hegemonic center that created and depends on academic dependency from other nation-states. As noted by Marginson (2008), the United States includes three aspects of dominance within the field of global higher education: flows of knowledge, the global dominance of the English language, and U.S. universities as top academic destinations.

Specifically related to international students and scholars, the United States has created an academic dependency over the years for what is considered an exemplary quality education and opportunities for English language immersion because of the role of English as a lingua franca.

For international students and scholars, attending U.S. institutions contributes to the development of an overall global cultural capital, related to the above-referenced positional competition. As a result, students may choose to attend U.S. higher education institutions in search of the global capital that comes from a perceived high-quality education and destination, as evidenced by Kim's (2011) study on South Korean graduate students' motivation for selecting the United States. The rhetoric of U.S. education being the "best in the world" was echoed by participants in my research on Chinese international students (Yao, 2014), who withstood discrimination and interpersonal difficulties from U.S. domestic students for a degree that would bring them greater advancement within the global economy. As a result of these narratives that have spread across the globe, the United States has established itself as the top destination for mobile students over the past decade (IIE, 2018), which contributes to the perceived academic dependency from other countries.

Another contribution to academic dependency is the use of English as the operating language around the globe and as the primary academic language (Altbach, 2016). English language instruction is used to attract tuition-paying international students and increase global prestige (Ferguson, 2007), and because many students want to improve their English skills within a predominantly English-speaking context, international students are attracted to English-speaking countries like the United States (OECD, 2020a). As a result, English as a lingua franca creates an academic dependency from students who seek to improve their English skills as a way to join the academic elites, despite having to withstand negative and discriminatory experiences at their U.S. institutions (Jon and Kim, 2011; Kim, 2011; Yao, 2014, 2018). Thus, this academic dependency based on the English language contributes to the U.S. hegemonic and imperialistic categorization as being a top destination for international students.

Academic dependency is also visible in U.S. study abroad practices and initiatives, although I would argue that economic dependency is more readily apparent. The unequal relationship between the United States and study abroad locations is apparent in the discourse related to how international education benefits the United States. For U.S. students, study abroad can perpetuate the academic and economic dependency of other nations. In particular, the nature of short-term study abroad may lend itself to "issues of consumerism, postcolonial practices, cultural tourism, and commodification of experiences" (Kortegast and Kupo, 2017, p. 151). The relationships between sojourning students and their host countries can propagate the United States as a dominant force, as evidenced by issues in international service learning related to increased dependency on the income from hosting traveling students (Smaller and O'Sullivan, 2018). Study abroad, including international service learning, has been critiqued by multiple scholars (e.g., Andreotti, 2006; Jefferess, 2008; Smaller and O'Sullivan, 2018) as contributing to an unequal dependency from the Global South.

Tourism can be dangerous for the host country's society and environment, and it typically affects more vulnerable nation-states (Archer, Cooper, and Ruhanen, 2005). Yet the effects of short-term study abroad on the host community are often ignored as the focus is typically on the outcomes and benefits of the touring student (Schroeder, Wood, Galiardi, and Koehn, 2009). As a result, the emphasis of study abroad has continued to be on how it benefits the United States and its students, again contributing to academic dependency and academic imperialism.

Interest Convergence

Interest convergence is a term that has its roots in critical legal studies and critical race theory to address how decisions to serve subordinate groups of individuals are created to serve the interests of the dominant group (Bell, 1980). Although interest convergence may benefit the disadvantaged group in some way, the dominant group will always benefit the most, and their desires will remain the priority for advancement. As stated by Bell (1980) and by Delgado and Stefancic (2017), the desires and needs of the majority group are always going to impose dominance and supremacy over the subordinate group, despite interest convergence benefiting all actors.

The foundations of interest convergence are rooted in critical race theory and the experiences of people of color in the United States; however, interest convergence should be extended to include international student mobility as it benefits the overall power of U.S. higher education (Yao and Viggiano, 2019). In addition, the majority of international students and scholars to the United States may be considered people of color based on the top sending countries (Yao, George Mwangi, and Malaney Brown, 2019). As a result, the interests of the United States are served by the global mobility of students, which benefits the United States through financial profits, global competition, and international reputation (Altbach, 2016).

There is no question that multiple push-pull factors exist for international students to study abroad, such as language development (e.g., Xing and Bolden, 2019; Yao, 2016) and academic prestige (e.g., Lee, 2008; Yan and Berliner, 2011). However, although international students may perceive benefits from attending college in the United States, the primary purpose for recruiting this population is often to serve the interests of the soft-power development of the United States as a means for garnering diversity, contributing to foreign policy, producing knowledge, and generating economic gains (Yao and Viggiano, 2019).

The OECD (2016, 2020a) also touts the economic value of international student mobility, because for host countries such as the United States, international students bring benefits in both economic development and innovation (OECD, 2020a). In addition, international students contribute to knowledge development and may be more likely to find employment in their host countries (OECD, 2020a), both of which benefit the United States as the host country. Yet at the same time, the immigration and foreign policy rhetoric by the current presidential administration is leaving U.S. higher education institutions, policy organizations, and professional associations scrambling to control the potential damage to international student enrollment. For example, current political tensions between the United States and China have led to warnings from China's Ministry of Education of potential difficulties for Chinese students seeking visas to study in the United States (Redden, 2019a). Such tensions have led university officials and higher education leaders to be concerned about potential problems related to student and scholar mobility from China, as evidenced by statements from institutions such as the Massachusetts Institute of Technology (MIT News, 2019) and the University of California-Berkeley (Berkeley News, 2019). In these statements, campus leaders reaffirmed their commitment to maintaining a welcoming community for international students and scholars. Yet embedded within the words about being open and welcoming is interest convergence of why and how international students and scholars from China benefit the United States. Thus, the interests of welcoming Chinese scholars primarily benefit MIT in the sense of demonstrating a welcoming institution, and also benefit the United States as a way to make global gains.

Yet at the same time, when considering the reverse flow of U.S. students studying abroad, the financial and talent infusion rarely leaves the United States for other countries as a result of the proliferation of short-term study abroad programs. In addition, short-term study abroad brings significant benefits to the United States, as stated by NAFSA (2019a) in an issue brief lobbying for the Senator Paul Simon Study Abroad Program Act. Study abroad and "global learning helps American students succeed in their careers, and collectively, these international experiences lead to a more innovative, secure, and prosperous United States" (NAFSA, 2019a). The strength of the United States is once again highlighted by former First Lady Michelle Obama, who stated that study abroad helps build up the United States when discussing the 100,000 Strong Initiative during the Obama administration. In addition, Michelle Obama praised the diplomacy benefits of students studying abroad by stating that "with every friendship you make, and every bond of trust you establish, you are shaping the image of America projected to the rest of the world" (Schulman, 2011). Thus, as indicated by some contemporary discourse, study abroad goes beyond mere cultural immersion for the participating student. Rather, U.S. students studying abroad also serve some diplomacy roles as ambassadors of the United States as well as being able to contribute to their country by strengthening it. Although the interests of students who are seeking international experiences are served, the interests of the United States are also served in relation to maintaining its position in global academic imperialism.

DISCUSSION AND RECOMMENDATIONS FOR FUTURE DIRECTIONS

Using positional competition, academic dependency, and interest convergence as analytical lenses reveals a troubling commodities narrative that dominates the discourse and actions of U.S. higher education. The view of students as commodities is problematic because it dehumanizes individuals and promotes self-centered priorities. Identifying students as imports and exports should bring discomfort to higher education stakeholders, and yet the current discourse on students indicates that the commodification is rarely problematized, especially when discussing international students in the United States. In fact, the economic emphasis of international students on the United States has grown increasingly more frequent as a result of the two-year decline of new international student enrollment (IIE, 2018), as evidenced by recent news reports such as Redden's (2019b) *Inside Higher Ed* article on the increase of Chinese students enrolling in the UK. In the article, the marketization and commodification of international students is apparent, as exemplified by a director of an Oxford-based think tank stating that "the global market for international students is growing" (Redden, 2019b), indicating a global discourse of students as commodities. Thus, the challenge here is perhaps facing the reality that viewing students as commodities may not slow down in the near or distant future.

Up until spring 2020, student mobility showed little sign of abating; in fact, the number of mobile students globally had continued to grow over the years. Yet when COVID-19 was first identified as an infectious disease in Wuhan, China, countries all around the world scrambled to manage the effects of the virus. U.S. higher education institutions shut down all on-campus operations in an attempt to mitigate the spread of the virus while simultaneously bringing study abroad students back to the United States (Fischer, 2020a; Redden, 2020b). Despite the country being in the midst of the pandemic, much of the current discourse related to international higher education focuses on how U.S. higher education will lose millions in revenue owing to low international student enrollment in post-COVID-19 times (Fischer, 2020b; Redden, 2020a). NAFSA (2020) recently released a report on the financial impact of COVID-19 on higher education, stating that "U.S. higher education overall has potentially lost nearly $1 billion due to shortened or canceled study abroad programs and spent approximately $638 million in financial support for international students, scholars, faculty, and staff who remained on campus when courses moved online. Responses further estimate that U.S. higher education will lose at least $3 billion due to anticipated international student enrollment declines for fall 2020" (p. 2). At the current time, the projected effects of COVID-19 appear to be relatively bleak for U.S. institutions, especially when considering the financial impact. The pandemic illustrates that students, both international students and students studying abroad, continue to serve an economic purpose in higher education.

There is no question that sojourning students bring economic, cultural, and political benefits to most participants and stakeholders. Yet as evidenced by its global positional competition and academic dependency, the United States will likely continue to remain a dominant academic force within the international education arena despite COVID-19, and will seek to maintain its global positioning. As stated by NAFSA (2020), the purpose of its recent financial report was "to better understand the needs of the field and share this information with the U.S. Congress as future economic stimulus packages and additional policy changes are considered" (p. 1). Thus, efforts are already being made to recoup U.S. institutions' interests in international education. The United States as well as its institutions has invested too much time, money, and resources to maintain its dominant position only to lose power as the result of a health pandemic. Continuing to prioritize their interests by commodifying students will contribute to maintaining and likely increasing academic imperialism despite the projected effects of COVID-19.

So the question arises of, now what? What are ways to move forward in regard to student mobility? How can praxis come from acknowledging the tools that contribute to academic imperialism? First, an understanding of how global forces affect the institutional practices that affect students, especially international students and students studying abroad, is key to gaining perspective on the importance of student mobility to an institution. Also, acknowledging the dehumanization of viewing students as exports and imports may lead to a shift in thinking and practice. Asking reflective questions may assist higher education stakeholders in moving beyond the discourse that commodifies students.

For international student recruitment to the United States as well as other leading countries, some questions for institutions and leaders to ask include the following:

- Does our organization talk about international students in humanizing ways?
- Do we always lead with the economic benefits when discussing their importance to our campus and nation?
- Do we discuss ways to better support and engage international students on our campus?
- Do we avoid essentializing international students into one homogenous group?

Overall, higher education stakeholders must go beyond viewing international students as simply numbers that pay full tuition, contribute to the local economy, and create jobs, which falls within an interest convergence lens. Many associations, institutions, and academic leaders have voiced their support of international students in the United States; however, the narrative is situated within academic imperialistic ways that dehumanize students into commodities. In the discourse, international students become othered and subordinated, without much concern for their learning and well-being. As a result, higher education institutions and associations focus primarily on the recruitment; however, stakeholders must go beyond naming national interests as the primary reasons to support international students.

Not only are international students viewed as imports, but U.S. students are commodified as well and become exports for dominance and political gain. In order to address the imperialistic approach to study abroad, higher education stakeholders should consider some questions related to study abroad:

- How does our organization talk about the purpose of study abroad?
- How do we make short-term study abroad experiences more meaningful and go beyond academic tourism?

- Do we critically examine our current study abroad practices to ensure that study abroad is accessible to all students?
- Do we have best practices and/or policies on how to work in responsible ways with host countries?

The discourse related to study abroad must go beyond that of perpetuating the colonial and imperial ways of human exploration. Some unintended outcomes of study abroad may negatively affect host countries, as demonstrated through academic dependency and positional competition lenses. In addition, the Senator Paul Simon Study Abroad Program Act, which is heavily supported by associations such as NAFSA (2019a) and the American Council on Education (2019), includes lofty goals such as increased representation from diverse students in regard to gender, ethnicity, and income level, as well as sending students to more nontraditional destinations that are outside Western Europe. Yet despite the support for increasing study abroad, there is little discussion among higher education stakeholders on how to deconstruct current study abroad practices to attract more underrepresented students, as well as how to avoid creating additional academic dependency from nontraditional host countries. How can study abroad be more accessible to all students, including minoritized students who experience racism and discrimination while abroad (Green, 2017)? Addressing these nuances related to study abroad would move toward avoiding the use of sojourning students as exports to spread U.S. academic imperialism.

Overall, higher education stakeholders have established a discourse that commodifies students for the purpose of the United States' overall pursuit of academic imperialism through economic gain, institutional visibility, and international prestige. Specifically, the use of tools such as positional competition, academic dependency, and interest convergence contributes in both subtle and explicit ways toward the United States' quest for global academic dominance. Thus, it is essential for higher education stakeholders to question how the discourse on student mobility contributes to academic imperialism, and to move toward a more humanizing perspective in discussing global student mobility.

REFERENCES

Alatas, S. F. (2003). Academic dependency and the global division of labour in the social sciences. *Current Sociology*, 51(6), 599–613.

Alatas, S. H. (2000). Intellectual imperialism: Definition, traits, and problems. *Asian Journal of Social Science*, 28(1), 23–45.

Altbach, P. G. (1977). Servitude of the mind? Education, dependency, and neocolonialism. *Teachers College Record*, 79(2), 187–204.

———. (2016). *Global perspectives on higher education*. Baltimore, MD: Johns Hopkins University Press.

Altbach, P. G., and Knight, J. (2007). The internationalization of higher education: Motivations and realities. *Journal of Studies in International Education*, 11(3–4), 290–305.

American Council on Education. (2019, April 15). Senator Paul Simon Study Abroad Program Act introduced in Senate. Retrieved from https://www.acenet.edu/news-room/Pages/Senator-Paul-Simon-Study-Abroad-Program-Act-Introduced-in-Senate.aspx

American Council on Education, Association of American Universities, Association of Public and Land-grant Universities, and the Council on Governmental Relations. (2018). *Joint statement of the American Council on Education, Association of American Universities, Association of Public and Land-grant Universities, and the Council on Governmental Relations.* Retrieved from http://www.acenet.edu/news-room/Documents/Joint-Statement-AAU-APLU-ACE-COGR-Senate-Judiciary.pdf

Andreotti, V. (2006). Soft versus critical global citizenship education. *Policy & Practice: A Development Education Review, 3*, 40–51.

Archer, B., Cooper, C., and Ruhanen, L. (2005). The positive and negative impacts of tourism. In W. F. Theobald (Ed.), *Global Tourism* (pp. 79–102). New York, NY: Elsevier.

Bell, D. A. (1980). Brown v. Board of Education and the interest-convergence dilemma. *Harvard Law Review, 93*(3), 518–533.

Berkeley News. (2019, February 21). Reaffirming our support for Berkeley's international community. Retrieved from https://news.berkeley.edu/2019/02/21/reaffirming-our-support-for-berkeleys-international-community/

Brief for American Council on Education et al., as Amicus Curiae Supporting Respondents, Donald J. Trump, President of the United States, et al. v. State of Hawaii, et al., (2018) (no. 17-965).

Brown, P. (2000). The globalisation of positional competition? *Sociology, 34*(4), 633–653.

Brown, P., Lauder, H., and Ashton, D. (2008). Education, globalisation and the future of the knowledge economy. *European Educational Research Journal, 7*(2), 131–156.

Delgado, R., and Stefancic, J. (2017). *Critical race theory: An introduction* (3rd ed.). New York: New York University Press.

Ferguson, G. (2007). The global spread of English, scientific communication and ESP: Questions of equity, access and domain loss. *Ibérica: Revista de la Asociación Europea de Lenguas para Fines Específicos, 13*, 7–38.

Fischer, K. (2017, November 13). International student enrollment is slowing—and it isn't all Donald Trump's fault. *The Chronicle of Higher Education.* Retrieved from https://www.chronicle.com/article/International-Student/241737

———. (2020a, March 6). With coronavirus keeping them in U.S., international students face uncertainty. So do their colleges. *The Chronicle of Higher Education.* Retrieved from https://www.chronicle.com/article/With-Coronavirus-Keeping-Them/248201?cid=cp275

———. (2020b, May 22). To keep international students during the pandemic, colleges get creative. *The Chronicle of Higher Education.* Retrieved from https://www.chronicle.com/article/To-Keep-International-Students/248838

Green, Q. (2017). *Feeling to see: Black graduate student women (re)membering Black womanhood through study abroad* (Doctoral dissertation). Retrieved from ProQuest (UMI 10605022).

Hirsch, F. (1977). *Social limits to growth.* London, England: Routledge and Kegan Paul.

Institute of International Education. (2017, November 13). IIE releases Open Doors 2017 data. Retrieved from https://www.iie.org/Why-IIE/Announcements/2017/11/2017-11-13-Open-Doors-Data

———. (2018, November 13). Number of international students in the United States reaches new high of 1.09 million. Retrieved from https://www.iie.org/en/Why-IIE/Announcements/2018/11/2018-11-13-Number-of-International-Students-Reaches-New-High

———. (2020a). 2020 "Fast facts." Retrieved from https://opendoorsdata.org/wp-content/uploads/2020/11/Open-Doors-2020-Fast-Facts.pdf

———.(2020b, November 16). United States hosts over 1 million international students for the fifth consecutive year. Retrieved from https://opendoorsdata.org/wp-content/uploads/2020/11/Open-Doors-2020-Press-Release.pdf

Jefferess, D. (2008). Global citizenship and the cultural politics of benevolence. *Critical Literacy: Theories and Practices*, 2(1), 27–36.

Jon, J. E., and Kim, E. Y. (2011). What it takes to internationalize higher education in Korea and Japan: English-mediated courses and international students. In J. D. Palmer, A. Roberts, Y. H. Cho, and G. S. Ching (Eds.), *The internationalization of East Asian higher education* (pp. 147–171). New York, NY: Palgrave Macmillan.

Kim, J. (2011). Aspiration for global cultural capital in the stratified realm of global higher education: Why do Korean students go to US graduate schools? *British Journal of Sociology of Education*, 32(1), 109–126.

———. (2016). Global cultural capital and global positional competition: International graduate students' transnational occupational trajectories. *British Journal of Sociology of Education*, 37(1), 30–50.

Knight, J. (2012). Student mobility and internationalization: Trends and tribulations. *Research in Comparative and International Education*, 7(1), 20–33.

Kortegast, C., and Kupo, V. L. (2017). Deconstructing underlying practices of short-term study abroad: Exploring issues of consumerism, postcolonialism, cultural tourism, and commodification of experience. *The International Journal of Critical Pedagogy*, 8(1), 149–172.

Lee, J. J. (2008). Beyond borders: International student pathways to the United States. *Journal of Studies in International Education*, 12(3), 308–327.

Lewin, R. (2009). Introduction: The quest for global citizenship through study abroad. In R. Lewin (Ed.), *The handbook of practice and research in study abroad: Higher education and the quest for global citizenship* (pp. xiii–xxii). New York, NY: Routledge.

Marginson, S. (2008). Global field and global imagining: Bourdieu and worldwide higher education. *British Journal of Sociology of Education*, 29(3), 303–315.

Marginson, S., and Rhoades, G. (2002). Beyond national states, markets, and systems of higher education: A glonacal agency heuristic. *Higher Education*, 43(3), 281–309.

MIT News. (2019, June 25). Letter to the MIT community: Immigration is a kind of oxygen. Retrieved from http://news.mit.edu/2019/letter-community-immigration-is-oxygen-0625

NAFSA. (2018a). International students contribute to our economy and American innovation. Retrieved from https://www.nafsa.org/sites/default/files/ektron/files/underscore/infographic_econ_value_2018.pdf

———. (2018b). U.S. at risk of losing the benefits of talented international students. Retrieved from http://www.nafsa.org/Policy_and_Advocacy/Policy_Resources/Policy_Trends_and_Data/U_S__at_Risk_of_Losing_the_Benefits_of_Talented_International_Students/

———. (2019a). Issue brief: Senator Paul Simon Study Abroad Program Act. Retrieved from http://www.nafsa.org/_/File/_/issue_brief_simon.pdf

———. (2019b). Losing talent: An economic and foreign policy risk America *can't* ignore. Retrieved from http://www.nafsa.org/_/File/_/nafsa-losing-talent.pdd

———. (2020). NAFSA financial impact survey. Retrieved from https://www.nafsa.org/sites/default/files/media/document/2020-financial-impact-survey.pdf

Naidoo, R. (2011). Rethinking development: Higher education and the new imperialism. In R. King, S. Marginson, and R. Naidoo (Eds.), *Handbook on globalization and higher education* (pp. 40–58). Cheltenham, UK: Edward Elgar.

Naidoo, R., and Jamieson, I. (2005). Knowledge in the marketplace: The global commodification of teaching and learning in higher education. In P. Ninnes and M. Hellsten (Eds.), *Internationalizing higher education* (pp. 37–51). Dordrecht, Netherlands: Springer.

Okahana, H., and Zhou, E. (2019). *International graduate applications and enrollment: Fall 2018*. Washington, DC: Council of Graduate Schools.

Organisation for Economic Co-operation and Development. (2016). *OECD science, technology and innovation outlook 2016*. Paris, France: Author.

———. (2020a). *What is the profile of internationally mobile students? Education at a glance 2020: OECD Indicators*. Paris, France: Author.

———. (2020b). *Education at a glance 2020: OECD indicators*. Paris, France: Author.

Ramírez, G. B. (2013). Learning abroad or just going abroad? International education in opposite sides of the border. *The Qualitative Report, 18*(31), 1–11.

Redden, E. (2017, November 13). An end to years of growth for new international enrollments. *Inside Higher Ed*. Retrieved from https://www.insidehighered.com/admissions/article/2017/11/13/after-years-growth-us-colleges-see-decline-number-new-international

———. (2019a, June 4). China issues warning to U.S.-bound students. *Inside Higher Ed*. Retrieved from https://www.insidehighered.com/news/2019/06/04/chinese-officials-warn-students-visa-problems-if-they-come-us

———. (2019b, July 15). In the U.K., a surge of Chinese applicants. *Inside Higher Ed*. Retrieved from https://www.insidehighered.com/admissions/article/2019/07/15/surge-chinese-applicants-british-universities

———. (2020a, May 26). A bleak picture for international enrollment. *Inside Higher Ed*. Retrieved from https://www.insidehighered.com/news/2020/05/26/colleges-expect-few-new-international-students-will-make-it-their-campuses-fall

———. (2020b, March 24). Stranded abroad. *Inside Higher Ed*. Retrieved from https://www.insidehighered.com/news/2020/03/24/study-abroad-students-caught-international-border-closures

Rhee, J. E., and Sagaria, M. A. D. (2004). International students: Constructions of imperialism in the Chronicle of Higher Education. *The Review of Higher Education, 28*(1), 77–96.

Said, E. W. 1993. *Culture & imperialism*. London, England: Vintage.

Schroeder, K., Wood, C., Galiardi, S., and Koehn, J. (2009). First, do no harm: Ideas for mitigating negative community impacts of short-term study abroad. *Journal of Geography, 108*(3), 141–147.

Schulman, K. (2011, January 19). First Lady Michelle Obama: "When you study abroad, you're helping to make America stronger." Retrieved from https://obamawhitehouse.archives.gov/blog/2011/01/19/first-lady-michelle-obama-when-you-study-abroad-you-re-helping-make-america-stronger

Smaller, H., and O'Sullivan, M. (2018). International service learning: Decolonizing possibilities? *Journal of Global Citizenship & Equity Education, 6*(1), 1–23.

U.S.-China Strong. (2019). 100,000 strong. Retrieved from https://100kstrong.org/initiatives/100k-strong/

Välimaa, J. (2004). Nationalisation, localisation and globalisation in Finnish higher education. *Higher Education, 48*(1), 27–54.

Xing, D., and Bolden, B. (2019). Exploring oral English learning motivation in Chinese international students with low oral English proficiency. *Journal of International Students, 9*(3), 834–855.

Yan, K., and Berliner, D. C. (2011). Chinese international students in the United States: Demographic trends, motivations, acculturation features and adjustment challenges. *Asia Pacific Education Review, 12*(2), 173–184.

Yao, C. W. (2014). *Being and belonging: A critical phenomenological study of undergraduate Chinese international students' sense of belonging in residence halls* (Doctoral dissertation). Retrieved from ProQuest (UMI 3620602).

———. (2016). "Better English is the better mind": Influence of language skills on sense of belonging in Chinese international students. *Journal of College and University Student Housing, 43*(1), 74–88.

———. (2018). "They don't care about you": Chinese international students' experiences with neo-racism and othering on a U.S. campus. *Journal of the First-Year Experience and Students in Transition, 30*(1), 87–101.

Yao, C. W., George Mwangi, C. A., and Malaney Brown, V. K. (2019). Exploring the intersections of transnationalism and critical race theory. *Race, Ethnicity, and Education, 22*(1), 38–58.

Yao, C. W., and Viggiano, T. (2019). Interest convergence and the commodification of international students and scholars in the United States. *Journal Committed to Social Change on Race and Ethnicity, 5*(1), 81–109.

Yao, C. W., and Vital, L. M. (2018). Reflexivity in international contexts: Implications for U.S. doctoral students' international research preparation. *International Journal of Doctoral Studies, 13*, 193–210.

10 • GLOBAL COMPETENCE
Hidden Frames of National Security and Economic Competitiveness

CHRIS R. GLASS

The aim of developing global competence in college students parallels the rise of a tumultuous period of globalization marked by the intensification of economic competition, unprecedented migration, asynchronous warfare, and income inequality (Olson and Kroeger, 2001). The "global competence" imperative has intermingled with nation-states' concerns and anxieties related to their national security and economic competitiveness, as well as concerns about global climate change. Most discussions about global competence tend to center on the strengths and limitations of various conceptions of global competence that reflect the question, What does a globally competent college graduate look like? The dictionary definition of competence, after all, suggests "the ability to do something successfully or efficiently" (Lexico, n.d.).

It is not that debates about the normative ideals of globally competent graduates are unimportant. It is that such intense, and often exclusive, focus on normative aspects of global competence tends to obscure critical assumptions about whether changing individuals' beliefs and values through educational processes actually produces the world envisioned—or, more concerning, may even reproduce the geopolitical realities that education for global competence aims to address (Aktas, Pitts, Richards, and Silova, 2017; Balarin, 2011). This chapter argues that we ignore our responsibilities if we challenge the content but not the "hidden" structural frames of national security and economic competitiveness present within the discourse on global competence (Stein, Andreotti, Bruce, and Suša, 2016). The aim of this chapter is to draw attention to these oft-overlooked structural frames. The first part presents a brief history of education for global competence in the United States, and the link between global competence and U.S. economic competitiveness and national security. The second part highlights further how global competence is often framed "globally" without reference to geography, stratification, politics, and non-Western views of the self.

FOUR WAVES OF EDUCATION FOR GLOBAL COMPETENCE

The history of education for global competence in the United States parallels a series of four overlapping waves of development within the field of international education more broadly (Kondakci, Bedenlier, and Zawacki-Richter, 2018). The first wave reflects the delineation of the term "global competence" (1997–2001); the second wave focused on the assessment of global competence as an essential learning outcome of a U.S. college education (2002–2006); the third wave reflected the need to develop a more coherent and coordinated U.S. internationalization strategy with the growing worldwide interconnectedness of U.S. universities (2007–2015); and the fourth and current wave reflects nationalist and populist reactions to the emphasis placed on global competence that reflect the anxieties and concerns regarding the effects of globalization on working-class Americans (2016–present).

First Wave: Delineation of "Global Competence" (1997–2001)

Efforts to add an international dimension to the U.S. college curriculum can be traced to a seminal report published by the American Council on Education (ACE, 1998), *Educating for Global Competence: America's Passport to the Future*, which international educators describe as the Magna Carta of the field. The report links education for global competence with U.S. economic competitiveness and national security, arguing that colleges and universities must "develop new forms of education appropriate to a global economy" to address "new realities of economic competitiveness and national security in a global context" (p. 6). It warned of "massive, traumatic, and sweeping transformations" to come with dire language that presaged the realities many middle-class American families would experience in the coming decades, including the trauma of the 9/11 terrorist attacks, the outsourcing of U.S. manufacturing jobs, and long-term unemployment faced by Americans without a college degree after the Great Recession.

The trauma of the terrorist attack on the World Trade Center in New York City on September 11, 2001, further solidified the link between education for global competence and U.S. economic leadership and geopolitical power (Mario and DeSouza, 2007), as business, political, and university leaders became concerned that Americans lacked knowledge and skills needed for success in a globalized world. Two months after 9/11, President Bush (2001) released a statement in honor of International Education Week, in which he described how "America's leadership and national security rest on our commitment to educate and prepare our youth for active engagement in the international community" (para. 4). The post-9/11 ACE report (2002) echoed President Bush's sentiments that "the tragic events of September 11, 2001 crystallized in a single, terrible moment, the challenges of globalization and the importance of international research and education to our national security" (p. 7). There is little doubt that after 9/11 the priority given to global competence was driven by deep anxiety over a perceived lack of readiness for the United States to ensure its national security and compete in a global economy. Global competence was no longer optional, but how it would be defined and assessed would be a matter of intense disagreement for years to come.

Second Wave: Definition and Assessment of Global Competence (2002–2006)

A report by the Association of American Colleges & Universities (AAC&U), *College Level Learning for a New Global Century*, gave U.S. political, business, and civic leaders further reason to be alarmed about Americans' readiness for a new global era. AAC&U's national survey found that one in eight U.S. college students achieved basic competence in a language other than English, less than one-third of U.S. college students earned credit for an international studies class, and less than one in ten students participated in any type of cross-cultural study abroad experience. The report emphasized the need for colleges and universities to prepare graduates for the "important civic responsibilities to their communities, their nation, and the larger world" (AAC&U, 2007, p. 37). Although AAC&U struck a far more humanistic tone of education for "a world lived in common with others" (Greene, 1988, p. 4), the association maintained the link between education for global competence and U.S. economic leadership and geopolitical power: "The world is being dramatically reshaped by scientific and technological innovations, global interdependence, cross-cultural encounters, and changes in the balance of economic and political power" (p. 2).

Global competence as an essential learning outcome was framed as providing U.S. college graduates a "competitive edge" because "competitors lurk not just around the corner in the home market but increasingly in distant and often little-understood regions of the world as well" (Gupta and Govindarajan, 2002, p. 116). Global competence was also envisioned as enhancing national security through the use of soft power in global business partnerships, multinational engineering firms, and international development projects. Hunter, White, and Godbey (2006) synthesized conceptions of global competence among human resource managers of transnational corporations, United Nations officials and diplomats, and international educators at higher education institutions: "Colleges and universities have a special interest in, and capacity to contribute to, soft power—a form that permits win-win situations through intercultural borrowings and synthesis and the global extrapolation of the work of nonprofit, humanitarian organizations" (p. 269).

Once global competence began to be viewed as an imperative for U.S. global competitiveness and national security, the need to measure and assess it became acute for higher education administrators eager to demonstrate institutional change to accreditation agencies as part of university quality enhancement plans. The most widely used instruments to measure global competence are largely student self-assessments fraught with measurement issues related to self-reported data (Bowman and Hill, 2011). Some of the most popular include the Global Perspective Inventory (GPI), used by nearly 200 U.S. colleges, universities, and educational organizations to examine the relationship between educational experiences and development of a global perspective (Merrill, Braskamp, and Braskamp, 2012); the Global Citizenship Scale, primarily used in U.S. study abroad programs (Morais and Ogden, 2011); the Beliefs, Events, and Values Inventory (BEVI) (developed in partnership with the Forum on Education Abroad), designed to assess how life experiences, culture, and context affect our beliefs, values, and worldview (Wandschneider et al., 2015); and the Intercultural Development Inventory (IDI), designed to measure a student's progression through developmental stages (Hammer, Bennett, and Wiseman, 2003). The IDI, one of the most widely used instruments in international education, connected intercultural competence with to U.S. global leadership such that it would provide a competitive edge to college graduates:"[A] competitive edge in the 21st century will not derive from simple technological dominance; rather, it will accrue to those organizations that can deploy their global human resources effectively" (Bennett, 2001, p. 2).

Third Wave: U.S. Internationalization Strategy (2007–2015)

Once global competence had been established as essential for the personal and political development of all U.S. students (Mansilla and Jackson, 2013), there was an immediate urgency for policymakers to outline a national strategy to support the highly decentralized, state-driven U.S. higher education system. The Lincoln Commission (2005), in its report *Global Competence, National Needs*, established the goal of sending 1 million U.S. undergraduates abroad annually by 2017 and made a direct link between globalization, education abroad, and U.S. economic competitiveness: "Making study abroad the norm and not the exception can position this and future generations of Americans for success in the world in much the same way that establishment of the land-grant university system and enactment of the GI Bill helped create the 'American century'" (p. v).

In 2012, the U.S. Department of Education (USDOE), under the Obama administration, established its first-ever international strategy, published in the report *Succeeding Globally through International Education and Engagement*. The strategy emphasized global competence as being essential to the economic security of U.S. students, with a heightened emphasis on global competence for students from traditionally disadvantaged groups: "Global competencies comprise the knowledge and skills individuals need to be successful in today's flat, interconnected world and to be fully engaged in and act on issues of global significance" (USDOE, 2012, p. 5). The three major emphases in the report parallel the prominent strands highlighted so far: economic competitiveness and jobs, global challenges, and national security and diplomacy.

The national-level scope of the measurement and assessment of global competence is illustrated by the creation of the Global Learning VALUE rubric introduced by AAC&U in 2014, as well as the new Global Learning Topical Module in the widely used, U.S.-based National Survey of Student Engagement (NSSE) instrument, which assesses student experiences and coursework that emphasize global affairs, world cultures, nationalities, religions, and other international topics. The *Mapping Internationalization on U.S. Campuses* report by the ACE (2017) provides evidence that significant progress has been made in the operationalization and assessment of global competence: "Compared to 2011, more institutions have delineated broad-based global learning outcomes, and have implemented academic policies (e.g., general education requirements) that extend the reach of internationally focused content to a larger proportion of students" (p. 15).

Four Wave: Nationalist and Populist Reactions (2016–present)

In 2016, the Brexit referendum in the United Kingdom and the election of Donald J. Trump as president of the United States set the tone and tenor of rhetoric about global competence with more antagonism toward globalism. At a rally on December 1, 2016, President-elect Trump told a crowd of supporters: "There is no global anthem, no global currency, no certificate of global citizenship" (quoted in Hains, 2016, para. 4). Likewise, UK prime minister Theresa May, in her post-Brexit referendum speech to the Conservative Party conference, declared, "If you believe you are a citizen of the world, you're a citizen of nowhere" (quoted in Bearak, 2016, para. 4). The Trump administration would maintain the two-decades-long focus on Americans' succeeding globally through international education but would foreground nationalistic economic rationales and strategic interests.

In late 2018, the USDOE, under the Trump administration, updated its internationalization strategy with a new report, *Framework for Developing Global and Cultural Competencies to Advance Equity, Excellence and Economic Competitiveness*, and removed the previous report entirely from the department's website. In the press release for the new strategy, Secretary Betsy DeVos emphasized the need for the United States to "fundamentally rethink education so that each student, at every age is prepared for whatever comes next" and to prepare "all of our students for careers in the global economy." Devos continued: "We need more individuals with an entrepreneurial mindset to foster a new generation of innovators, inventors, and job creators who will unleash their ingenuity worldwide" (USDOE, 2018, para 4).

Efforts to measure and assess global competence have continued to grow unabated on a global scale. Global competence is now on the global education policy agenda with impetus largely generated by the U.N. Sustainable Development Goals and the increasing desire for data that allow for worldwide comparisons and benchmarking of global competence. A focus on "global citizenship" was introduced in the 2015 U.N. declaration *Transforming Our World: The 2030 Agenda for Sustainable Development*. The bellwether for this new wave is the introduction of the Global Competence Framework by the Organisation for Economic Co-operation and Development (OECD) as part of its Programme for International Student Assessment (PISA) (OECD, 2016). For the first time, PISA included an assessment of global competence in the 2018 administration of the widely used educational assessment instrument. The PISA Global Competence Framework, developed by a team of three U.S.-based scholars and one UK-based scholar, combines a cognitive test focused on knowledge of global issues and a set of self-reported items where students rate their awareness of global issues and cultures, cognitive and social skills, and attitudes, as well as identify the activities used to promote global competence in their school and in the classroom. The data from over half a million fifteen-year-olds in eighty countries have the potential to influence educational policy and practice. Mansilla, one of the U.S.-based scholars who developed the new framework, emphasized the power of the findings to inform educational practice worldwide: "What makes the new OECD PISA framework exciting, in my view, is not only its clear potential to help us gauge how 15-year-olds today think about pressing issues of local, global, and intercultural significance, but also its power to inform educational practice in every region of the world" (Bayer, 2017, para. 2).

THE HIDDEN FRAME OF GLOBAL COMPETENCE

The first part of this chapter presented a brief history of education for global competence in the United States, and the link between global competence and U.S. national security and economic competitiveness. Much of the debate has focused on the definition and assessment of global competence with an inherent belief that changing individuals' beliefs and values through educational processes is a force for producing new generations of citizens of the world (Stein et al., 2016). This section further scrutinizes the "hidden" structural frame by highlighting how discussions of global competence are often framed "globally" without reference to geography, stratification, politics, or non-Western views of the self. First, I highlight the variegated geographies of global competence that contrast with the worldwide, universal ideals that normalize Western superiority. Next,

I consider how discussions of global competence often fail to recognize the economic aspects of mobility that reflect social stratification and economic inequalities. I then highlight the depoliticized nature of global competence in terms of "soft" and "hard" belonging. Finally, I consider how global competence often lacks relational perspectives that decenter the individual and deconstruct Cartesian forms of subjectivity.

Global Competence without Geography

The geography of global competence is a particularly useful place to begin, in part because "global" is defined as "relating to the whole world," but the whole world has not had a voice in creating the normative ideals students are measured against. For example, the OECD countries that created the new PISA framework represent 80 percent of world trade and investment but only about 18 percent of the world's population. And the Global South has been "largely excluded from the debates about the concept" (Jooste and Heleta, 2017, p. 39). Reimers (2006) captured the impulse to universalize global competence, arguing: "If educating for global competence is desirable . . . then why is it not happening on a massive scale around the world?" (p. 192). The universalistic emphasis on the "global" normalizes Western superiority and decontextualizes the particulars of what it means to live in an unequal but interconnected world (Aktas et al., 2017).

Global competence acts as "one manifestation of a 'global cultural frame' that is affecting education in diverse ways" (Buckner, 2019, p. 2), where the outcomes and expected benefits of global competence are influenced by a country's position in the geopolitical context. Goren and Yemini (2017) provide a comprehensive review that highlights vast differences in the antecedents that have driven the call to educate students for global competence and the outcomes such an education aims to produce. European scholars tend to frame global competence as a response to population changes due to immigration in order to promote new forms of citizenship that produce greater social cohesion. European studies focus on how global and European forms of citizenship could exist alongside national citizenship to foster the inclusion of minorities and immigrants, but rarely feature social, critical, or environmental forms of advocacy (Oxley and Morris, 2013). Global competence in the United States is often framed as a strategic response to the shifting economic and political landscape in order to preserve its status as a global leader, with only an occasional emphasis on global climate change or economic inequality. Global competence is focused on the personal development of students with little emphasis on collective advocacy for human rights or deep-rooted historical injustices (Buckner and Stein, 2019). As in the United States, scholarship in the Asia-Pacific region tends to frame global competence as a response to the shifting economic and political landscape but adds an emphasis on stronger ties with the West and the role of English in order to compete in the global economy (Pan, 2011). In general, human rights, as well as ecological and humanitarian aspects of global competence, are often overlooked (Goren and Yemini, 2017), and the recognition that aspirations for global competence are rooted in the advantages of membership in particular nation-states tends to be glossed over entirely (Koyama, 2015).

Although regional and national differences are important to recognize, it is also important to recognize that many studies of global competence focus on relatively homogenous populations within otherwise diverse societies. Poststructuralist perspectives illustrate how globalization reshapes nation-based views of geography (Beech and Larsen, 2014). As Deresiewicz (2014) argues: "Kids at schools like Stanford think that their environment is diverse if one comes from Missouri and another from Pakistan, or if one plays the cello and the other lacrosse. Never mind that all of their parents are doctors or bankers" (para. 20). The same holds true on the other end of the economic spectrum. As Selasi (2014) illustrates: "A Mexican gardener in Los Angeles and a Nepali housekeeper in Delhi have more in common in terms of rituals and restrictions than nationality implies" (para. 24). Nation-based views of geography obfuscate that these students are "locals of the same milieu" (Selasi, 2014, para. 24). Students do not just move from one country to another, they occupy spaces and places that shape their identities and human experiences. Thus, the almost exclusively normative focus on dimensions of global competence often evades questions about minoritized groups who exist outside the national economic and security interests of a country (Shahjahan and Kezar, 2013). Global competence is imagined for the kid from Missouri whose STEM (science, technology, engineering, and mathematics) degree advances national interests, but the Mexican gardener in Los Angeles is included and valued only to the extent that their existence advances those interests.

Global Competence without Stratification

Economic globalization reflects conflicting realities: income inequality between countries has been reduced as economic inequality for individuals within those countries has increased (Bourguignon 2017; Marginson 2018). The educational literature tends to focus on the development of global competence as a matter of changing individuals' beliefs and values through educational processes (Balarin, 2011), but often fails to recognize the economic aspects of mobility that reflect social stratification and economic inequalities within and across nations (Glass, Streitwieser, and Gopal, 2019; Maksim, 2016). The assumption that education changes individuals' beliefs and values ignores the fact that the distribution of those experiences for students from various socioeconomic backgrounds remains chronically and unevenly distributed (Glass et al., 2019). Thus, it creates a two-faced reality where universities may espouse a commitment to global competence but the distribution of opportunities to those educational experiences across the world remains highly stratified. Universities are positioned as central to the economic and political competitiveness of nation-states, which then compete against each other for dominance and reinforce hierarchies of countries at the core and periphery of higher education (Shahjahan and Kezar, 2013). As Igarashi and Saito (2014) powerfully argue: "Education systems legitimate cosmopolitanism as a desirable disposition at the global level, while simultaneously distributing it unequally among different groups of actors according to their geographical locations and volumes of economic, cultural, and social capital their families possess" (p. 222).

Thus, global competence may not be a matter of an individual's beliefs and values, but simply a proxy for their social status that reflects the privilege of students who happen to live within wealthy and well-connected university spaces across the globe (Larsen, 2016). Mobility, after all, is linked to classical forms of social inequality, such as the differential distribution of wealth, income, and educational attainment and status, as well as new forms of inequality that interconnect with various mobilities due to the market-like quality of education across the world. Much like standardized tests, where wealthier students score much higher than their low-income peers (Wermund, 2017), measures of global competence often reflect the network capital that students accumulate at their institutions (Larsen, 2016), thus rendering institutions unequal in their ability to provide this type of capital, and creating further stratification and structuring of inequality between universities (Waters, 2012). Measures of global competence may simply identify—and reify—those students privileged enough to inhabit the spaces that have allowed for interactions and opportunities to demonstrate such competence (Koyama, 2015).

Global competence may be a cultural status symbol of the cosmopolitan elite and dangled before the working class as something attainable by hard work and individual effort without a recognition of the spatial and institutional contexts that produce inequalities of opportunity. Education abroad, for example, is championed as the ticket for middle-class U.S. students to gain an edge in a competitive job market; and appeals are made that focus on the cash value of global competence (Lilley, Barker, and Harris, 2015). For example, the Institute for International Education (IIE) report, *Gaining an Employment Edge: The Impact of Study Abroad on 21st Century Skills and Career Prospects*, ties education abroad to economic opportunity: "Longer periods of study abroad have a high impact on subsequent job offers and the development of most skills. Short term programs are most effective at developing teamwork skills" (Farrugia and Sanger, 2017, p. 6).

Global Competence without Politics

Global competence is often framed in depoliticized terms that minimize unequal power relations and their historical precedents. This view from nowhere emphasizes a flattened global economy that paints a picture of campus internationalization void of ethical and political dimensions (Buckner and Stein, 2019; Stein, 2015). For example, the means to develop global competence is often viewed through an apolitical lens of U.S. students' opportunities to interact with international students' (Page and Chahboun, 2019). Traditional notions of college student involvement and engagement frame any lack of interaction as inherently problematic (Page and Chahboun, 2019). The emphasis on "integration," which dominates the field, lacks full recognition of racialized patterns of dominance (Lee and Rice, 2007; Yao, George Mwangi, and Brown, 2019) and often results in deficit framing of international students' lack of involvement in "effective educational practices" compared with their American counterparts (Zhao, Kuh, and Carini, 2005). From a depoliticized college student development perspective, international students are valued as "resources" on campus to help U.S. students develop global competence (Abe, Talbot, and Geelhoed, 1998).

Research on "belonging" offers a counterpoint to an "integration" perspective. Belonging involves membership and participation (Bittencourt, Johnstone, Adjei, and Seithers, 2019). Belonging "to what" (something) is linked to belonging "with whom" (others). It is created in spaces and places where people are accepted as members or feel that they are members (Bittencourt et al., 2019). It is shaped by the dynamics of power of these identities and the ability to participate in and shape the living traditions of a place. It requires the right to participate in the development of the "living tradition" or the reflexive arguments of that society (May, 2011).

Belonging, however, involves a pair of opposites—what I refer to as "soft" and "hard" belonging. The "soft" aspects of belonging are relational with an emotional component of "feeling at home" or "yearning for a home"; the "hard" aspects of belonging are "political" with an element of claim-making for space and recognition. Apolitical perspectives of global competence prize the soft aspects of belonging but eschew its hard aspects; they ignore the ability of a dominant group or society to impose its beliefs and standards on less powerful groups (Sue, 2004). Hard belonging, also known as the politics of belonging, is "the dirty work of boundary maintenance" (Crowley, 1999, p. 15). Research shows that the perception of symbolic threats (international students represent a threat to the values, beliefs, and culture of the majority population) and social dominance (strong belief in the superiority of one group's cultural heritage over another) are the two biggest predictors of prejudice against international students (Charles-Toussaint and Crowson, 2010).

The "integration" imaginary makes Western higher education a desirable product in the global higher education market and shapes the reception of international students (Stein et al. 2016). Hard belonging recognizes that recruitment and racism are framed by a dominant global imaginary rooted in Western supremacy (Mario and DeSouza, 2007; Stein, 2015). International students make headlines when they challenge the "integration" frame and, instead, take political action in claim-making for space and recognition (Redden, 2019). Universities are derelict in their educational responsibilities if they maintain a depoliticized approach to global competence where ethnocentric notions may be manifested in the programs, policies, and structures of the institution (Buckner and Stein, 2019; Sue, 2004).

The almost exclusive concern with the normative aspects of competence—that is, with defining new, better models of global competence—hinders warranted consideration of the social and political structures that impede individuals acting on those ideals and produces marginalization in the first place (Balarin, 2011). Positionality recognizes the importance of body, time, and space and how "subjectivities shift and evolve as our bodies move through time and space" (Torres-Olave and Lee, 2019, p. 137). Embodied perspectives join "body and mind in a physical and mental act of knowledge construction . . . and entail thoughtful awareness of body, space, and social context" (Nguyen and Larson, 2015, p. 332). Social identity is influenced by a multiplicity of voices and counter-voices—personal voices of individuals or collective voices of groups—emanating from local and global sources and exercising social dominance (Hermans and Dimaggio, 2007). We may be marginalized in one social context, marginalized differently in others, or not marginalized at all. Thus, the lived experience of global competence is not a fixed "ability to do something successfully or efficiently" that the dictionary definition of competence implies. Rather, competence is better characterized as constantly shifting performance that involves reconstructing knowledge and identities in each new situation we encounter.

Global Competence without Relationality

Global competence is portrayed as highly individualistic, leaving students to their own devices to focus on their personal development (Balarin, 2011). In the widely cited paper "The Neglected 95%: Why American Psychology Needs to Become Less American," Arnett (2008) argues that much of U.S.-based published research reflects an "understanding of psychology that is incomplete and does not adequately represent humanity" (p. 602). Research on global competence is no different. Competence is viewed as some "thing" (knowledge, skill, or attitude) that a person "builds," "develops," or "possesses" and, thus, can be measured, typically on a self-reported individualized assessment instrument. It is an outcome-to-be-achieved (and measured) rather than a lifelong process-to-be-lived through continuous self-reflection and self-critique (Tervalon and Murray-Garcia, 1998). This individualistic focus suggests a degree of autonomy and self-determination that ignores the ways thought and behavior are influenced by context, and how the structures and dynamics of connections produce places where social identities are both contested and fluid (Larsen, 2016).

The implicit metaphors of learning and development found in rubrics and assessments also suggest a type of linear progress that reflects the assumption that individual human development occurs in a sequence of stages, structured around the belief that individuals develop global competence the same way they would climb a ladder: straight up, one step at a time. But learning is more like a developmental web with changes in direction, forks, and intersections of the strands (Fischer, Yan, and Stewart, 2012). Learning as a developmental web suggests many different pathways constructed from one's own knowledge and experience rather than a single pathway. More importantly, learning as a developmental web recognizes that knowledge and behavior are socially constructed moment-to-moment as people interact in ensembles. Rather than the linear progress of individuals toward a normative ideal, experience suggests that our global competence is embodied and is constantly shifting with our position within various social contexts (Torres-Olave and Lee, 2019).

Counter to this individualistic approach are more relational perspectives that decenter the individual and deconstruct Cartesian forms of subjectivity (Larsen, 2016). A relational translocalist approach, for example, challenges both the frame and content of global competence (Stein et al., 2016). It is disenchanted with the definitional-focused discussion of global competence and, instead, foregrounds how global competence is framed within Cartesian forms of subjectivity measured by tests of knowledge as some "thing" acquired, and thus risks reproducing the very realities that education for global competence espouses to address (Aktas et al., 2017). Relational translocalist perspective also challenges "the binary of people and place, or objects and place, seeing a complex relationality of places, objects, and persons connected through performances" (Larsen, 2016, p. 25). A relational translocalist perspective runs counter to the dominant framing of global competence that advances the economic and national security interests of a nation-state. Global competence is not simply a matter of knowledge about systemic inequality; it operates from a different set of ontological assumptions that recognize one's complicity in the reproduction of these realities. Non-Western views of the self also call into question Cartesian forms of subjectivity that reframe global competence. The commitment to Western-defined concepts of the self-privileges an individual as a "thinker of thoughts, the doer of deeds, and the feeler of feelings." However, the psychology of Buddhism, for example, proposes a radically different view that rejects this agentive, separate self (Orr, 2018). Global competence cannot be some "thing" possessed by an individual, because there is no separate self who possesses it.

CONCLUSION

This chapter highlights the hidden frame that structures much of the discourse on global competence. It also highlights the historical link between global competence and U.S. national security and economic competitiveness. It then argues that popular discourses of global competence obscure critical assumptions that frame the discussion: universalistic impulses that decontextualize the particulars of life in an unequal but interconnected world, failure to recognize social stratification and economic inequality, minimization of deep-rooted power relations and historical injustices, and individualistic emphases over relational perspectives that deconstruct Cartesian forms of subjectivity.

REFERENCES

Abe, J., Talbot, D. M., and Geelhoed, R. J. (1998). Effects of a peer program on international student adjustment. *Journal of College Student Development*, 39(6), 539–547.

Aktas, F., Pitts, K., Richards, J. C., and Silova, I. (2017). Institutionalizing global citizenship: A critical analysis of higher education programs and curricula. *Journal of Studies in International Education*, 21(1), 65–80. https://doi.org/10.1177/1028315316669815

American Council of Education. (1998). *Educating for global competence: America's passport to the future*. Washington, DC: Author.

———. (2002). *Beyond September 11th: A Comprehensive Policy on International Education*. Washington, DC: Author.

———. (2017). *Mapping internationalization on U.S. campuses*. Washington, DC: Author.

Arnett, J. J. (2008). The neglected 95%: Why American psychology needs to become less American. *American Psychologist*, 63(7), 602–614. https://doi.org/10.1037/0003-066X.63.7.602

Association of American Colleges & Universities. (2007). *College learning for the new global century*. Washington, DC: Author.

Balarin, M. (2011). Global citizenship and marginalisation: Contributions towards a political economy of global citizenship. *Globalisation, Societies and Education*, 9(3–4), 355–366. https://doi.org/10.1080/14767724.2011.605321

Bayer, C. (2017). PISA 2018 Test to Include Global Competency Assessment. Retrieved from https://www.gse.harvard.edu/news/17/12/pisa-2018-test-include-global-competency-assessment

Bearak, M. (2016, October 5). Theresa May criticized the term 'citizen of the world.' But half the world identifies that way. *Washington Post*. Retrieved from https://www.washingtonpost.com/news/worldviews/wp/2016/10/05/theresa-may-criticized-the-term-citizen-of-the-world-but-half-the-world-identifies-that-way/

Beech, J., & Larsen, M. A. (2014). Replacing old spatial empires of the mind. *European Education*, 46(1), 75–94. https://doi.org/10.2753/eue1056-4934460104

Bennett, M. J. (2001). *Intercultural competence for global leadership*. Gig Harbor, WA: The Intercultural Development Research Institute. Retrieved from https://www.idrinstitute.org/wp-content/uploads/2018/02/Global_ICC_IDRI.pdf

Bittencourt, T., Johnstone, C., Adjei, M., and Seithers, L. (2019). "We see the world different now": Remapping assumptions about international student adaptation. *Journal of Studies in International Education*. https://doi.org/10.1177/1028315319861366

Bourguignon, F. (2017). *The globalization of inequality*. Princeton, NJ: Princeton University Press.

Bowman, N. A., and Hill, P. L. (2011). Measuring how college affects students: Social desirability and other potential biases in college student self-reported gains. *New Directions for Institutional Research*, 150, 73–85. https://doi.org/10.1002/ir.390

Buckner, E. (2019). The internationalization of higher education: National interpretations of a global model. *Comparative Education Review*, 63(3), 315–336. https://doi.org/10.1086/703794

Buckner, E., and Stein, S. (2019). What counts as internationalization? Deconstructing the internationalization imperative. *Journal of Studies in International Education*, 24(2), 151–166. https://doi.org/10.1177/1028315319829878

Bush, G. W. (2001). International Education Week. Retrieved from https://web.archive.org/web/20011130075222/http://exchanges.state.gov/iew2001/message.htm

Charles-Toussaint, G. C., and Crowson, H. M. (2010). Prejudice against international students: The role of threat perceptions and authoritarian dispositions in U.S. students. *Journal of Psychology: Interdisciplinary and Applied*, 144(5), 413–428. https://doi.org/10.1080/00223980.2010.496643

Crowley, J. (1999). The politics of belonging. Some theoretical considerations. In A. Geddes and A. Favell (Eds.), *The Politics of Belonging: Migrants and Minorities in Contemporary Europe* (pp. 15–41). Aldershot, UK: Ashgate. https://doi.org/10.1109/LAWP.2012.2208092

Deresiewicz, W. (2014, July 21). Don't send your kid to the Ivy League. *The New Republic*. Retrieved from http://www.newrepublic.com/article/118747/ivy-league-schools-are-overrated-send-your-kids-elsewhere

Farrugia, C., and Sanger, J. (2017). *Gaining an employment edge: The impact of study abroad on 21st century skills & career prospects*. New York, NY: Institute of International Education. Retrieved from https://www.iie.org/Research-and-Insights/Publications/Gaining-an-employment-edge—The-Impact-of-Study-Abroad

Fischer, K., Yan, Z., and Stewart, J. (2012). Adult cognitive development: Dynamics in the developmental web. In *Handbook of Developmental Psychology* (pp. 491–516). New York, NY: SAGE. https://doi.org/10.4135/9781848608306.n21

Glass, C. R., Streitwieser, B., and Gopal, A. (2019). Inequities of global mobility: Socioeconomic stratification in the meanings of a university education for international students. *Compare*. https://doi.org/10.1080/03057925.2019.1590180

Goren, H., and Yemini, M. (2017). Citizenship education redefined: A systematic review of empirical studies on global citizenship education. *International Journal of Educational Research*, 82, 170–183. https://doi.org/10.1016/j.ijer.2017.02.004

Greene, M. (1988). *The dialectic of freedom*. New York, NY: Teachers College Press.

Gupta, A., and Govindarajan, V. (2002). Cultivating a global mindset. *Academy of Management Perspectives*, 16(1), 116–126.

Hains, T. (2016). Trump: There is no global flag, no global currency, no global citizenship. Retrieved from https://www.realclearpolitics.com/video/2016/12/01/trump_there_is_no_global_flag_no_global_currency_no_global_citizenship_we_are_united_as_americans.html

Hammer, M. R., Bennett, M. J., and Wiseman, R. (2003). Measuring intercultural sensitivity: The intercultural development inventory. *International Journal of Intercultural Relations*, 27(4), 421–443. https://doi.org/10.1016/S0147-1767(03)00032-4

Hermans, H.J.M.M., and Dimaggio, G. (2007). Self, identity, and globalization in times of uncertainty: A dialogical analysis. *Review of General Psychology*, 11(1), 31–61. https://doi.org/10.1037/1089-2680.11.1.31

Hunter, B., White, G. P., and Godbey, G. C. (2006). What does it mean to be globally competent? *Journal of Studies in International Education*, 10(3), 267–285. https://doi.org/10.1177/1028315306286930

Igarashi, H., and Saito, H. (2014). Cosmopolitanism as cultural capital: Exploring the intersection of globalization, education and stratification. *Cultural Sociology*, 8(3), 222–239. https://doi.org/10.1177/1749975514523935

Jooste, N., and Heleta, S. (2017). Global citizenship versus globally competent graduates: A critical view from the South. *Journal of Studies in International Education*, 21(1), 39–51. https://doi.org/10.1177/1028315316637341

Kondakci, Y., Bedenlier, S., and Zawacki-Richter, O. (2018). Two decades of research into the internationalization of higher education: Major themes in the *Journal of Studies in International Education* (1997–2016). *Journal of Studies in International Education*, 22(2), 108–135. https://doi.org/10.1177/1028315317710093

Koyama, J. (2015, January). *The elusive and exclusive global citizen* (Mahatma Gandhi Institute of Education for Peace and Sustainable Development Working Paper 2015-02). UNESCO, New Delhi, India.

Larsen, M. A. (2016). Constructing a theoretical framework: Space, networks, and mobilities. In *Internationalization of higher education: An analysis through spatial, network, and mobilities theories* (pp. 15–31). London, UK: Palgrave Macmillan. https://doi.org/10.1057/978-1-137-53345-6

Lee, J. J., and Rice, C. (2007). Welcome to America? International student perceptions of discrimination. *Higher Education*, 53(3), 381–409. https://doi.org/10.1007/s10734-005-4508-3

Lexico (n.d.). Competence. In Oxford English and Spanish Dictionary. Retrieved December 26, 2020, from https://www.lexico.com/definition/competence

Lilley, K., Barker, M., and Harris, N. (2015). Exploring the process of global citizen learning and the student mind-set. *Journal of Studies in International Education*, 19(3), 225–245. https://doi.org/10.1177/1028315314547822

Lincoln Commission. (2005). *Global competence and national needs: One million Americans studying abroad.* Commission on the Abraham Lincoln Study Abroad Fellowship Program. Washington, DC: Author.

Maksim, H. (2016). *Mobilities and inequality.* London, UK: Routledge. https://doi.org/10.4324/9781315595719

Mansilla, V. B., and Jackson, A. (2013). Educating for global competence: Learning redefined for an interconnected world. In V. Boix Mansilla, A. W. Jackson, H. H. Hacobs, W. Kist, H. S. Tavangar, & S. R. Tolisano (Eds.), *Mastering Global Literacy, Contemporary Perspectives* (pp. 1–24). New York, NY: Solution Tree.

Marginson, S. (2018). *The new geo-politics of higher education: Global cooperation, national competition and social inequality in the world-class university (WCU) sector* (Centre for Global Higher Education Working Paper No. 34). Retrieved from CGHE website: https://www.researchcghe.org/perch/resources/publications/wp34final.pdf

Mario, L., and DeSouza, T.M.E. (2007). Global citizenship and study abroad: It's all about U.S. *Critical Literacy*, 1(2), 16–28.

May, V. (2011). Self, belonging and social change. *Sociology*, 45(3), 363–378. https://doi.org/10.1177/0038038511399624

Merrill, K. C., Braskamp, D. C., and Braskamp, L. A. (2012). Assessing individuals' global perspective. *Journal of College Student Development*, 53(2), 356–360. https://doi.org/10.1353/csd.2012.0034

Morais, D. B., and Ogden, A. C. (2011). Initial development and validation of the global citizenship scale. *Journal of Studies in International Education*, 15(5), 445–466. https://doi.org/10.1177/1028315310375308

Nguyen, D. J., and Larson, J. B. (2015). Don't forget about the body: Exploring the curricular possibilities of embodied pedagogy. *Innovative Higher Education*, 40(4), 331–344. https://doi.org/10.1007/s10755-015-9319-6

Olson, C., and Kroeger, K. R. (2001). Global competency and intercultural sensitivity. *Journal of Studies in International Education*, 5(2), 116–137. https://doi.org/10.1177/102831530152003

Organisation for Economic Co-operation and Development. (2016). *Preparing our youth for an inclusive and sustainable world.* Paris, France: Author. Retrieved from https://www.oecd.org/education/Global-competency-for-an-inclusive-world.pdf

Orr, D. (2018). Ethics, mindfulness, and skillfulness. In S. Stanley, R. E. Purser, and N. N. Singh (Eds.), *Handbook of ethical foundations of mindfulness* (pp. 121–140). Cham, Switzerland: Springer. https://doi.org/10.1007/978-3-319-76538-9_7

Oxley, L., and Morris, P. (2013). Global citizenship: A typology for distinguishing its multiple conceptions. *British Journal of Educational Studies, 61*(3), 301–325. https://doi.org/10.1080/00071005.2013.798393

Page, A. G., and Chahboun, S. (2019). Emerging empowerment of international students: How international student literature has shifted to include the students' voices. *Higher Education, 78*(5), 871–885. https://doi.org/10.1007/s10734-019-00375-7

Pan, S. (2011). Multileveled citizenship and citizenship education: Experiences of students in China's Beijing. *Citizenship Studies, 15*(2), 283–306.

Redden, E. (2019, February 5). Not an isolated incident. *InsideHigherEd*. Retrieved from https://www.insidehighered.com/news/2019/02/05/weighing-duke-case-experts-discuss-discrimination-against-international-students-and

Reimers, F. (2006). Citizenship, identity and education: Examining the public purposes of schools in an age of globalization. *Prospects, 36*(3), 275–294. https://doi.org/10.1007/s11125-006-0009-0

Selasi, T. (2014). Don't ask where I'm from, ask where I'm a local. Retrieved from https://www.ted.com/talks/taiye_selasi_don_t_ask_where_i_m_from_ask_where_i_m_a_local/transcript

Shahjahan, R. A., and Kezar, A. J. (2013). Beyond the "national container." *Educational Researcher, 42*(1), 20–29. https://doi.org/10.3102/0013189x12463050

Stein, S. (2015). Mapping global citizenship. *Journal of College and Character, 16*(4), 242–252. https://doi.org/10.1080/2194587x.2015.1091361

Stein, S., de Andreotti, V., Bruce, J., and Suša, R. (2016). Towards different conversations about the internationalization of higher education. *Comparative and International Education, 45*(1), 2–20.

Sue, D. W. (2004). Whiteness and ethnocentric monoculturalism: Making the "invisible" visible. *American Psychologist, 59*(8), 761–769. https://doi.org/10.1037/0003-066X.59.8.761

Tervalon, M., and Murray-Garcia, J. (1998). Cultural humility versus cultural competence: A critical distinction in defining physician training outcomes in multicultural education. *Journal of Health Care for the Poor and Underserved, 9*(2), 117–125.

Torres-Olave, B., and Lee, J. J. (2019). Shifting positionalities across international locations: Embodied knowledge, time-geography, and the polyvalence of privilege. *Higher Education Quarterly, 74*(2), 136–148. https://doi.org/10.1111/hequ.12216

U.S. Department of Education. (2012). *Succeeding globally through international education and engagement*. Washington, DC: Author.

———. (2018). *Succeeding globally through international education and engagement*. Washington, DC: Author.

Wandschneider, E., Pysarchik, D. T., Sternberger, L. G., Ma, W., Acheson, K., Baltensperger, B., and Hart, V. (2015). The Forum BEVI Project: Applications and implications for international, multicultural, and transformative learning. *Frontiers: The Interdisciplinary Journal of Study Abroad, 25*, 150–228.

Waters, J. L. (2012). Geographies of international education: Mobilities and the reproduction of social (dis)advantage. *Geography Compass, 6*(3), 123–136. https://doi.org/10.1111/J.1749-8198.2011.00473.X

Wermund, B. (2017, September 10). How U.S. News college rankings promote economic inequality on campus. *Politico*. Retrieved from https://www.politico.com/interactives/2017/top-college-rankings-list-2017-us-news-investigation/

Yao, C. W., George Mwangi, C. A., and Malaney Brown, V. K. (2019). Exploring the intersection of transnationalism and critical race theory: A critical race analysis of international student experiences in the United States. *Race Ethnicity and Education*, 22(1), 38–58. https://doi.org/10.1080/13613324.2018.1497968

Zhao, C.-M., Kuh, G. D., and Carini, R. M. (2005). A comparison of international student and American student engagement in effective educational practices. *The Journal of Higher Education*, 76(2), 209–231. https://doi.org/10.1353/jhe.2005.0018

11 • INTERNATIONALIZING THE CURRICULUM

Conceptual Orientations and Practical Implications in the Shadow of Western Hegemony

SHARON STEIN

Internationalization of the higher education curriculum is often justified through the perceived imperatives to prepare graduates for an increasingly interconnected world by providing an avenue for "internationalization at home" (Clifford and Montgomery, 2015; Leask, Beelen, and Kaunda, 2013). Efforts to internationalize higher education curricula can indeed create important opportunities for reimagining inherited approaches to teaching and learning. Yet while it is increasingly common to find agreement that curriculum internationalization is important, the concept means different things to different people, and thus is variously "the cause of fascination, frustration, confusion, and fulfillment" (Leask, 2015, p. 3). This, in turn, reflects more general contestation around the meaning of internationalization itself, as well as its orienting principles, values, and purposes (e.g., Buckner and Stein, 2019; de Wit, 2014; Knight, 2014; Stein, Andreotti, Bruce, and Suša, 2016; Stier, 2004). Rather than advocate for a particular approach to curriculum internationalization, in this chapter I invite readers to deepen their engagement with the tensions and complexities of this work, particularly in relation to national hegemony and a dominant global imaginary that has been largely naturalized through centuries of colonization.

In the context of this edited book and its concern to denaturalize enduring power relations in general, and U.S. power in particular, it is important to consider that the practice of curriculum internationalization does not necessarily interrupt or challenge "business as usual." In fact, it can reinforce national power and exceptionalism in the context of an increasingly interconnected world. Mainstream approaches add selected international content to existing curricula, but leave the underlying frames of knowledge untouched. This approach instrumentalizes epistemic difference toward continued political and economic hegemony, which contrasts with approaches that mobilize epistemic difference toward "global social justice" (Santos, 2007). While internationalization's use as a vehicle for national power is not new, it takes on renewed relevance in the context of concerns about growing global uncertainty and competition, which in turn prompts varied proposed responses that range from shoring up national power, to redistributing power, to fundamentally reimagining how we relate to one another and the world. This range of responses suggests the need for more nuanced engagements regarding the orientations and implications of divergent approaches to curriculum internationalization. In this chapter I offer a framework for distinguishing between and assessing these different approaches using U.S. higher education as an example. I do so with a social cartography methodology that offers not an objective representation of reality but rather a situated, post-representational depiction of relevant tensions and complexities that invites people to identify and learn from contrasting approaches to a particular issue (Andreotti, Stein, Pashby, and Nicolson, 2016; Paulston, 2009).

I begin the chapter by reviewing trends in curriculum internationalization, and how these relate to larger trends of internationalization. Next, I consider the relationship between curriculum internationalization today and earlier eras of this work. My purpose in doing so is not only to denaturalize current approaches but also to link the present to a history of instrumentalizing higher education in the service of national hegemony—and an even longer history of efforts to universalize a particular global imaginary and mode of existence through processes of colonization. Then, rather than advocate for a universal approach to curriculum internationalization, I suggest the need to develop critical literacy around different possibilities. To do so, I offer a map of four different approaches to curriculum internationalization that will help clarify what each approach might offer those who mobilize them in their own context. This will prepare scholars and practitioners working on curriculum internationalization to assess the gifts and limitations of *all* approaches and to make their own critically informed, context-specific, and socially accountable choices about what to do in a particular time and place.

CURRENT TRENDS

Internationalizing the curriculum is a staple in the suite of common practices of internationalization, even as it often falls behind international student recruitment, study abroad, and international partnerships in terms of institutional priorities (Helms and Brajkovic, 2018). In practice, it can entail the inclusion of more international scholars on a course syllabus, addressing international topics in the content of a course itself, or in some cases, adding an entirely new "internationally focused" course to an existing program or degree. Transforming the curriculum is often understood as a form of "internationalization at home"—that is, international engagements that are not premised on physical mobility—and is a primary dimension of the "comprehensive internationalization" advocated by NAFSA: Association of International Educators, the American Council on Education (ACE), and others. Comprehensive internationalization "sees [internationalization] as pervading the institution and affecting a broad spectrum of people, policies and programs, leads to deeper and potentially more challenging change ... [and is] a broad, deep and integrative international practice that enables campuses to become fully internationaliz[ed]" (ACE, as cited by Hudzik, 2011, p. 5).

However, as Crosling, Edwards, and Schroder (2008) note, "curriculum internationalization is a multidimensional concept that can be defined and, therefore, approached in several ways" (p. 107). Some of these differences have primarily to do with the differences between disciplines; for instance, NAFSA offers resources and trainings around "global learning" in areas including business, health professions, STEM (science, technology, engineering, and mathematics), and teacher education. Other differences have more to do with distinctions in orienting assumptions, hopes, political horizons, and investments, which I will review in detail later in this chapter. Yet despite these differences in the approaches of individual people, offices, and institutions, in order to understand the broader trend of curriculum internationalization, it is important to situate it within the larger current social, political, and economic context. This context, and in particular the configuration of local and global power relations in the United States, arguably sets the stage for curriculum internationalization to be on the table at all, regardless of the approach one takes. Grasping this context is therefore important for assessing different possible approaches and their practical and ethical implications.

Contemporary curriculum internationalization, as with internationalization more generally, can be understood in part as a response to "wicked problems" that can only be adequately grasped when placed within a global frame; these problems include climate change, biodiversity loss, large-scale migration, economic insecurity and austerity, employment precarity, public health crises, and political instability and polarization. Some suggest that these problems cannot be addressed using only existing knowledge paradigms and problem-solving approaches (Andreotti et al., 2018). However, these problems are often narrowly framed in terms of their implications for the relative position of a nation-state and its citizens in this increasingly interconnected and interdependent world. In other words, a growing sense of interconnection does not necessarily prompt a greater sense of social and ecological accountability; it can also prompt a greater sense of perceived threat and competition. When these concerns become the orienting approach to internationalizing the curriculum, higher education can serve as an instrument to reinforce national power. It is important to note that while the emphasis of this chapter is on the U.S. context, similar trends take place in many other wealthy, Western nation-states. Thus, the United States can be viewed as a telling example of a larger pattern. I invite readers outside the United States to consider how this pattern manifests (or not) in their own national context.

It is also important to note that nationalistic concerns and strategic interests take many forms. In other words, it is not only in blatantly xenophobic discourses, or even in economistic discourses that emphasize national competitiveness, but also in many of the more seemingly benevolent discourses of inclusion that we find concern to maintain the advantage of the nation-state and/or its citizens. These articulations differ in some ways, overlap in others, and are often mixed with other concerns, which can result in complex and even contradictory discourses. Thus, even more inclusive approaches to curriculum internationalization can paradoxically reproduce nationalism. Lest we think that concern for national interests is a novel development in the context of internationalizing higher education, it is vital to consider that there is a longer history behind it. In order to review that history, I first briefly review the notion of U.S. exceptionalism.

HISTORICAL PRECEDENTS

To some extent, all modern nation-states are premised on narratives of exceptionalism, which make up a key component of the binding glue through which different citizens are held together under a uniform national umbrella. However, the exceptionalism of certain countries is particularly notable when they have global—rather than only their national—influence, and indeed imperial reach (Pease, 2009). The United States is one such nation-state, given that its post–World War II rise to global hegemony followed its pursuit of domestic continental hegemony.

From its very beginnings the United States framed itself as exceptional in its celebration of individual rights and freedoms and formal equality, a narrative whose coherence required a disavowal of the nonfreedoms and inequalities inherent in the foundational role of settler colonialism (Arvin, Tuck, and Morrill, 2013; Byrd, 2011) and slavery (Rodriguez, 2018; Silva, 2014) in the making of the U.S. nation-state. Constituting exceptionalism through disavowal has also created a sanctioned ignorance of these numerous contradictions of celebrated values (Pease, 2009), first domestically, then globally with the creation of new colonies in the nineteenth century (e.g., Puerto Rico, the Philippines, Hawaii), and later imperial interventions throughout Latin America, Asia, and Africa via the means of war, economic coercion, and covert operations (e.g., support for right-wing coups during the twentieth century). Rather than view these actions as contradictory to the United States' exceptionalist narrative, we can instead view them as conditions of possibility for the United States itself—and certainly for its global economic and geopolitical dominance. In other words, the United States would not exist were it not for these constitutive racial/colonial violences.

Narratives of U.S. exceptionalism, including disavowal of U.S. violence, are highly relevant to internationalization. Once we start to think more broadly about the ways that U.S. advantage has been sought, reproduced, and rationalized across time and space, and through many seemingly different approaches to internationalization, then we can also start to see that the contemporary era of internationalization has many continuities with the past—in particular the post–World War II era, with which it is often compared. It is common to lament that we have seen a historical break in the orienting concerns of internationalization, which is often articulated as a shift from "aid to trade"-based orientations (Knight, 2014). The former orientation was presumably guided by more benevolent and cooperative concerns than the more immediate economic and competitive concerns that predominate in the present. While this narrative is one way to frame the distinction, another way would be to consider that in both cases, U.S. national interests guided internationalization efforts, and it is in fact the shifting global landscape that has driven the change in approaches to internationalization, rather than changing values.

The international dimensions of U.S. higher education were strongly affected by World War II itself as well as the postwar transition to the United States' position of geopolitical influence and economic power (Goodwin and Nacht, 1991). U.S. concerns were oriented by the Cold War struggle for hegemony between the United States (and its allies) and the USSR (Union of Soviet Socialist Republics) (and its allies), including the contest for influence in the Global South and the desire to combat the "spread" of communism (Kapoor, 2014). For instance, the National Defense Education Act was passed in response to the Soviet launch of Sputnik to help fund the sciences and area studies centered on the study of language and culture in "strategic" global regions (Trilokekar, 2015), and federal agencies such as the Pentagon and the CIA (Central Intelligence Agency) funded social science research about communist countries in fields such as sociology and geography (Kamola, 2014). Thus, internationalization of the curriculum during the Cold War often took the form of transmitting essentialized notions of cultural difference for the purpose of ensuring U.S. global military, political, and economic advantage—part of the classic colonial strategy of mobilizing knowledge as power. At the same time, collaborations between higher education and the military became the object of critique on campus, both in more traditional fields and in burgeoning ethnic studies departments (Hong, 2008). Hence, critical approaches to curriculum internationalization also have historical roots.

Meanwhile, many internationalization efforts at the time were also framed as humanitarian efforts. This involved sending faculty to institutions in the Global South to provide "technical assistance" and hosting international students. International students during this time often came from elite families seeking tools for the "building of modern, robust nation-states" (Kramer, 2009, p. 792). For its part, the United States positioned itself as generously imparting these students with "universal" knowledge and technical expertise, so that the students might lead their home countries on the Western-led linear path of human development—specifically, toward capitalist economic growth. The hope was that these students would also foster political goodwill and positive trade relationships. Thus, in the "aid" era of internationalization, the U.S. curriculum was not so much internationalized as instrumentalized to export its domestic curriculum abroad.

These efforts to export knowledge served not only to extend U.S. power but also to further universalize a particular global imaginary with colonial roots— including the political organization of the world into nation-states, the economic organization of the world into capitalist markets, the epistemic organization of the world into a single (Western) rationality, and the fostering of an ethos of individualism and anthropocentrism (Stein and Andreotti, 2017). In this way, the Cold War role of U.S. higher education in naturalizing this imaginary and its accompanying mode of existence on a global scale was an extension of earlier efforts to do so. The United States was not only projecting outward what it had already done "at home" in its own settler colony and its external colonies, but also extending legacies of colonialism elsewhere in former colonies of other European empires—albeit under a different name and flag (Kapoor, 2014).

INTERNATIONALIZATION IN THE SHADOW OF DECLINING HEGEMONY?

Today internationalization looks different from how it did during the Cold War— at least on the surface. However, I suggest that this has less to do with shifts in values and more to do with efforts to sustain the United States' position within a larger global context—especially given increasing challenges to its geopolitical and economic dominance. Some suggest that declining U.S. global hegemony began as early as the 1970s, with the oil crisis, end of the Bretton Woods consensus, and defeat in Vietnam (Wallerstein, 2004). Others emphasize the end of the Cold War as a turning point. As Pease (2009) notes, "During the Cold War, the discourse of American exceptionalism had legitimated America's dominance within a dichotomized world order by supplying the rationale for America's moral superiority to Russian communism" (p. 19). After the fall of the USSR, this rationale started to have significantly less global influence.

The events of September 11, the 2007/2008 financial crisis, and even the election of Donald Trump have been cited as more recent indicators of U.S. global decline. This is not to suggest that the United States does not remain a forebodingly powerful global entity, but rather that its unquestioned position of dominance has faltered. The recent decrease in the number of international students (Redden, 2018) may be symptomatic of this decline. While some might argue that the size and strength of the United States' global military presence indicates its enduring power, others suggest this is proof of the increasing imperative to use brute force to reassert power in light of declines in the less coercive dimensions of political and economic influence (Mendes, 2018). Parallels can be drawn domestically, given that the growth of prisons and other dimensions of the more overtly violent carceral state followed the decline of the postwar consensus premised on a widened social safety set (including free or low-cost public higher education) (Rodriguez, 2018).

I have suggested that contemporary internationalization efforts should be broadly understood in relation to the potential decline in U.S. global hegemony, and to a larger set of global challenges that we collectively face, albeit with highly uneven levels of intensity and vulnerability. That said, there are many possible ways to respond to this conjuncture. In the remainder of this chapter, I will consider how different approaches to curriculum internationalization can be understood in relation to the current context—including how each approach frames national hegemony, and more broadly, whether it reproduces or interrupts the universalization of a particular global imaginary and related mode of being that has been naturalized through successive waves of European colonization over the past six centuries.

SOCIAL CARTOGRAPHY OF CURRICULUM INTERNATIONALIZATION

The methodology of social cartography produces maps of multiple ways of framing a shared issue of concern. In turn, this enables those who engage the resulting maps to trace the implicit political and theoretical investments and assumptions about each of the different approaches, to better understand the relationships between these different approaches, and to more fully appreciate the possibilities and limitations that each approach can produce (Paulston, 2009. However, unlike representational mapping, which claims to capture every existing possibility, social cartographies are situated translations of "reality" that emphasize particular dimensions and de-emphasize others; they can also map absences as a means of gesturing toward possibilities that are viable but currently unimaginable or unintelligible to most people (Andreotti et al., 2016). The resulting map is always partial and provisional, and in this sense, it invites further engagement and an endless practice of critical, self-reflexive conversations rooted in humility about one's own assumptions about the root causes and possible solutions to shared problems. Thus, rather than fostering consensus, social cartographies are produced with the assumption that any practical decisions or solutions that are derived from engaging with a map will be situated, limited, and strategic, rather than universal. Because of this, cartographies can serve as powerful tools for scholars and practitioners who are seeking to meet the immediate challenges of their context without collapsing the complexity and uncertainty inherent to the challenge at hand—and thus, without foreclosing the possibility of dissent and future revisions.

When it comes to curriculum internationalization, there are multiple ways to approach its conceptualization and implementation. In this chapter I focus on differing possible objectives and conceptual orientations, and specifically how these relate to national hegemony as well as the wider issue of a hegemonic global imaginary. That does not mean that other kinds of cartographies of curriculum internationalization would not be useful—for instance, one that maps the contrasting approaches of different disciplines or different stakeholders on campus. It also does not mean that this map is the only possible way to trace the relationships between curriculum internationalization, national hegemony, and a hegemonic global imaginary. Like all social cartographies, the map I present here is oriented by a particular set of concerns, which were partially outlined in the preceding sections and are further elaborated here.

Since I have already addressed in some detail the dimensions of national hegemony in relation to higher education internationalization, here I want to consider in more detail the global imaginary toward which curriculum internationalization can take different orientations. Through its organizing logics, practices, common sense, and social relations, a social imaginary makes certain things intelligible/imaginable (Taylor, 2002). In turn, this tends to make other things unintelligible/unimaginable, which then circumscribes the available and viable possibilities for knowing, being, relating, imagining, and hoping (Kamola, 2014; Santos, 2007). Social imaginaries are often described at the level of a nation, or even more locally, but they can also be understood on a global scale (Byrdon and Dvorak, 2012), which I emphasize here. In my analysis, the currently hegemonic global imaginary is specifically a modern/colonial imaginary (Stein et al., 2016; Stein and Andreotti, 2017). That is, this imaginary was initiated with the onset of European colonization and the trans-Atlantic slave trade in the fifteenth century, and though it has morphed considerably over time, often in response to resistance to it, its primary dimensions have been in place for several centuries. In their current formation, these dimensions naturalize the following social and ecological organization of life on the planet into the following systems:

- *Global capitalism (economic system),* which promises progress and development through endless growth and accumulation, and which is enabled through the racialized expropriation and exploitation of humans and other-than-human beings (including the earth itself) (Coulthard, 2014; Silva, 2014)

- *Nation-state (political system)*, which promises social cohesion through a shared national identity, and social order and protection of property through the state's monopoly on violence, and which is enabled by domestic policing, militarism, and border policing (Arvin et al., 2013; Byrd, 2011)
- *Universal reason (knowledge system)*, which promises that a single (Eurocentric) rationality and set of values can describe and order the world as a means to predict and control it, and which is enabled by devaluing/suppressing other ways of knowing and reducing being to knowing (Ahenakew, 2016; Santos, 2007)
- *Individualism and anthropocentrism (basis of existence)*, which promises unrestricted autonomy and places (white male) humans at the center of the world, and which is enabled through the denial of relationships and responsibilities to other beings (Alexander, 2005)

During the Cold War, the United States led the project of spreading and universalizing this global imaginary throughout the world, particularly in the newly independent former colonies of Europe. Thus, efforts to secure national hegemony were not mutually exclusive from efforts to ensure the hegemony of a particular mode of existence that is naturalized within this global imaginary. Although U.S. hegemony has arguably declined, just as UK hegemony declined before it, it is not yet clear which nation-state(s)—if any—will replace it (Parnreiter, 2018). Additionally, while the global imaginary itself certainly remains hegemonic, its endurance has come under question in the context of today's many wicked problems. For instance, there are growing questions about the sustainability of the mode of social and ecological organization that is supported through this global imaginary in light of the existing and future threat of climate change (Baskin, 2019; Bendell, 2018). More generally, people have questioned the ability of the knowledge and practices produced within the existing global imaginary to address the problems we face, given the complexity and unprecedented scope and scale of these problems—as well as the analysis by some that it is precisely this global imaginary that has led to many of the problems we now face (Andreotti et al., 2018). In reviewing each approach to curriculum internationalization below (summarized in table 11.1), I therefore consider the implications of each approach not only for national hegemony in Western countries but also for this global imaginary.

Curriculum Internationalization for National Hegemony in the World

The primary orienting concern of this approach to internationalization is an instrumental one intended to maintain or reclaim national political and economic advantage on a global scale. Thus, while it may offer opportunities to learn about different peoples and places, this learning is always directed toward the assessment of threats and opportunities. This not only forecloses the possibility

TABLE 11.1 Different orientations and implications of curriculum internationalization

	Curriculum internationalization for national hegemony in the world	Curriculum internationalization for improving the world	Curriculum internationalization for radically remaking the world	Curriculum internationalization "for the end of the world as we know it"
Orienting concerns	Maintain or reclaim national political and economic advantage	Help make the world a more equitable and sustainable place	Change the world based on oppressed peoples' knowledge	Prepare for transformative shifts without knowing what will come after
Implications for learning	Learn about different peoples and places in order to understand (and neutralize) threats and maximize opportunities for the nation-state	Learn about more different peoples and places in order to appreciate human diversity and make the world a better, more peaceful place	Challenge dominant frameworks and learn different ways of knowing (especially what is marginalized) to find new blueprints	Learn to ethically encounter different ways of knowing without projecting onto, appropriating, or consuming them for one's own ends
Implications for knowledge	Knowledge should be perpetually accumulated to arrive at fuller truths and certainties with which to predict, order, and organize the world	Knowledge is a collective resource that should be made available to all but should be adapted to the specificities of local contexts	Because Eurocentric knowledge cannot solve the problems it has created, we need suppressed knowledges to craft different futures	All knowledges have contextual (rather than universal) relevance, both gifts and limitations; knowledge is important but does not define existence
Implications for the Western nation-state	The nation-state has earned its position of global power and economic advantage and should defend/reclaim it	The nation-state should wield its influence in more positive ways (e.g., international aid)	The nation-state should enact redress for its historical wrongs by redistributing power and resources	The nation-state was founded and continues to be sustained through colonial violence, and thus it cannot be reformed
Implications for the dominant global imaginary	Organizing the world according to the dominant global imaginary is the most advanced/evolved form of human existence	The dominant global imaginary should be adjusted depending on the local context to ensure respect for cultural difference	The dominant global imaginary should be replaced by the imaginaries of marginalized communities	The dominant global imaginary needs to end so that we can welcome other possibilities for collective existence

of noninstrumental learning, but also forecloses the possibility that some things may be uncertain or unknown as well as unknowable. Rather, the assumption is that knowledge is the most reliable way to understand (universal) reality, and the intention is to acquire as much knowledge as possible in order to gain a fuller picture of the world with the assumption that this will enable rational planning to engineer the maximization of resources and opportunities for securing national advantages in the "global knowledge economy." The knowledge economy framework positions higher education as vital to national economic growth and competitiveness by preparing graduates and producing research and innovations. Thus, internationalizing the curriculum means including more knowledge *about* difference for strategic purposes, while maintaining a basic orientation of Western epistemic and economic supremacy.

This approach to curriculum internationalization presumes that it is natural and healthy to seek national economic advantage (competition), and that the nation-state has a right to defend its global position of power. In Western countries, this is justified through the colonial notion that these nations are the most advanced and evolved forms of human existence and social organization. Thus, this tends to reproduce the dominant global imaginary. As Stehr and Ufer (2009) caution, "Normative visions, promising business plans, decrees of global worlds of knowledge and first empirical observations are often . . . Eurocentric prejudices that deny non-western actors the ability to govern themselves successfully" (p. 13). Wealthy Western nation-states continue to have the most political, economic, and epistemic power, largely owing to the ongoing legacies of colonialism, and thus it is these countries that I emphasize here. However, they are certainly not the only countries (re)framing their curricula toward the imperative of national advantage.

Questions derived from this approach to curriculum internationalization might include the following: *What do students need to know in order to successfully compete as individuals and employees of national corporations within the global knowledge economy? What do we need to know about other parts of the world in order to contain possible military, economic, or political threats to national power? How can we incentivize students to major in areas that serve national strategic interests, such as STEM, and the languages of countries positioned as enemies of the country? What data or information do we need in order to predict and plan for future global challenges?*

Curriculum Internationalization for Improving the World

Curriculum internationalization for improving the world presumes that the existing curriculum is generally robust but needs supplementation to better reflect human diversity. This approach emphasizes learning about different peoples or places, not necessarily for a direct political or economic purpose but because it is assumed that by understanding human differences as well commonalities, the world will become more equitable, sustainable, and peaceful. Further, if we can include more voices in a shared global vision, then we will be better prepared to face today's global challenges, and we will do so in a more harmonious way. Thus, learning about difference is oriented toward preparing students to lead more inclusive global projects and initiatives that will benefit those beyond their national borders. This approach to curriculum internationalization cultivates a more globalized sense of responsibility than explicit efforts to internationalize the curriculum for national hegemony. However, this approach ultimately tends to take the form of tokenistic additions to an underlying Western framework; rarely does it shift the framework itself or challenge the presumption of Western students as natural and benevolent global leaders and change agents (Zemach-Bersin, 2007). This then reproduces Western exceptionalism and paternalistic relationships, even though it is not directly oriented toward national gain.

Thus, including non-Western knowledges in the curriculum can have recolonizing effects if not done in a way that challenges the ethical and political assumptions that frame the curriculum itself (Ahenakew, 2016). In other words, this approach to curriculum internationalization assumes that the dominant global imaginary should be adapted to particular local contexts, but that the imaginary itself is universally valid. In this way, it is presumed that Western higher education is the primary site at which "solutions" to the problems of the entire world should be formulated. This is further framed as an ethical responsibility of the "more developed" nations to assist those that are "less developed," which reproduces a linear and ethnocentric imaginary of human progress that frames the West as the natural global leader.

Questions derived from this approach to curriculum internationalization might include the following: *How can students develop a sense of responsibility and leadership beyond national borders? What information do domestic students need to have in order to serve as effective global change makers in relation to pressing global issues like climate change and income inequality? How can we include more voices in the curriculum to expose students to cultural differences? How can we prepare students to adapt global policies and universal scientific knowledge/innovations to different local contexts and needs? What kind of learning will inspire students to leverage their national advantage to help less advantaged countries develop more sustainably?*

Curriculum Internationalization for Radically Remaking the World

Curriculum internationalization for radically remaking the world is oriented by a concern to make the world more just by dismantling various interlocking oppressive systems, including racism, colonialism, capitalism, sexism, heterosexism, and ableism (Stein et al., 2016). In terms of learning, it has two primary intentions: challenge existing curricula by problematizing how it tends to either rationalize or provide simplistic/depoliticized solutions to injustice and inequality; and make space for marginalized (e.g., Black, Indigenous, feminist, Global South) knowledges as part of the search for different guiding frameworks of knowing, being, and relating. Further, it is assumed that cognitive justice will prompt greater social, political, economic, and ecological justice (Santos, 2007). The orienting anti-oppressive framework of this approach posits that if we continue to rely on Eurocentric curricula, we will likely reproduce the same harmful political, economic, and ecological system that these curricula have fostered. Thus, what is envisioned is a radical remaking of the curricula to not only include but also center different (non-Western) perspectives and entire knowledge systems. This challenges nation-centric curricula and substitutes a new, alternative global imaginary for the existing dominant global imaginary.

This approach offers a strong and necessary interruption of the presumption of Western epistemic supremacy and forces learners to reckon with the historical and ongoing entanglement of knowledge with power. This includes attending to the violences perpetrated by Western nation-states and asking how that can be redressed (e.g., reparations, debt forgiveness). However, this approach also risks unwittingly reproducing some dimensions of a Western epistemic framework— in particular, the search for universality. In this case, historically marginalized knowledges are now the ones being universalized, but this can mean swapping one hegemony for another, and can result in romanticizing, homogenizing, and imposing a colonial agenda onto marginalized knowledges in ways that betray the knowledges' internal integrity and instrumentalize their gifts (Ahenakew, 2016). This approach also potentially feeds the search for a position of epistemic purity, innocence, and privilege (Shotwell, 2016), ultimately reproducing notions of (reformed) hierarchy and contingent forms of human worth. Further, it can reproduce desires for certainty, and thus, for a predetermined alternative that precludes the emergence of what is currently unimaginable and risks projecting our current limitations onto the future.

Questions derived from this approach to curriculum internationalization might include the following: *How can we ensure that when nonhegemonic knowledges are included in curricula, they are not merely tokenized but contextualized, centered, and supported with adequate resources? How can we go beyond simply deconstructing canonical knowledge toward introducing and centering previously marginalized knowledges? Which knowledges should students use to develop a more just vision for the future? How can internationalized curricula prepare students to engage the world in consideration of their structural positions, and with a concern to not only critique but also challenge and dismantle centuries of accumulated structural inequalities?*

Curriculum Internationalization for "The End of the World As We Know It"
The "end of the world" approach to curriculum internationalization is oriented by the assumption that the current world system is organized in an inherently

violent and unsustainable way, and is only made possible through ongoing colonial genocide and ecocide. While it is understood that contemporary challenges—political, economic, and ecological—have roots in the dominant global imaginary, they are also viewed as symptoms of its potential decline. Further, it is believed that the knowledge that was developed within this imaginary will be insufficient for facing the challenges that the imaginary itself has created. This does not mean entirely dismissing Western knowledge, but rather shrinking its influence and integrating it into what Santos (2007) describes as an "ecology of knowledges," which provides an alternative to both the mainstream tendency to seek universal relevance and the mirror response of asserting absolute relativism. In such an ecology, all knowledges are understood to be relevant to particular contexts, meaning they are partial and limited, as well as indispensable.

This approach is oriented by diagnoses of the inherent colonial violence and ecological unsustainability of modern systems and institutions (including the nation-state). Inspired by the notion that decolonization requires nothing less than "the end of the world as we know it" (Silva, 2014), and that the world as we know it will likely not survive impending climate catastrophe (Bendell, 2018), this approach to curriculum internationalization asks how we might prepare for a world that is ending in order to welcome what will emerge in its place (Stein et al., 2020). This approach is therefore less about including particular content or knowledge frameworks and more about denaturalizing the curricula we have, without dismissing its gifts, and learning how to encounter other knowledges with reverence and respect but without reproducing old patterns premised on the consumption and romanticization of difference and the search for new universals. Thus, this approach also seeks to develop learners' capacity, self-reflexivity, humility, and stamina to face complexity, uncertainty, and conflict. This approach can be frustrating for those looking for immediate answers, but important for those looking for something beyond currently available possibilities. Further, this approach to curriculum has not only intellectual but also affective and relational dimensions, as facing the end of the only system many people have ever known is an overwhelming task, and doing so in a generative way would require developing (or regenerating) new modes of not just knowing but also being, feeling, desiring, and relating.

Questions derived from this approach to curriculum internationalization might include the following: *How can we shift dominant relationships to knowledge from the search for absolute truth to appreciation of contextual relevance? What curricula could prepare students to responsibly navigate complexity and uncertainty in a rapidly changing, unequal, and deeply interdependent world with no clear epistemic authorities? What curricular changes can prompt people to denaturalize dominant modes of ecological, political, and economic organization and open themselves up to new possibilities (without projecting old patterns onto those new possibilities)? How can we support students to develop the humility, stamina, and intellectual, affective, and relational capacities that are needed in order to face "the end of the world as we know it" in a generative way? How can we invite learners to create space for futures that are viable but unimaginable from within dominant frames of reference?*

CONCLUSION

In this chapter I examined the social and historical contexts surrounding contemporary curriculum internationalization in higher education, particularly in light of the potential waning of national hegemony. Although I emphasize the U.S. context, similar patterns can be observed in many wealthy Western nation-states. I also offered a social cartography of four different approaches to curriculum internationalization, and the extent to which each reproduces or challenges ideas of national hegemony and exceptionalism, as well as the extent to which it reproduces or challenges a dominant global imaginary. I did not advocate for any particular approach to curriculum internationalization but rather showcased the contributions and limitations of each, including offering a glimpse of the kinds of questions that they can prompt us to ask about practice. I contend that, however it is framed, internationalization of the curriculum should serve as an invitation for students as well as practitioners and professors to encounter the world in its full complexity, expand their sense of social and ecological accountability, and develop a deepened critical literacy and capacity for discernment so as to be better prepared to make difficult decisions about what kinds of changes and international engagements are possible and desirable for their own educational contexts. These capabilities will be crucial for facing the coming challenges in our increasingly uncertain, unequal world.

REFERENCES

Ahenakew, C. (2016). Grafting indigenous ways of knowing onto non-Indigenous ways of being: The (underestimated) challenges of a decolonial imagination. *International Review of Qualitative Research, 9*(3), 323–340.

Alexander, M. J. (2005). *Pedagogies of crossing: Meditations on feminism, sexual politics, memory, and the sacred*. Durham, NC: Duke University Press.

Andreotti, V., Stein, S., Pashby, K., and Nicolson, M. (2016). Social cartographies as performative devices in research on higher education. *Higher Education Research & Development, 35*(1), 84–99.

Andreotti, V., Stein, S., Sutherland, A., Pashby, K., Suša, R., and Amsler, S. (2018). Mobilising different conversations about global justice in education. *Policy & Practice: A Development Education Review, 26*, 9–41.

Arvin, M., Tuck, E., and Morrill, A. (2013). Decolonizing feminism: Challenging connections between settler colonialism and heteropatriarchy. *Feminist Formations, 25*(1), 8–34.

Baskin, J. (2019). Global justice and the anthropocene: Reproducing a development story. In F. Biermann & E. Lövbrand (Eds.), *Anthropocene Encounters: New Directions in Green Political Thinking* (pp. 150–168). Cambridge: Cambridge University Press. doi:10.1017/9781108646673.008

Bendell, J. (2018). Deep adaptation: A map for navigating climate tragedy. Retrieved from http://www.lifeworth.com/deepadaptation.pdf

Brydon, D., and Dvorák, M. (Eds.). (2012). *Crosstalk: Canadian and global imaginaries in dialogue*. Waterloo, Ontario, Canada: Wilfrid Laurier University Press.

Byrd, J. (2011). *The transit of empire: Indigenous critiques of colonialism*. Minneapolis: University of Minnesota Press.

Buckner, E., and Stein, S. (2019). What counts as internationalization? Deconstructing the internationalization imperative. *Journal of Studies in International Education*, 24(2), 151–166.

Clifford, V., and Montgomery, C. (2015). Transformative learning through internationalization of the curriculum in higher education. *Journal of Transformative Education*, 13(1), 46–64.

Coulthard, G. (2014). *Red skin, white masks: Rejecting the colonial politics of recognition*. Minneapolis: University of Minnesota Press.

Crosling, G., Edwards, R., and Schroder, B. (2008). Internationalizing the curriculum: The implementation experience in a faculty of business and economics. *Journal of Higher Education Policy and Management*, 30(2), 107–121.

de Wit, H. (2014). The different faces and phases of internationalisation of higher education. In A. Maldonado-Maldonado and R. M. Bassett (Eds.), *The forefront of international higher education* (pp. 89–99). Dordrecht, Netherlands: Springer Science+Business Media.

Goodwin, C. D., and Nacht, M. (1991). *Missing the boat: The failure to internationalize American higher education*. Cambridge, UK: Cambridge University Press.

Helms, R. M., and Brajkovic, L. (2018). Internationalization in the United States: Data, trends, and Trump. *International Briefs for Higher Education Leaders*, 7, 4–6.

Hong, G. K. (2008). "The future of our worlds": Black feminism and the politics of knowledge in the university under globalization. *Meridians: Feminism, Race, Transnationalism*, 8(2), 95–115.

Hudzik, J. K. (2011). *Comprehensive internationalization: From concept to action*. Washington, DC: NAFSA: Association of International Educators.

Kamola, I. (2014). US universities and the production of the global imaginary. *The British Journal of Politics & International Relations*, 16(3), 515–533.

Kapoor, I. (2014). Psychoanalysis and development: Contributions, examples, limits. *Third World Quarterly*, 35(7), 1120–1143.

Knight, J. (2014). Is internationalisation of higher education having an identity crisis? In *The forefront of international higher education* (pp. 75–87). Dordrecht: Springer.

Kramer, P. A. (2009). Is the world our campus? International students and US global power in the Long Twentieth Century. *Diplomatic History*, 33(5), 775–806.

Leask, B. (2015). *Internationalizing the Curriculum*. Abington, UK: Routledge.

Leask, B., Beelen, J., & Kaunda, L. (2013). Internationalisation of the curriculum: international approaches and perspectives. In H. Wit, F. Hunter, L. Johnson, & H. Liempd (Eds.), *Possible Futures: The Next 25 Years of the Internationalisation of Higher Education* (pp. 187–205). The Netherlands: European Association for International Education (EAIE).

Mendes, M. V. I. (2018). Is it the end of North-American hegemony? *Brazilian Journal of Political Economy*, 38(3), 434–449.

Parnreiter, C. (2018). America first! Donald Trump, the demise of the US hegemony and chaos in the capitalist world-system. *Zeitschrift für Wirtschaftsgeographie*, 62(1), 1–13.

Paulston, R. G. (2009). Mapping comparative education after postmodernity. In R. Cowen and A. M. Kazamias (Eds.), *International handbook of comparative education* (pp. 965–990). Dordrecht, Netherlands: Springer.

Pease, D. (2009). Re-thinking "American Studies after US exceptionalism." *American Literary History*, 21(1), 19–27.

Redden, E. (2018, November 13). New international enrollments decline again. *InsideHigherEd*. Retrieved from https://www.insidehighered.com/news/2018/11/13/new-international-student-enrollments-continue-decline-us-universities

Rodriguez, D. (2018). Abolition as praxis of human being: A foreword. *Harvard Law Review*, 132, 1575.

Santos, B. S. (2007). Beyond abyssal thinking: From global lines to ecologies of knowledges. *Review (Fernand Braudel Center)*, 30(1), 45–89.

Shotwell, A. (2016). *Against Purity: Living Ethically in Compromised Times*. Minneapolis, MN: University of Minnesota Press.

Silva, D.F.D. (2014). Toward a Black feminist poethics: The quest(ion) of Blackness toward the end of the world. *The Black Scholar*, 44(2), 81–97.

Stehr, N., and Ufer, U. (2009). On the global distribution and dissemination of knowledge. *International Social Science Journal*, 60(195), 7–24.

Stein, S., Andreotti, V., Suša, R., Ahenakew, C., & Čajková, T. (2020). From "education for sustainable development" to "education for the end of the world as we know it". *Educational Philosophy and Theory*, 1–14.

Stein, S., and Andreotti, V. (2017). Higher education and the modern/colonial global imaginary. *Cultural Studies ↔ Critical Methodologies*, 17(3), 173–181.

Stein, S., Andreotti, V., Bruce, J., and Suša, R. (2016). Towards different conversations about the internationalization of higher education. *Comparative and International Education*, 45(1), 1–18.

Stier, J. (2004). Taking a critical stance toward internationalization ideologies in higher education: Idealism, instrumentalism and educationalism. *Globalisation, Societies and Education*, 2(1), 1–28.

Taylor, C. (2002). Modern social imaginaries. *Public Culture*, 14, 91–124.

Trilokekar, R. D. (2015). *From soft power to economic diplomacy? A comparison of the changing rationales and roles of the US and Canadian federal governments in international education* (Center for Studies in Higher Education Research and Occasional Paper Series, UC Berkeley). Retrieved from https://cshe.berkeley.edu/publications/soft-power-economic-diplomacy-comparison-changing-rationales-and-roles-u-s-and-canadian

Wallerstein, I. M. (2004). *World-systems analysis: An introduction*. Durham, NC: Duke University Press.

Zemach-Bersin, T. (2007). Global citizenship and study abroad: It's all about US. *Critical Literacy: Theories and Practices*, 1(2), 16–28.

PART 5 CONCLUDING THOUGHTS

12 • WHERE DO WE GO FROM HERE?

JENNY J. LEE AND SANTIAGO CASTIELLO-GUTIÉRREZ

The main objective of this book is to shed light on the current geopolitical and globally unequal nature of international higher education by centering the role of power in how internationalization is understood. As explained in chapter 1, Jane Knight's (2004) highly cited definition was extended as follows: *the power* and process of integrating an international, intercultural or global dimension into the purpose, functions or delivery of post-secondary education While the preceding chapters provide a critical examination of a range of practices in how power operates, the accounts do not end here. Additional areas may include branch campuses and other forms of transnational education, professional associations and networks, and international organizations, as well as the particular dynamics between or within regions, countries, or groups, to name some. Furthermore, power does not reside in the United States or the Global North alone. The choice to focus on the United States was made not only to demonstrate the geopolitical strengths associated with a single case country but also to highlight the immense responsibilities that the United States, especially through its higher education institutions, possesses. Other countries are not exempt but may relate to the U.S. example depending on their relative position to their international partners or in their respective region. With the book's national focus, readers should be careful in taking an ambivalent position between seeing the United States as either "an exceptional model for other nations to follow . . . [or] as a dystopia that should be strongly avoided" (O'Connor, 2020, p. xiii).

Some readers may disagree that geopolitical tensions exist, at least in relation to their own institutions. Clearly, there are exceptions as there is no shortage of best-practice texts and conferences devoted to institutions showcasing how they are doing it right. But we encourage these same readers to at least be aware of the potential ways that power might operate, even when programmatic goals are achieved. All too often it is erroneously assumed that simple mutual agreement is the correct and sufficient means for internationalization to occur. Sometimes framed as public diplomacy in geopolitical contexts (Castells, 2008), diverse voices can be heard and respected in an effort to identify shared values. Consensus becomes idealized as the most humane effort to internationalize. While a diplomatic approach is certainly a step in the right direction, it is not the last. As these chapters clearly lay out, mutual agreement is already present. For example, institutions that strategize to rise in the global rankings, compete for the best and brightest students, and expand global partnerships are able to do so because there is built-in soft power that enables them to reach their immediate targets while also sustaining the current world order. Participating leaders, faculty, and administrators are effective only to the extent that they are able to identify willing individuals and institutions from abroad to cooperate with. But still, the status quo and power imbalance in interinstitutional relations remain unchanged.

Yet, all is not lost. Rather, what is needed is critical awareness as the foundational baseline for more global responsibility in the internationalization process. Beyond pursuing more and more internationalization activities or identifying win-wins, the preceding chapters evoke questions such as: What is the cost of internationalization, culturally and for local communities? Who is being left out? What are the consequences for those uninvited to participate? Another important missing piece is the (dis)connection between discourses (and literature) and practice. Asking the right questions and critically reflecting on issues of inequality and on potential consequences are fundamental. And while geopolitics is clearly embedded, internationalization must transcend national and even institutional interests. As Roopa Desai Trilokekar concluded in chapter 2, governments can support global education, but this "is only feasible when national governments invest in a geopolitical ideology, which is first and foremost global and international in orientation." When higher education becomes a geopolitical tool for country-first agendas, such as domestic growth or international competitiveness, internationalization outcomes are then narrowly measured by human capital and economic returns. In doing so, immigration policies become more about the consequences for the national economy and less about humanitarian goals. In higher education, targets to increase international enrollments while creating an unwelcoming climate should not coexist. Similarly, public statements about providing, for example, a "world-class education" may run counter to isolationist practices and policies that narrowly measure "excellence" by research funding and publication citations. As proposed by the updated definition, internationalization must extend beyond functionalism. Acknowledgment of power and how it operates is a requisite to internationalizing responsibly, as well as fulfilling higher education's purpose toward a greater common good.

CRITICAL ACTION

In order to move forward and realize the full potential of internationalization, critical awareness must be accompanied by critical action (Freire, 2018). Although many of the issues previously discussed are systemic, individual actions are the basis of collective actions—and ultimately they are the basis for social change. Therefore, given the manifold issues troubling internationalization as expressed in the preceding chapters, this concluding chapter offers further reflections and some possible directions institutions can strategically implement to transform their internationalization approach into one that is more globally responsible. Some of these recommendations could be adopted, as a starting point, by individuals within the organizations. As shown by Dale LaFleur in chapter 8, the effect of individual managerial professionals who are on the front lines of implementing internationalization initiatives is highly influential in establishing institutionalized practices. Other recommendations need to be implemented at national policy and organizational levels since they require a shift of priorities and discourses, as expressed by Christina W. Yao in chapter 9.

Different scholars throughout this book have argued for the need to envision alternative futures that make plain the unevenness of internationalization and call for greater social responsibility in the process. Additionally, caution should be exercised when considering who should design these new practices or where they should come from. It is easy to assume that a single dominant country, such as the United States, or its peers can and should "fix" these issues. This presumption only reinforces the superiority of certain actors by centering them while negating or marginalizing the agency of others. Therefore, we call for change that simultaneously takes different forms, from different actors, and across different locations. These proposals are for individuals and collectivities in both the United States and elsewhere. We summarize some recommendations from the previous chapters as well as offer some additional suggestions. They are not intended as a straightforward recipe; rather, they represent an invitation to critically reflect on and innovate current internationalization approaches.

Rankings and Accreditations

Both global rankings and university accreditations shape global norms, and thereby shape national education policies and, in turn, institutional behaviors (Blanco Ramírez, 2015; Hazelkorn, 2015). They also extend Anglo-American academic colonialism and imperialism. But again, their influence is not solely determined by the United States or other dominant countries. The rest of the world, for the most part, is a willing participant, further legitimizing these powerful mechanisms. Beyond replicating U.S. or Anglo-based practices, governments and their institutions have an opportunity to innovate by generating alternative ideas and forms of knowing (Lee and Maldonado-Maldonado, 2018b). With the

United States and the United Kingdom (UK) looking more inward (via America-first and Brexit policies), other countries can rescript current discourses and rules. Given such global shifts, we have an opportunity to leave behind practices that reinforce the current imaginary, and start focusing on building a new global reality together.

As Ellen Hazelkorn stated in chapter 3, the world is indeed becoming more multipolar and interconnected. Although new contestants are appearing on the rankings stage, the rules for the pageant have not considerably changed. While a convenient tool, global rankings tend to place a higher premium on research and reputational factors than on student learning. Governments, organizations, and higher education stakeholders can respond to the global rankings in different ways. Among these, ministries of education could provide greater incentives and evaluation schemes toward local impact. University leaders could minimize the global rankings' importance in developing university strategies. This is especially true when institutions might shortchange their local commitments and the needs of their communities in favor of aligning with ranking metrics (Lee, Vance, Stensaker, and Ghosh, 2020).

Alternatively, institutions might opt out of participation. A number of African universities, for example, have considered withdrawing their participation in global rankings as a way to resist global pressures to imitate the West and instead focus their resources on local matters (Teferra, 2017). Rather than conforming to the dominant narrative, each country/region/institution is urged to move from "archaic and 'dumb' decolonisation monologues to contemporary and 'smart' internationalisation dialogues" by inserting itself into the conversation while preserving its own essence (Teferra, 2020, para. 8). Both efforts require a different global norm that values and recognizes a broader range of institutions for their intrinsic importance and diverse social benefits, not just the outcomes compared against a prescribed standard.

Similarly, when discussing the prominence of international accreditations, Gerardo L. Blanco (chapter 4) argues that these standards originated in specific contexts but have globally generalized and now exert tremendous influence. By definition, standards are fixed and hardly questioned; therefore, the measured unit (i.e., university) must adapt in order to fit the particular standard. While benchmarking has some value for comparison purposes, there is a danger when legitimacy is determined by imitation. Although there is momentous international pressure and funding toward university and program accreditation, there should also be a consideration of the consequences that various measurements might have in deepening the stratification within their own national context. As Blanco recommends, quality indicators and standards should reflect local and regional values. These institutions could thus invest greater time, knowledge, and resources toward strengthening their own national accreditation system over disqualifying it for failing to meet U.S. assumptions about quality.

Research

When it comes to the creation and dissemination of knowledge, research productivity and publication impact have become primary measures of faculty worth and institutional value (i.e., rankings). While knowledge production is essential in the current knowledge society, national policies and professional norms about the type of research, the outlets (and therefore language) of where it should be published, epistemologies and methodologies, and the backgrounds and number of collaborators have helped perpetuate the hegemony of Western knowledge. Even when the United States and other highly resourced countries are importing top talent from every corner of the world, these scholars are tacitly forced to "publish or perish" and channeled toward Science Citation Index journals. Therefore, one consideration, which institutions have already begun to adopt, is to rethink the value of journal metrics so that publications that are more inclusive of different languages, locations, and forms of knowledge are also valued and rewarded.

Similarly, given the rise of exploitative academic publishers that charge hefty fees to authors without peer-review or editorial services—often referred to as predatory publishers—simply publishing more is not the answer (Altbach and de Wit, 2018). Nor is reserving research for the few (Lee and Maldonado-Maldonado, 2018b). As discussed throughout this book, the risks of maintaining a narrow definition of world-class, or what counts as quality research, are enormous in terms of perpetuating current patterns that favor the Global North. Only a handful of already dominant institutions in mostly English-speaking countries benefit based on current metrics. Besides rethinking publication metrics, establishing or transforming academic journals into multiple languages, having globally diverse editorial boards, and expanding knowledge production to encompass broader viewpoints and frameworks are additional ways to address current inequities (Lee and Maldonado-Maldonado, 2018a).

Even despite geopolitical tensions, collaborative research does not have to follow suit. As explained by John P. Haupt and Jenny J. Lee in chapter 5 and Brendan Cantwell in chapter 6, collaboration and mobility between China and the United States arguably benefit both countries—albeit in different forms—but with comparable impacts. Beyond research to simply serve geopolitical agendas, Haupt and Lee find that there is considerable research that supports global science, such as current efforts to address the COVID-19 pandemic. However, the conditions for research are not universally secure or supported. When scholars are pushed out by conditions of violence and attacks on their academic freedom, other countries play a key role in creating safe spaces for their research to continue.

When it comes to the mobility of graduate students and scholars, inequality is also present. As mentioned by Cantwell in chapter 6, the push-pull model remains a dominant framework that conveys a gravitational pull toward places with the most resources. Indeed, a vast majority of these academics are moving to a handful of the wealthiest economies. From the perspective of the host countries, there needs to be greater recognition of what they offer culturally, beyond their immediate skill set, and how to be more inclusive as a vital part of the university community. From the perspective of these scholars' countries of origin, the narrative is not narrowly about losing talent, but about critically investigating the conditions that led them to leave as well as how to maintain networks across borders.

Institutional Strategies and Partnerships

Geopolitics exerts particular influence on how international partnerships between higher education institutions develop. As Chrystal A. George Mwangi, Sean Jung-Hau Chen, and Pempho Chinkondenji show in chapter 7, institutions in the United States tend to take either an altruistic or a prestige (self-benefiting) discourse when showcasing their internationalization plans. This aligns with the overall representation of how the United States, as the most dominant economy in the world, engages with other countries. Thus, both representations of internationalization in this context position the U.S. institution as the sole "savior" in addressing the global grand challenges. This approach only exacerbates hegemonic practices and impedes dialogue among institutions.

Therefore, under this premise, partnerships between U.S. institutions (or others in dominant countries) and the rest of the world's majority can be imbalanced. When these institutions refer to their partnerships as win-win relations, exactly what, how, and at what cost does each partner win? While it is true that in most cases each institution benefits in some form from an international project, existing power disparities may only be reinforced and further dependencies created. In chapter 8, among the author's recommendations is for institutions to collaborate with their partners in developing internationalization plans. As Dale LaFleur further recommends in this chapter, economics-based programs need to shift toward values-based ones. She also advises institutions to place greater attention on the assessment mechanisms that center on students' experiences and outcomes while also supporting the long-term sustainability of the programs. At the same time, institutions on the other side of the power spectrum are advised to identify the intangible reputational factors of being associated with a "prestigious" institution. Likewise, universities, not just those based in the United States but also those outside the United States, could consider how current power imbalances might be reduced via internationalization.

Such efforts for fairer partnerships are currently under way. A number of organizations are inviting higher education institutions to be more aware of the responsibilities and consequences of establishing partnerships abroad. For example, the Forum on Education Abroad has issued a Standards of Good Practice document as well as a Code of Ethics for Education Abroad, in which it encourages its member institutions to be "aware of and sensitive to host community cultural norms and expectations in program planning and execution"

(Forum on Education Abroad, 2011, sec. 3).[1] These standards, as well as other calls for more ethical partnerships (e.g., Global Dialogues [International Education Association of South Africa, 2014]), help to decenter the nation-state as a container for internationalization practices (Shahjahan and Kezar, 2013).

Student Mobility and Learning

A key policy issue for student mobility is immigration. During the writing of this book, there were numerous attempts by the federal government to limit immigration into the United States, which had a direct impact on international students and scholars. These included travel bans against those from Muslim-majority countries, Chinese students in sensitive fields of study, and those with ties to China's military, as well as the suspension of new work visas. Among the more drastic policies was the U.S. Immigration and Customs Enformcement guidance during the COVID-19 pandemic, which would have led to the deportation of up to a million international students should their universities pivot to fully online. Although the rule was eventually rescinded, such anti-immigration steps continue to hinder current as well as prospective students from attending U.S. universities.

Thus, open and flexible immigration rules that allow international students to remain in the country, even in the event of global crises, are key. While the United States was tightening its immigration criteria, Canada and Australia were loosening theirs. However, resistance is also possible. In response to the July 2020 ICE policy, numerous universities took legal action against the government. Members of Congress, business leaders, and U.S. citizens openly denounced the policy, demonstrating their support for affected students. Besides the immediate policy reversal, this example demonstrates the power of collective action in support of internationals.

While the benefits that international students bring to both the country and host institutions are indisputable, policymakers and organizational leaders should be especially mindful of any dehumanizing language in referring to student mobility. As explained by Christina W. Yao in chapter 9, the commodification of students seen as numbers of imports/exports "expressly contributes to the overall global power that sustains a nation-state's positioning as a world leader in education, economics, and politics." In this chapter, Yao calls for a different discourse that promotes the human side of international students instead. This shift helps garner more support toward their academic success than mere enrollment. For example, universities can shift the focus from promoting the head count of participants to measuring the programmatic impact. Furthermore, creating safe spaces for international students and scholars to thrive is vital, especially amid rising nationalistic and neo-racist expressions on campuses. Thus, higher education institutions can expend at least the same effort to support international students upon arrival as they expend to attract them (Castiello-Gutiérrez, 2019a; Lee, 2013).

Another key area for critical inquiry is on the level of student learning. As Chris R. Glass warns in chapter 10, learning outcomes—typically in the form of intercultural competencies—have the potential to reproduce the same geopolitical hierarchies since these measures often reflect other forms of capital possessed by already affluent and cosmopolitan students. Thus, instead of focusing on how to educate *global citizens*, universities need to shift the perspective toward educating "global selves ... to make their way among diverse others on the basis of a critical awareness of the impact of their actions" (Killick, 2015, p. 33). According to Glass, this means recognizing global competency as a "developmental web," which is lifelong, nonlinear, and shaped by self-determination and context. To do so, Sharon Stein, in chapter 11, presents a social cartography for internationalizing the curriculum. According to Stein, U.S. national hegemony can be present even in "seemingly benevolent discourses of inclusion." In order to move from U.S. national hegemony to a more critical and context-specific approach to internationalizing that allows for more voices, she presents a series of key reflective questions that could lead to a new global imaginary.

CONCLUDING REMARKS

In closing, we invite readers to reflect on how international higher education has been and continues to be intrinsically linked to the geopolitical context and remains governed by U.S. interests abroad. Ironically, the United States has long been praised as a bastion of democracy and free market competition; but at the same time its higher education institutions have been criticized for being too immersed in—and even driven by—these same economic liberalism norms (Koch, 2014). However, the current nationalistic context represents an "anomaly in the history of the U.S. federal government's use of soft power as an aspect of its foreign policy" (Trilokekar, chapter 2, this volume), and as such, it presents an opportunity for the higher education sector to decouple its internationalization strategies from the geopolitical interests of the country and from the neoliberal motivations that have driven many international higher education endeavors thus far. While universities have worked and should continue to work alongside governments, they are not federal arms. Rather, universities can lead the way in reimagining a more sustainable, equitable, and ethical approach to how they engage with the rest of the world. By moving beyond self-interested and revenue-driven strategies, higher education institutions can start creating an environment that enhances intercultural engagement both within their campuses (i.e., between "local" and "international" students) and outside their campuses (i.e., between international partners) (Castiello-Gutiérrez, 2019b). When it comes to learning, U.S. approaches need not or should not be seen as the assumptive "standard" or "norm" or as "universal" (Blanco, chapter 4; Glass, chapter 10; Stein, chapter 11). By disentangling colonial legacies, more voices and perspectives are included.

And while most of the recommendations in this chapter are directed toward readers in the United States and other Western countries, they should also serve as lessons for all. Indeed, the world is shifting geopolitically. For example, the rise of China as an economic superpower will certainly alter how and with whom universities around the world engage as well as the flows of international students. Other countries should also take note on the consequences of policies and politics used to alienate international students and scholars in the United States. Also, as more universities from outside the United States and the United Kingdom strengthen their research capacities, international cooperation and funding for such research will keep expanding. However—for higher education—this new world order needs to be an evolution from the previous one and not a mere update (or increase in the number) of players. Regardless of which country possesses the most geopolitical power, internationalization discourses and practices should extend beyond the nation-state. The risks associated with a country losing its position as a top destination for international students should not be solely framed in revenue returns inasmuch as the reasons for other countries to start recruiting more international students should not only be about the human capital benefits. The decision to partner with an institution abroad or to seek international accreditation should also shift from being driven by achieving a particular status to being driven by a more conscious decision about its potential to help fulfill their greater social mission. Otherwise, the same systemic issues are sustained, albeit being led from different countries or regions. What we suggest is for institutions throughout the world to observe the pervasiveness and the effects of geopolitical power in informing their internationalization strategies, and to consider ways that are better aligned with their unique missions oriented toward a greater common good (Castiello-Gutiérrez, 2020).

At the time of writing of this book, the world of higher education was still struggling to prepare for the future ramifications that the COVID-19 pandemic will bring. So far, we have witnessed institutions facing financial downturns, due in part to their dependency on tuition revenue from international students (Altbach and de Wit, 2020; Marinoni and Van't Land, 2020; Mitchell, 2020). While we have seen some shifts in destination countries before, this time the challenge is global and, therefore, almost every country has been affected. The post-COVID world will most certainly be one where the physical international mobility of students will be reduced significantly, at least for the medium term (Fischer, 2020; Marginson cited in Mitchell, 2020). Or we may be entering a post-mobility world in which physical mobility remains reduced because of its inherent limitations and inequities (White and Lee, 2020) or because of the high environmental impact it represents (Shields, 2019). In the meantime, international affairs will be forced to shift its attention inward, which presents further opportunities for universities to develop international and intercultural education at their own institutions.

We have also witnessed the titanic efforts of institutions in pivoting from face-to-face instruction to remote instruction using technology. Administrators and professionals were also using those same technologies to cooperate with their peers abroad. Countless webinars and virtual conferences were organized during 2020 to discuss international collaboration in a world where almost everyone was suddenly forced into home confinement. Instead of traveling to visit a potential partner to discuss a new study abroad program, universities were talking about virtual exchanges for their students; instead of planning where to open new program sites, institutions were rolling out plans to be "everywhere" (e.g., University of Arizona, 2020). But while the world applauded how the use of information and communication technologies (ICT) "rescued" the academic year, these technologies also remind us of the great inequities that still remain. Just as the chapters in this book have argued that internationalization is defined by power and politics, ICT is also not neutral. Who has access to which technologies? In what language are those tools developed? What kinds of new partnerships will develop? Recent data have shown that moving instruction online left many students without any education at all (Organisation for Economic Co-operation and Development, 2020). How will those students and their institutions engage internationally? So even if the future of internationalization—including international student mobility—is virtual, how will this remote shift perpetuate and even enlarge the existing gaps? Just as mobility programs were leaving behind the less affluent students, virtual mobility programs may also leave many students out.

Finally, after reflecting on these issues, it is our desire that not only national or institutional strategies evolve, but the overall approach toward the ways we collectively analyze and critique internationalization of higher education evolve as well. We hope that this book serves as a starting point toward said refreshment in the critique. For higher education scholars, practitioners, and policymakers to aspire to a more equitable and just approach to international higher education, a consideration of power must be among the guiding principles.

NOTE

1. The Forum on Education Abroad is a 501(c)(3) nonprofit, membership association recognized by the U.S. Department of Justice and the Federal Trade Commission as the Standards Development Organization for the field of education abroad in the United States.

REFERENCES

Altbach, P. G., and de Wit, H. (2018, September 7). Too much academic research is being published. *University World News*. Retrieved from https://www.universityworldnews.com/post.php?story=20180905095203579

———. (2020, April 4). Post pandemic outlook for HE is bleakest for the poorest. *University World News.* Retrieved from https://www.universityworldnews.com/post.php?story=20200402152914362

Blanco Ramírez, G. (2015). International accreditation as global position taking: An empirical exploration of U.S. accreditation in Mexico. *Higher Education, 69*(3), 361–374. https://doi.org/10.1007/s10734-014-9780-7

Castells, M. (2008). The new public sphere: Global civil society, communication networks, and global governance. *The ANNALS of the American Academy of Political and Social Science, 616*(1), 78–93. https://doi.org/10.1177/0002716207311877

Castiello-Gutiérrez, S. (2019a, April 8). Beyond the melting pot: International students on campus. *Inside Higher Education: The World View.* Retrieved from https://www.insidehighered.com/blogs/world-view/beyond-melting-pot-international-students-campus

———. (2019b, March 1). Reframing internationalisation's values and principles. *University World News.* Retrieved from https://www.universityworldnews.com/post.php?story=20190225085141576

———. (2020). Purposeful internationalization: A common-good approach of global engagement. *Journal of Comparative & International Higher Education, 11*(Winter), 93–95. https://doi.org/https://doi.org/10.32674/jcihe.v11iWinter.1539

Fischer, K. (2020, May 22). To keep international students during the pandemic, colleges get creative. *The Chronicle of Higher Education.* Retrieved from https://www.chronicle.com/article/To-Keep-International-Students/248838

Forum on Education Abroad. (2011). Code of ethics. Standards of Good Practice. Retrieved from https://forumea.org/resources/standards-of-good-practice/code-of-ethics/#3

Freire, P. (2018). *Pedagogy of the oppressed (50th anniversary edition)* (4th ed.). New York, NY: Bloomsbury.

Hazelkorn, E. (2015). *Rankings and the reshaping of higher education: The battle for world-class excellence* (2nd ed.). London, UK: Palgrave Macmillan. https://doi.org/10.1057/9781137446671

International Education Association of South Africa. (2014). *Nelson Mandela Bay global dialogue declaration on the future of internationalisation of higher education.* Retrieved from https://www.eaie.org/dam/jcr:86722ac9-fc8f-44c7-bc41-8dce7e290258/Global Dialogue 2014 Declaration.pdf

Killick, D. (2015). *Developing the global student: Higher education in an era of globalization.* Abington, UK: Routledge, Taylor & Francis Group.

Knight, J. (2004). Internationalization remodeled: Definition, approaches, and rationales. *Journal of Studies in International Education, 8*(1), 5–31.

Koch, N. (2014). The shifting geopolitics of higher education: Inter/nationalizing elite universities in Kazakhstan, Saudi Arabia, and beyond. *Geoforum, 56,* 46–54. https://doi.org/http://dx.doi.org/10.1016/j.geoforum.2014.06.014

Lee, J. J. (2013). The false halo of internationalization. *International Higher Education, 72,* 5–7.

Lee, J.J., and Maldonado-Maldonado, A. (2018a, September 30). The dangers of limiting research to elite universities. *University World News.* Retrieved from http://www.universityworldnews.com/article.php?story=20180927104004479

Lee, J. J., and Maldonado-Maldonado, A. (2018b, September 14). Not enough diverse academic research is being published. *University World News.* Retrieved from https://www.universityworldnews.com/post.php?story=20180913095151857

Lee, J. J., Vance, H., Stensaker, B., and Ghosh, S. (2020). Global rankings at a local cost? The strategic pursuit of status and the third mission. *Comparative Education,* online first, 1–21. https://doi.org/10.1080/03050068.2020.1741195

Marinoni, G., and Van't Land, H. (2020). The impact of COVID-19 on global higher education. *International Higher Education, Spring 102*, 7–9.

Mitchell, N. (2020, March 25). COVID-19 crisis will change HE forever, IHEF hears. *University World News*. Retrieved from https://www.universityworldnews.com/post.php?story=20200325235602611

O'Connor, B. (2020). *Anti-Americanism and American exceptionalism: Prejudice and pride about the USA*. London, UK: Routledge. https://doi.org/10.4324/9780429277436

Organisation for Economic Co-operation and Development. (2020). *Learning remotely when schools close: How well are students and schools prepared? Insights from PISA*. Retrieved from https://read.oecd-ilibrary.org/view/?ref=127_127063-iiwm328658&title=Learning-remotely-when-schools-close

Shahjahan, R. A., and Kezar, A. J. (2013). Beyond the "national container": Addressing methodological nationalism in higher education research. *Educational Researcher, 42*(1), 20–29. https://doi.org/10.3102/0013189X12463050

Shields, R. (2019). The sustainability of international higher education: Student mobility and global climate change. *Journal of Cleaner Production, 217*, 594–602. https://doi.org/https://doi.org/10.1016/j.jclepro.2019.01.291

Teferra, D. (2017, September 8). Tempest in the rankings teapot—an African perspective. *University World News*. Retrieved from https://www.universityworldnews.com/post.php?story=20170905085216591

University of Arizona (2020, May 4). University of Arizona launches unprecedented global network. Tucson, AZ: University of Arizona. Retreived from https://global.arizona.edu/news/university-arizona-launches-unprecedented-global-network

White, B., and Lee, J. J. (2020, April 18). The future of international HE in a post-mobility world. *University World News*. Retrieved from https://www.universityworldnews.com/post.php?story=20200417105255362

NOTES ON CONTRIBUTORS

JENNY J. LEE is a professor at the Center for the Study of Higher Education at the University of Arizona. She was formerly a NAFSA senior fellow, associate editor of the *Review of Higher Education*, chair for the Council of International Higher Education, and member of the board of directors for the Association for the Study of Higher Education (ASHE). Lee's research encompasses a range of key higher education issues that center on the internationalization of higher education. Her past research studies have included student engagement, community outreach, and organizational behaviors in the United States as well as abroad. Her ongoing research on international students' mobility and experiences in the United States, South Africa, Mexico, and Korea over the past decade has been cited widely. Lee has authored and co-authored over one hundred publications in the aforementioned research areas, which regularly appear in the top journals of higher education. *Nature, Science,* the *New York Times,* ABC News, *Al Jazeera,* and many other news outlets have quoted Lee and featured her research. Lee was a global professor at Korea University, an honorary visiting scholar at City University, London, and a Fulbright Scholar to South Africa at the University of Pretoria. She is currently a visiting scholar at the University of Cape Town, South Africa.

GERARDO L. BLANCO is an associate professor of higher education and associate director of the Center for International Higher Education at Boston College. His research explores the intersections of quality and internationalization in higher education and is motivated by a commitment to global social justice and a deep curiosity for the ways higher education institutions define, improve, and communicate their value to different stakeholder groups. His teaching, research, and consulting have taken place in fifteen countries and five continents. An interdisciplinary scholar, theoretically informed by postcolonial theory and poststructuralism, Gerardo has published his research in leading journals, such as *Higher Education, Studies in Higher Education,* the *Comparative Education Review,* and the *Review of Higher Education.* He has held leadership roles in the Comparative and International Education Society (CIES) and the Association for the Study of Higher Education Council for International Higher Education. He serves on several editorial boards, including International Higher Education and Quality in Higher Education. In 2017 he received the "Best Research Article Award" from the Comparative & International Education Society's Higher Education SIG. In 2014 and 2020 his work received honorable mentions from the same organization. Gerardo has been a visiting faculty member at Shaanxi Normal University (China) and a visiting expert at the International Centre for Higher Education Research (INCHER) at the University of Kassel (Germany), and he was selected as an Erasmus+ teaching fellow at the John Paul II Catholic University of Lublin (Poland).

BRENDAN CANTWELL is an associate professor of higher, adult, and lifelong education in the Department of Education at Michigan State University. Brendan is focusing on how higher education organizations' systems reflect and contribute to social, political, and economic processes and outcomes. He is co-author of *Unequal Higher Education* and co-editor of *High Participation Systems of Higher Education, Handbook on the Politics of Higher Education*, and *Academic Capitalism in the Age of Globalization*. Brendan's research has appeared in several journals, including *Higher Education, Studies in Higher Education, Journal of Higher Education, Research in Higher Education, Comparative Education*, and *Harvard Educational Review*. Brendan is co-editor of *Higher Education* and sits on the review boards of several other journals.

SANTIAGO CASTIELLO-GUTIÉRREZ earned his PhD at the University of Arizona's Center for the Study of Higher Education. He is the coordinator for the Consortium for North American Higher Education Collaboration's mobility programs. His research interests are in internationalization of higher education, intercultural competence development, and organization and administration of higher education institutions. He is a co-author of several publications including refereed articles, book chapters, and encyclopedia entries. Before moving to the United States, Santiago worked for nine years in Mexico as director for international cooperation at the Tecnológico de Monterrey (ITESM), where he later served as director for international programs of ITESM's shared services center. Santiago is also a CONACyT fellowship recipient and has been distinguished as an Erasmus Circle Scholar by the University of Arizona College of Education. He is a 2019 recipient of the Harold Josephson Award for Professional Promise in International Education of the Association of International Education Administrators (AIEA).

SEAN JUNG-HAU CHEN is a junior researcher at the Language Training and Testing Center (LTTC) in Taipei, Taiwan. His research uses a critical lens to focus on (1) international student experiences and the heterogeneity of the international student population and (2) the internationalization of higher education, with an emphasis on geopolitical and power dynamics. He is also interested in second language education and assessment, particularly the social impacts of large-scale language tests/assessments. He has published in the *Journal of Student Affairs* at New York University and presented research at national higher education conferences including NASPA and NACADA. Sean has worked in higher education administration in the United States and Taiwan, including positions in academic affairs, admissions, and student health services with a peer sexuality education troupe. He has also worked with Fulbright Taiwan's Foundation for Scholarly Exchange to help facilitate communications and interactions between scholarship grantees from the United States and local communities in Taiwan. Sean received his MEd in higher education at the University of Massachusetts Amherst and his BA in English language and literature at Fu Jen Catholic University.

PEMPHO CHINKONDENJI is a PhD student at the University of Massachusetts Amherst, and she is pursuing a degree in international education policy and development. Her research focuses on women and girls' education, particularly on pregnancy-related policies and the relationship among gender, education, and development in sub-Saharan African contexts. Pempho also looks at the power and gender dynamics in higher education, in both the Global North and the Global South. She recently published a media review in *Comparative Education Review*, titled "Sex for Grades: Undercover in West African Universities," which was produced by the BBC Africa Eye in 2019. Pempho is a co-founder of Loving Arms Malawi, a nonprofit that supports rural girls' education and raises awareness about sexual violence in Malawi. She also serves as the youth delegate to the United Nations for Pan-Pacific and South-East Asian Women's Association, USA. Pempho received her MA in cross-cultural and international education from Bowling Green State University and her BA in mass communications from African Bible College.

CHRIS R. GLASS, PhD, is an associate professor in the Department of Educational Foundations & Leadership at Old Dominion University, Virginia. His research and writing focus on issues of equity and sustainability in international higher education and community colleges. He is the editor of the *Journal of International Students* and the co-editor of the Routledge Studies in Global Student Mobility book series. He was the recipient of the NAFSA Innovative Research in International Education Award in 2016, and he currently serves as vice president of the Comparative and International Education Society (CIES) Study Abroad and International Students SIG. His research has been published in the *International Journal of Educational Development, Studies in Higher Education, Compare, Community College Journal of Research and Practice*, and the *Journal of Studies in International Education*.

JOHN P. HAUPT is a PhD student in the Center for the Study of Higher Education at the University of Arizona. He has over a decade of experience in international education as an instructor and administrator in the United States and abroad. His research focuses on topics within comparative and international education that are related to student and scholar mobility, transnational education, international research collaboration, and international development. His most recent work has focused on U.S.-China research collaboration and the impact of COVID-19 on global research networks.

ELLEN HAZELKORN is joint managing partner at BH Associates education consultants. She is professor emerita at Technological University Dublin (Ireland) and joint editor of *Policy Reviews in Higher Education*. She is also international co-investigator for the Centre for Global Higher Education (CGHE) in London, and research fellow at the Centre for International Higher Education at Boston College. Ellen is a member of the Quality Board for Higher Education in Iceland and the Commission for the College of the Future (UK), as well as various university and government boards. She has written numerous reports and led evaluations and reviews for the Organisation for Economic Co-operation and Development, European Commission, and United Nations Educational, Scientific and Cultural Organization, as well as for governments, government agencies, and universities. She was policy advisor and board member of the Higher Education Authority of Ireland (HEA) and vice president of the Dublin Institute of Technology (now TU Dublin) for twenty years. Ellen publishes widely on higher education policy and global rankings: *Research Handbook on Quality, Performance and Accountability in Higher Education* (2018); *Global Rankings and the Geopolitics of Higher Education* (2016); *The Impact and Future of Arts and Humanities Research* (2016); *The Civic University: Meeting the Leadership and Management Challenges* (2016); *Rankings and the Reshaping of Higher Education: The Battle for World-Class Excellence*, 2nd ed. (2015); *Rankings and Accountability in Higher Education: Uses and Misuses* (2013). Forthcoming publications include the following: *Research Handbook on University Rankings: History, Methodology, Influence and Impact* (2021) and *Global Governance of International Higher Education and Global Science: Rethinking Multilateralism* (2022). Ellen was awarded a BA and PhD from the University of Wisconsin, Madison, and the University of Kent, UK, respectively.

DALE LAFLEUR is the senior director of academic affairs and internationalization at NAFSA: Association of International Educators. In this role, she leads the association's strategies to support global learning and higher education internationalization by producing, planning, and delivering programs, publications, and services for use by the international education community. Before joining NAFSA, Dale worked in the field of international education for over twenty years, focusing on the development of institutional partnerships, student mobility, and leadership programs at both the University of Arizona and Seattle University. She received her PhD in higher education from the University of Arizona and served as an instructor for Leadership Strategies and a guest lecturer in Comparative Education. She is also a part-time faculty member in the International Education Leadership master's program at Northern Arizona University. Professionally, in 2013 she was selected as a member of the Fulbright International Education Administrator Program to Japan and in 2014 was invited to participate in the Baden-Württemberg Administrator Seminar in Germany. Dale has written several articles and leads workshops on international partnership development and joint and dual degree programs.

CHRYSTAL A. GEORGE MWANGI is an associate professor of higher education and research associate at the Center for Student Success Research at the University of Massachusetts Amherst. Her scholarship broadly centers on (1) structures of opportunity and issues of inequity that impact the trajectory of minoritized students into and through college; (2) internationalization efforts within higher education, the transnational nature of universities, and the use of higher education as a tool for international mobility/migration; and (3) African and African Diaspora populations in higher education with a specific emphasis on the impact of race, racism, and coloniality on their educational experiences. Her work has been published in journals including *Harvard Educational Review, Higher Education, Review of Higher Education, and Teachers College Record*. George Mwangi was a recipient of NAFSA's Innovative Research in International Education Award and has also received a Comparative & International Education Society (CIES) Study Abroad and International Student SIG Best Article Award. She is an associate editor for the *Journal for Diversity in Higher Education* and serves on the editorial board for the *Journal of College Student Development*. Before her faculty position, she worked for nearly a decade as a college administrator. She has also served as a research consultant for the American Council on Education (ACE) and USAID. George Mwangi received her PhD in higher education administration from the University of Maryland, College Park, and her MS in higher education and student affairs administration from Florida State University.

SHARON STEIN is an assistant professor in the Department of Educational Studies at the University of British Columbia. Her research addresses patterns of intellectual, affective, relational, political, economic, and ecological injustice in the study and practice of higher education, especially in relation to issues of internationalization, decolonization, and sustainability. Her scholarship has been published in *Review of Higher Education, Critical Ethnic Studies, Studies in Philosophy and Education,* and *Critical Studies in Education*. She is the founder and convener of the Critical Internationalization Studies Network, and a founding member of the Gesturing Towards Decolonial Futures arts/research collective.

ROOPA DESAI TRILOKEKAR is an associate professor in the Faculty of Education, York University, Canada. She comes to an academic career after twenty years of experience as a professional in the field of international education in Canada, India, and the United States, which includes ten years with the U.S. Educational Foundation in India (Fulbright Program). Her research interests are focused on government policy in the internationalization of higher education, student experiential learning through international education, and internationalizing pre-service teacher education. She has co-edited three volumes, *International Education as Public Policy in Canada*, *Making Policy in Turbulent Times: Challenge and Prospects for Higher Education*, and *Canada's Universities Go Global*, as well as published over twenty-eight book chapters and journal articles on international education. She has a strong record of successful research grants. She is currently engaged in the following research projects: "What Is 'International' about the International Student Experience in the Canadian Labour Market? A Study Examining the Similarities and Differences in Labour Market Experiences and Outcomes of International and Canadian Born Students" (funded by Immigration, Refugees and Citizenship Canada [IRCC]) and "International Students Are 'Ideal' Immigrants: A Critical Discourse Analysis of Study-Migration Pathways in Canada, Australia and Germany" (funded by the Social Science and Humanities Research Council). Most recently she has been awarded a Fulbright Research Chair in Public Diplomacy at the University of Southern California to complete a project titled "International Education as Soft Power: Its Relevance in a World of Changing US-Canada Relations and New Geopolitics."

CHRISTINA W. YAO is an assistant professor of higher education and program coordinator of the Higher Education and Student Affairs master's program at the University of South Carolina. She is a qualitative researcher who primarily studies undergraduate and graduate student engagement and learning in higher education. She operationalizes her research focus through three connected topical areas: international and comparative education, teaching and learning, and graduate education. Yao is involved in several professional organizations, including the Association for the Study of Higher Education (ASHE) and the Comparative and International Education Society (CIES). She also serves on the editorial board for several journals, including the *Journal of Diversity in Higher Education*, *Journal of Student Affairs Research and Practice*, and *Journal of International Students*.

INDEX

Note: References to figures and tables appear in italicized text; the following terms have been abbreviated:

International education: IE
Research & development: R&D
Scientific & technological innovation: S&T
9/11. *See* September 11 terrorist attacks
100,000 Strong in the Americas, 31, 155, 162

academic imperialism: characterized, 155–156; academic dependency, 159–160; interest convergence, 160–162; positional mobility, 156–158. *See also* geopolitics; hegemony
Academic Ranking of World Universities (ARWU), 7, *51, 52, 53*
academic tourism, 158, 160, 164
accountability: accountability agenda, 48–49; accreditation as, 61–62; university rankings, 49–54
accreditation: defined, 61–63; domestic confidence in US-based, 64–65; embracing change in, 70–72; geopolitical power and, 61, 68–70, 72, 125–126; globalization and, 63–64; post-colonial theory and, 61, 66; recommendations for critical action, 209–210; US standards in, 70; visual branding by accreditors, 66–68
Accreditation Board for Engineering and Technology (ABET), 64, *67–71*
Accreditation on the Edge, 64
Africa: global rankings and, 210; internationalization as coercion, 6, 8; trends in IE, *43, 52*, 119
America First policy, 32–35. *See also* foreign policy
American Council on Education (ACE), 115, 135, 158, 165, 171, 189, 223
Anglo-American supremacy. *See* Western dominance
anthropocentric & individualistic system, 195
anti-Asian sentiment, 33, 36, 77–78, 81–83
anti-communist ideology, 27–28, 190–192
Asiaweek, 53

Association for International Educators (NAFSA), 2, 14, 158, 165, 189
Association of American Colleges & Universities (AAC&U), 172
Association of American Universities, 158
Association of International Education Administrators, 116
Association of Public and Land-grant Universities, 158
Association to Advance Collegiate Schools of Business (AACSB), 64, *67–71*

Beliefs, Events, and Values Inventory (BEVI), 173
brain drain vs. technological nationalism, 104–105
Bretton Woods consensus, 192
Buchanan, John, 27
Bureau of Educational and Cultural Affairs (ECA), 10
Bureau of Public Affairs, 10
Bush, George Jr., 30, 171–172
Bush, George Sr., 28

Carter, Jimmy, 27
Cartesian forms of subjectivity, 180–181
Center for International Educational Cooperation, 26
China: ascendancy in R&D, 9, 46–47, 50–51, *52*, 107; economic growth in, 8, 37, 44, 46–47, 50, 215; relations with US, 3, 33, 36, 77–78, 81–83, 101–102, 161; in research collaboration, 84–87, 88–90, 211; transnational partnerships and, 133
Clinton, Bill, 29
Coalition for the Advancement of Foreign Languages and International Studies, 27
Cold War: IE and, 25–26, 27, 28–29; New Cold War, 3, 77; S&T capability advancement during, 77, 83, 96; US global hegemony and, 190–192

225

collaboration in research: recommendations for critical action, 211–212; scientific globalism vs. nationalism, 83–84, 88–90; in S&T innovation, 80–81, 84–90; trends in, 2, 42–48, 77–80, 84–85; US as world leader in, 7–10; US-China relations and, 77–79, 81–83, 84–90, 101–102, 211. *See also* research & development (R&D); transnational partnerships

colonialism, 3, 6, 190–192, 194–201. *See also* post-colonial theory

commercialization of IE, 29–32, 114, 125–128

Commission on Abraham Lincoln Study Abroad Fellowship Program, 31

Commission on Colleges of the Southern Association of Colleges & Schools, 67, 68

commodification of students, 31–32, 155–156, 162–165, 178–180

comprehensive internationalization, 115, 121, 123, 127, 189

Council for Higher Education Accreditation (CHEA), 60, 61, 64, 67

Council of Graduate Schools, 96

Council on Governmental Relations, 158

Covid-19: educational trends and, 2–3, 45, 47, 54, 152, 153, 154, 215; financial impact of, 163–164; internationalization strategies and, 45–47, 127, 128, 132, 140, 143–144; soft power and, 35–36, 37; US-China research collaboration, 78–79, 84–90, 211

Cox Report, 81

critical action, recommendations for: institutional strategies & partnerships, 212–213; rankings & accreditations, 209–210; research, 211–212; student mobility & learning, 213–214

Cultural Bridges Act (2002), 30

curriculum internationalization. *See* internationalization of curriculum

demographics, global trends in, 42–48, 45

Department of Education (DoED), 10, 27, 28, 32, 64, 173, 174–175

Department of Homeland Security, 30, 32, 36

Department of State (DOS), 26, 27, 29, 30, 31

dependency: in academic imperialism, 159–160; dependency theory, 102–104, 107; neo-nationalism vs., 105; transnational partnerships and, 3–4, 132–134. *See also* geopolitics; international students

developing nations: dependency and, 3–4, 102–104, 105, 107, 159–160; internationalization, impacts, 45–47, 102–104, 107, 124, 125–128, 132–134; in transnational partnerships, 3–4, 132–134; trends in education, 8, 42–48, 45

DeVos, Betsy, 174

diplomacy: under Clinton administration, 29; knowledge diplomacy, 138–141, 143; post–September 11 attacks, 29–31, 32, 34; study abroad as, 162; under Trump administration, 32–33, 34–36. *See also* foreign policy

discrimination, 12, 64, 105, 159

dual/joint degree programs, 135–136

ecology of knowledge, 200

economics: academic imperialism, 155–162; China, growth in, 37, 44, 46–47, 50, 215; commercialization of IE, 29–32, 114, 125–128; commodification of students, 31–32, 155–156, 162–165, 178–180; demand for higher education, 1, 42–44, 77, 100–102; global competence, competitiveness in, 170–175; global competence, inequality in, 176–178; income inequality, 3–5, 132–136, 144, 176–178, 211; protectionism vs. global engagement, 102–104; transnational partnerships and, 132–134; university rankings and, 48–49, 54; in US hegemony, 190–197, 199–201. *See also* geopolitics; soft power

Eisenhower, Dwight D., 25

English language: in academic imperialism, 4–5, 158, 160; accreditation practices and, 69–71; in global competence, 176; in transnational knowledge networks, 48

Enhanced Border Security Act (2002), 30

entrepreneurial internationalization. *See* transnational partnerships

European Association of International Education (EAIE), 14

exceptionalism, US, 190–192

Fascell, Dante, 27

Federal Bureau of Investigation (FBI), 78

federal government: IE, investment in, 10–13, 25–32; IE as soft power resource, 24–25;

national security, 25, 27–28, 29–30, 33, 36, 77–78, 81–83, 170–175, 181
Ford, Gerald R., 27
Foreign Affairs Reform and Restructuring Act (1998), 29
foreign policy: anti-communist ideology, 27–28, 190–192; globalization, emergence of, 28–29; IE, impact on, 24–25; IE as vital part of, 31–32; post–September 11 attacks, 29–31, 32, 34, 171–172; post–Vietnam War, 26–27; post–World War II, 25–26; scientific nationalism, 83–84, 88–90; soft power and, 34–37, 214; under Trump administration, 32–33, 34–36; US-China relations, 3, 33, 36, 77–78, 81–83, 88–90, 101–102, 161. *See also* geopolitics; immigration policy; internationalization; soft power
Fulbright, James William, 25
Fulbright Hays Act (1961), 10, 25, 26, 126

geography, nation-based views of, 176–177
geopolitics: commercialization of IE, 29–32, 114, 125–128; curriculum internationalization, 193–201; dependency and, 3–4, 102–104, 105, 107, 159–160; global competence, 170–175; human agency framework and, 106; IE as tool in, 10–13, 115–116, 117–119, 125–128; joint/dual degrees programs, 135–136; knowledge diplomacy and, 138–141; knowledge economy, 1, 24–25, 31, 42–44, 77, 100–102, 113–115; nationalism in, 83–84, 88–90, 104–105, 107; national security and, 25, 27–28, 29–30, 33, 36, 77–78, 81–83, 170–185; soft power and, 24–25, 33–37, 100–102, 207–208; US-based accreditation and, 61, 66, 68–70, 72; US-China relations, 3, 33, 36, 77–78, 81–83, 88–90, 101–102, 161; US exceptionalism, 190–192; US positional power, 7–10. *See also* foreign policy; internationalization; soft power
global capitalism system, 194
Global Citizenship Scale, 173
global competence: characterized, 170–171; assessment strategies, 172–173; delineating need for, 171–172; geography of, 176–177; individualistic vs. relational perspectives, 180–181; internationalization strategies, 173–174; nationalism & populism in, 174–175; politics of, 178–180; social stratification in, 177–178

Global Competence Framework, 175
global imaginary: characterized, 193–195; challenging dominant form of, 197–201; national hegemony and, 195, *196*, 197
globalism, scientific, 83–84, 88–90
globalization: academic imperialism, 155–162; higher education, impact on, 2–3, 42–48, 63–64, 134; investment in IE and, 29–32; wealth disparities and, 48. *See also* geopolitics; internationalization
Global Learning VALUE rubric, 174
global north & global south: defined, 66; dependency and, 3–4, 116, 159–160; global competence and, 176–177; internationalization, politics of, 6, 123–128, 190–192; standards of quality and, 125–126, 211–212. *See also* income inequality
Global Perspective Inventory (GPI), 173
global rankings, emergence of, 53
global talent pool: commodification of, 31–32, 155–156, 162–165, 178–180; trends in, 42–48

hegemony: curriculum internationalization for, 195, *196*, 197; decline of US, 192–193; hegemonic global imaginary, 193–195; historical precedents to US, 190–192; of ideas, 5. *See also* academic imperialism; geopolitics
Higher Education Act Title VI, 25, 27, 28, 30
higher education institutions (HEI): internationalization, approaches to, 114–115; internationalization, critique of, 115–116, 125–129; internationalization, implementation, 119–122; internationalization, purported benefits, 122–125; internationalization, strategic purposes, 117–119; knowledge diplomacy and, 138–141, 143; recommendations for critical action, 212–213, 214; transnational partnerships, 132–134, 135–138, 141–144. *See also* international education (IE)
higher education research & development (HERD). *See* research & development (R&D)
Homeland Security Act (2002), 30
Hughes, Karen, 31

Illegal Immigration Reform and Immigration Responsibility Act (1996), 29 immigration policy: higher education, impact on, 12–13, 95, 153–154, 157–158; recommendations for critical action, 213–214; September 11 attacks and, 29–30; under Trump administration, 3, 32–33, 35, 153–154, 161; World Trade Center bombings and, 29. *See also* foreign policy

inbound mobility, 153–154

income inequality: global competence and, 176–178; student mobility and, 3–5, 177–178, 211; transnational partnerships and, 132–136, 144. *See also* economics; global north & global south

individualistic & anthropocentric system, 195

individualistic vs. relational perspectives, 180–181

information and communication technologies (ICT), 1, 216

Institute for International Education (IIE), 178

institutional vs. programmatic accreditation, 62–63, 66–68

Intercultural Development Inventory (IDI), 173

interest convergence, 160–162

International Advisory Board, 30

International Association of Universities, 14

international education (IE): commercialization of, 29–32, 114, 125–128; globalization and, 28–29; immigration policy and, 12–13, 95, 153–154, 157–158; national security and, 25, 27–28, 29–30, 33, 36, 77–78, 81–83, 190–192; post–Vietnam War, 26–27; post–World War II, 25–26; September 11 attacks and, 29–31; as soft power resource, 10–13, 24–25, 31, 100–102; trends in, 42–48, 153–155; under Trump administration, 32–33, 34–36. *See also* research & development (R&D); scientific & technological (S&T) innovation

International Education Act (IEA) (1966), 26

internationalization: characterized, 3–7, 132–134; altruistic vs. status-based purposes, 117–119; approaches to successful, 114–115; comprehensive internationalization, 115, 121, 123, 127, 189; critique of, 115–116, 125–129; developing nations and, 45–47, 102–104, 107, 124, 125–128, 132–134; emergence of global rankings, 53–54; as geopolitical tool, 10–13; in global competence, 173–174; global trends reflecting, 42–48, 153–154; international collaboration in R&D, 47–48; joint/dual degree programs, 135–136; knowledge diplomacy in, 138–141, 143; purported benefits of, 122–125; technological nationalism and, 104–105; traditional vs. formulaic implementation, 119–122; transnational partnerships, 132–134, 136–144; university rankings reflecting, 50–51, 52; US-based accreditation practices, 63–72. *See also* geopolitics; globalization

internationalization of curriculum: current trends, 189–190; decline of US hegemony and, 192–193; global imaginary, characterized, 193–195; historical precedents to, 190–192; for improving the world, *196*, 197–198; for national hegemony, 195, *196*, *197*; for remaking the world, *196*, 198–199; for "the end of the world as we know it," *196*, 199–201

International Quality Group (IQG), 60

international students: academic dependency, 159–160; agency of, 106, 115–116; commodification of, 31–32, 155–156, 162–165, 178–180; dependency theory and, 102–104; educational trends, 1, 42–48, 153–155; geopolitical power and, 100–102; neo-nationalism as discrimination, 105; Ph.D. & postdoctoral degrees, 96–97, *99*, *100*, *101*; postdoctoral employment, *97*, 98–100; technological nationalism and, 104–105. *See also* international education (IE); scientific & technological (S&T) innovation

Iranian Revolution, 27

isolationism, 33, 54–55, 107, 208. *See also* nationalism

Johnson, Lyndon B., 26

joint/dual degree programs, 135–136

Kennedy, John F., 26–27

knowledge diplomacy, 138–141, 143

knowledge economy: academic imperialism and, 155–162; commercialization of IE, 29–32, 114, 125–128; commodification of students, 31–32, 155–156, 162–165, 178–180; curriculum internationalization and, 190–192, 195, *196*, 197; demand for higher education, 1, 24–25, 31, 42–44, 77, 100–102, 113–115; neo-nationalism and, 105. *See also* economics; international education (IE)

Lee, Wen Ho, 81, 82–83
Lincoln Commission (2005), 173

Maclean's magazine, 53
massification, 42, 43, 49. *See also* globalization
May, Theresa, 174
mobility, student: academic dependency, 159–160; academic imperialism, characterized, 155–156; Covid-19 and, 2–3, 144, 215; dependency theory and, 102–104; human agency framework, 106; inbound mobility, 153–154; interest convergence, 160–162; outbound mobility, 8–9, 154–155; positional competition, 156–158; recommendations for critical action, 162–165, 213–214; social stratification and, 177–178. *See also* global competence; international students
Mutual Educational and Cultural Exchange Act (1961), 26

National Defense Education Act (1958), 25, 28, 35, 191
nationalism: America First policy, 32–33; curriculum internationalization and, 187–190, 195, *196*, 197; in global competence, 174–175; IE & national interests, 10–13; international graduate enrollment and, 97, 100–102, 107; isolationism, 33, 54–55, 107, 208; neo-nationalism, 94, 105, 107; protectionism vs. global engagement, 102–104; scientific nationalism, 83–84, 88–90; technological nationalism, 104–105; US exceptionalism, 190–192. *See also* foreign policy; United States
national security: global competence as, 170–175, 181; IE as investment in, 25, 27–28, 190–192; IE as risk to, 29–30; scientific nationalism and, 83–84, 88–90; Travel Ban (2017), 153–154; US-China relations, 33, 36, 77–78, 81–83
National Security Education Act (1991), 28

National Survey of Student Engagement (NSSE), 174
nation-state system, 195
neoliberalism: institutional accreditation and, 69; internationalization processes and, 4, 7, 115–116; technological nationalism vs., 104–105; transnational partnerships and, 134, 140, 144
neo-nationalism, 94, 105, 107
neo-racism, 12, 105
New Cold War, 3, 77
Nixon, Richard M., 27

Obama, Barack, 31, 155, 173
Obama, Michelle, 162
Organization for Economic Co-operation and Development (OECD), 6, 43–46, 48, 53, 151, 175, 176
othering, 158
outbound mobility, 8–9, 154–155

peer-review. *See* accreditation
politics of belonging, 178–180
positional mobility, 156–158
post-colonial theory: internationalization processes and, 115–116, 125; US-based accreditation and, 61, 66. *See also* colonialism
poverty tourism, 158, 160, 164
Powell, Colin, 31
power: English language and, 4–5, 158, 160; internationalization defined and, 5–7, 207; knowledge and, 54, 77, 100–102, 194–201. *See also* colonialism; geopolitics; soft power
Programme for International Student Assessment (PISA), 44, 175, 176
protectionism: global engagement vs., 102–104; technological nationalism vs., 104–105; under Trump administration, 32–35. *See also* foreign policy; isolationism; nationalism

Quacquarelli Symonds World University Rankings, 8, 51, 53
quality assurance: accreditation, defined, 61–63; globalization and, 51, 53–54, 63–64, 115–116; global rankings, 48–54, 65; US influence on, 7–10, 61, 64–66, 68–70, 72, 125–126

rankings, university: accreditation and, 65; changes in, 51, 53; functions of, 49–50; global rankings, emergence of, 53–54; recommendations for critical action, 209–210; reflecting geopolitics, 50–51, 52; US as leader in, 7–10
Reagan, Ronald, 28
relational vs. individualistic perspectives, 180–181
research & development (R&D): developing nations and, 45–47; international collaboration in, 47–48; recommendations for critical action, 211–212; transformation from local to global, 42–43; US as world leader in, 7–10. *See also* collaboration in research; international education (IE)
Rice, Condoleezza, 31

science, engineering, and health-related (S&E) fields, 94
Science Citation Index (1961), 5, 9, 51
scientific globalism vs. nationalism, 83–84, 88–90
scientific & technological (S&T) innovation: "China Threat" and, 12, 77–79, 81–83, 86; Cold War and, 77, 83, 96; international contributions to, 80–81; research collaboration, leadership in, 86–87; research collaboration, trends in, 2, 42–48, 77–80, 84–85; scientific globalism vs. nationalism, 83–84, 88–90; US-China collaboration, value of, 85–86, 100–102, 211. *See also* collaboration in research; international education (IE)
Senator Paul Simon Study Abroad Foundation Act (2007), 31, 162, 165
September 11 terrorist attacks: diplomacy efforts following, 29–31, 32, 34; foreign policy and, 29–30; global competence initiatives and, 171–172; immigration policy and, 29–30; US global decline and, 192–193
Simon, Paul, 27
Simpson-Mazzoli bills, 28
Smith Act (1948), 26
social cartography of curriculum internationalization, 193–201
social imaginary, 194
Social Sciences Citation Index (1966), 51

social stratification, 177–178
soft power: academic imperialism as, 161; America First policy and, 32–35; China, economic growth, 8, 37, 44, 46–47, 50, 215; Covid-19 and, 35–36, 37; foreign policy and, 34–37, 214; global competence as, 172; IE as, 10–13, 24–25, 31, 100–102; immigration, role in, 35; US-China relations and, 33, 36, 101–102, 160–161. *See also* foreign policy; geopolitics
state government role in IE, 10, 24, 126
Student and Exchange Visitors Information System (SEVIS), 29
student mobility. *See* mobility, student

technological nationalism, 104–105
Thousand Talents Plan, 82
Times's World University Rankings, 7
transnational partnerships: characterized, 132–134; joint/dual degree programs, 135–136; key strategies, 136–138; knowledge diplomacy in, 138–141, 143; life cycle, defined, 141; life cycle, developmental, 142; life cycle, operational, 142–143; life cycle, assessment, 143–144; recommendations for critical action, 212–213. *See also* collaboration in research
Travel Ban (2017), 153–154
Truman, Harry S., 25
Trump, Donald J.: diplomacy under, 3, 32–35; global competence and, 174–175; international graduate enrollment under, 97, 153–154, 161; US global decline and, 192–193
Trump v. Hawaii, 154

United Nations: 2030 Agenda for Sustainable Development (2015), 47, 175; UNESCO, 6
United States: academic imperialism, 155–162; accreditation, geopolitical influence on, 7–10, 61, 64–66, 68–70, 72, 125–126; commodification of students, 162–165; decline of US hegemony, 192–193; exceptionalism, 190–192; Patriot Act (2001), 30; positional power of, 7–10; relations with China, 3, 33, 36, 77–78, 81–83, 101–102, 161; scientific nationalism, 83–84, 88–90; trends in education, 42–48, 77–80,

153–155; trends in university rankings, 51, 52. *See also* foreign policy; geopolitics; nationalism
universal reason system, 195
university rankings. *See* rankings, university
US Agency for International Development (USAID), 26, 28, 34
US Department of Education (USDOE). *See* Department of Education (DoED)
US Information Agency (USIA), 26
US International Communication Agency, 27
US News and World Report (USNWR), 51, 54
USNWR Best Global Rankings, 51, 53, 54
US State Department, 10, 34

Vietnam War, 27, 192
Visa Entry Reform Act (2002), 30

Wall Street Journal/Times Higher Education College Rankings, 53–54
wealth disparities. *See* income inequality
Webometrics, 53
Western Association of Schools and Colleges (WASC), 64, 67, 68, 69
Western dominance: academic imperialism, 155–162; curriculum internationalization and, 190–192, 195, *196*, 197; global competence and, 178–180; US-based accreditation and, 61, 66, 209–210. *See also* colonialism; geopolitics; hegemony
wicked problems, 189, 195
World Bank, 6
World Trade Center bombings, 29, 30
World War II: birth of IE following, 25–26, 135; US global hegemony and, 190–192

xenophobic politics, 95, 97, 190

Printed in the United States
by Baker & Taylor Publisher Services